AF690381

China's Age of Abundance

Between the 1980s and the present day, China has experienced one of the most consequential economic transformations in world history. One-fifth of the Earth's population has left behind a life of scarcity and subsistence for one of abundance and material comfort, while their nation has emerged as a preeminent economic and political power. In a systematic historical and sociological analysis of this unique juncture, Wang Feng charts the origins, forces, and consequences of this meteoric rise in living standards. He shifts the focus away from institutions and policies to offer new perspectives based on consumption among poorer rural populations as a driver of global economic change. But is this "Age of Abundance" coming to an end? Anticipating potential headwinds, including an aging population, increasing inequality, and intensifying political control, Wang explores whether this preeminence could be coming to a close.

Wang Feng is a professor of sociology at the University of California, Irvine.

China's Age of Abundance

Origins, Ascendance, and Aftermath

Wang Feng

University of California, Irvine

CAMBRIDGE
UNIVERSITY PRESS

CAMBRIDGE
UNIVERSITY PRESS

Shaftesbury Road, Cambridge CB2 8EA, United Kingdom

One Liberty Plaza, 20th Floor, New York, NY 10006, USA

477 Williamstown Road, Port Melbourne, VIC 3207, Australia

314–321, 3rd Floor, Plot 3, Splendor Forum, Jasola District Centre, New Delhi – 110025, India

103 Penang Road, #05–06/07, Visioncrest Commercial, Singapore 238467

Cambridge University Press is part of Cambridge University Press & Assessment, a department of the University of Cambridge.

We share the University's mission to contribute to society through the pursuit of education, learning and research at the highest international levels of excellence.

www.cambridge.org
Information on this title: www.cambridge.org/9781009444897

DOI: 10.1017/9781009444934

© Wang Feng 2024

This publication is in copyright. Subject to statutory exception and to the provisions of relevant collective licensing agreements, no reproduction of any part may take place without the written permission of Cambridge University Press & Assessment.

First published 2024

A catalogue record for this publication is available from the British Library

A Cataloging-in-Publication data record for this book is available from the Library of Congress

ISBN 978-1-009-44489-7 Hardback
ISBN 978-1-009-44492-7 Paperback

Cambridge University Press & Assessment has no responsibility for the persistence or accuracy of URLs for external or third-party internet websites referred to in this publication and does not guarantee that any content on such websites is, or will remain, accurate or appropriate.

To Max & Max

Contents

Figures

Tables

Preface

As someone who has had the privilege of living in this age and witnessing firsthand the historical transformations in China, I have often had a lingering desire to write a book documenting this remarkable chapter of human history. Two inspirations and one historical moment made this project a reality.

Reading economic history brought the first inspiration. Robert J. Gordon's masterful book on the rise and fall of the United States' growth reminded me of using consumption measures to document economic change. Two decades ago, when I did research for a book on rising income inequality in urban China, my data sources were mainly household income and expenditure surveys. So utilizing consumption data is rather familiar to me as a data source.

The second inspiration came from visiting Italy. Two academic visits, to the University of Padova in 2017 and the University of Florence in 2019, transported me away from focusing only on the two modern economic giants today: the United States and China. These visits sent me back into history. The center of the Roman Empire for over a millennium, Italy was also the birthplace of the Renaissance for two centuries from the fourteenth century. The beauties from that era of humanistic revival are still on full display today. Italy's historical glories reminded me that this era of Chinese material prosperity could also be only a fleeting moment in human history, albeit a magnificent moment that transformed the lives of the largest number of humans around the turn of the twenty-first century. I am deeply indebted to Massimo Livi Bacci, M. Giovanna Merli, Giovanni Zanalda, Maria Letizia Tanturri, and Gustavo De Santis, who made these visits possible and pleasurable.

Only a month after returning to California from Florence in December 2019, the Covid-19 pandemic broke out. That pandemic would soon engulf the whole world; a global pandemic that would last unexpectedly for three years. Suspension of travel and self-quarantine at home instilled a constant sense of apprehension and uncertainty, but they also brought a rare opportunity of quietness for research and writing, with undisturbed time and concentration. Forced separation from loved ones on the other side of the Pacific only intensified my desire to write, using it as a diversion from longing and boredom.

The list of acknowledgments for this book goes long and deep, dating all the way back to my graduate studies at the University of Michigan. Bill Lavely, my first academic adviser, has been a personal example to me with his meticulous scholarship as well as his grace and generosity. It was Bill who introduced me to James Lee – a colleague, dear friend, and a teacher who led me into economic history, among other fields. It is James with whom I had the most rewarding collaborations and lifelong intellectual conversations. I began my studies of China in graduate school through reading the works of Marty K. Whyte. For decades Marty has remained a most supportive mentor, serving as an example of a scholar, through his scholarship and by participating in his research projects. A one-year post-doctoral stay in 1987-88 at the University of California, Berkeley, turned out to be a life-changing experience, opening the doors to historical studies of population and economy. It was Gene Hammel who generously arranged for me to spend that precious year in Berkeley, after I had chosen Michigan over Berkeley for graduate training. It was only fate that Ron Lee, who was on the faculty at Berkeley then and throughout his later career, would be a cofounder of a global research consortium (National Transfer Accounts) that I became a participant in decades later. I had the good fortune of knowing and working with another cofounder, Andy Mason, while working at the East-West Center in Honolulu, Hawai‘i. For decades, Andy has been an intellectual and personal inspiration. His influences are documented in several parts of this book.

For a decade and half, I have also been fortunate to be affiliated with academic institutions in China, in particular Tsinghua University in Beijing and Fudan University in Shanghai. These affiliations availed me the opportunities to observe a fast-changing society close up and to benefit from collaborations and support from colleagues and students there. Between 2010 and 2013, I had the unique opportunity to be the director of Brookings-Tsinghua Center for Public Policy in Beijing. I am grateful that my home institution, the University of California, Irvine, granted me exceptional leave for three years. Ken Lieberthal, then the director of the John Thornton China Center at the Brookings Institution, recruited me to the position, supporting me with an open heart and open arms. Ken introduced me to a world entirely different from academia and influenced me with his profound knowledge of China and his unrivaled worldview. It was a genuine privilege to have worked with him. My over-a-decade-long affiliation with Fudan University in Shanghai allowed me to complete the work on China's demographic changes, work that contributed to ending the one-child policy, and to shift to new work on intergenerational economy. I am thankful to many colleagues at Fudan, in particular Peng Xizhe, Cheng Yuan, Liang Hong, and Liu Xin. It was at Fudan that I began collaborative work with Shen Ke on a number of topics, in particular on the economic and social consequences of population aging. Shen Ke has been a leader in our collaborative work, the work that forms the core of Chapter 6 in this book. She is indeed entitled to be a coauthor of that chapter. Shen Ke has also kindly read and commented carefully on the whole manuscript. Several graduate students, in particular Xu Wanting and Zhang Wenlei at Fudan University, also provided valuable assistance assembling data sources. I am indebted to them for all of their help.

Throughout the process of writing this book, and throughout the past two decades, Cai Yong has been a constant intellectual inspiration and collaborator. His brilliant mind and seemingly infinite knowledge and skills led to our many collaborations. As with Shen Ke, he should be another coauthor of Chapter 6. He was, however, much more than a collaborator on that chapter. Early in the process of writing this book, he read drafts, offered crucial insights, and made important corrections. He provided timely support numerous times, bringing data sources and producing some of the better graphs. I am extremely lucky to have had such a dear colleague and friend in my life.

Two other friends deserve special thanks. To break away from the self-imposed home isolation, Su Yang and Junling Ma arranged weekly hikes every Saturday morning for over a year and a half. Between May 2020 and January 2022, my log recorded over fifty such morning hikes around trails in Orange County and Los Angeles County, California, totaling over 330 miles. Had it not been for the Covid-19 pandemic, and for Junling and Su Yang, I might never have known about these trails. More than the much-needed weekly break from stay-at-home isolation, these weekly hikes turned into opportunities for intellectual discussions, allowing me to flesh out my ideas for the book. Su Yang and Junling pushed me to think beyond recording history and beyond China. Junling also read and provided detailed suggestions for the entire manuscript.

Special thanks also go to Claudia Shambaugh, who painstakingly read and edited the entire manuscript. Improving the language with more precise and readable words and sentences, Claudia was an editor in the truest sense. She questioned the arguments where she saw confusion or repetition and made numerous excellent suggestions with the organization of and approach to the book project. Our weekly meetings at her house to discuss the manuscript over tea and fruits provided much-needed intellectual rigor as well as spiritual uplifting during the time of the pandemic.

I am also grateful to Lucy Rhymer, senior commissioning editor at Cambridge University Press, and her colleagues. She had the vision and faith to take on this project and patiently guided me through the review process with her consummate professionalism. Two anonymous reviewers offered very helpful comments and suggestions, suggestions that helped highlight the unique contributions of the book and broaden its comparative scope. I am in deep debt to their kindness and help. In my long professional life, I have never before encountered such professional kindness as displayed by one of the reviewers, who in addition to substantive suggestions also went through every paragraph and offered detailed editorial suggestions.

There are many, many others. Their work has enabled and enriched this project, and my acknowledgments to them are documented in the references at the end of the book.

Over the course of writing this book, and over the entire course of my professional career, I have been most blessed by the love and support of my wife Haiou and my son Max. The pandemic made the preciousness of one's family more apparent than ever. When the whole world was shut down during a pandemic, home was always open and there for me.

This book is dedicated to Max & Max: Max Lummis and Maxwell Wang. Max Lummis forged our lifelong friendship soon after I arrived in Ann Arbor, Michigan, in 1983; our journey in life as friends and scholars paralleled the one of China's ascendancy to material abundance. Max Wang, my son, accompanied me for many humid summer field visits in China through the 1990s and 2000s. Whether he knew it or not at the time, he witnessed firsthand China's transformation into an entirely different society. This book is for his generation and for future generations to appreciate a remarkable chapter in human history.

1 Surprise

Regardless of its portrayal, the China miracle at the turn of the twenty-first century was not expected. Within four decades, over one-fifth of humanity left behind a life of subsistence, scarcity, and misery and moved to one of the abundance and material comforts. In the four short decades between 1979 and 2019, the size of China's portion of the world's total economic output shot up from less than 2 percent to over 16 percent.[1] With the arrival of the age of abundance, China reemerged as a preeminent global economic and political power, a status that had eluded it for centuries.

An economic miracle indeed, yet its emergence came largely as a surprise. It repeatedly amazed the leaders who presided over this part of history. As China's leaders set new and ambitious goals, those goals were surpassed repeatedly. Surprises came not because these leaders were timid or unambitious; to the contrary, mobilizing a nation with ambitious and grandiose goals was a constant political recipe. And yet these ambitious leaders continually underestimated the size of the economic boom.

Leaders in China were not the only ones who were surprised. The Chinese abundance eluded the world's most elite scholars specializing in the study of economics. Veteran analysts, living both in and outside of China, did not fully anticipate the arrival of China's age of abundance. Some of the world's leading economists outside of China also failed to anticipate the enormity or the rapidity of China's rise to prosperity.

This book offers a brief history of this extraordinary chapter in China's, as well as the world's, history. It offers an account of China's ascendance to material prosperity, or its age of abundance, and its future trajectory.

China's age of abundance was by no means preordained. A combination of unique forces and historical junctures led to this happy outcome. On the eve of its economic takeoff, China had not only a large but also a healthy

[1] In constant US$. According to the World Bank data, China's GDP was $178.28 billion in 1979, compared with the world's total of $9.97 trillion (China's share was 1.79 percent). In 2019, China's GDP rose to $14.34 trillion, against the world's $87.69 trillion. Measured in constant 2010 US$, China's share was only 1.16 percent in 1979 and 13.58 percent in 2019. https://data.worldbank.org/indicator/

and literate population. Living at the margins of subsistence and in the wake of the decade-long Cultural Revolution that had only worsened material scarcity, the Chinese people were eager and ready to improve their lives. That energy, coming from the bottom of society, was allowed and assisted to burst out by a generation of reform-minded leaders, in particular, Deng Xiaoping who was able to galvanize and navigate the country with his unique background, authority, determination, and political acumen as well as his artistry.

China has by no means reached the end of its economic rise at the time of writing. Yet its rapid growth rate peaked a decade ago and has been on a steady declining slope since. The onset of slowing down is not accidental. Nor is it temporary. The driving forces, as this book documents, have started to show signs of warning. Along with the headwinds that have accumulated over time, the age of abundance, remarkable by both its rapid rise and its length, is already largely history. Wealth will expand and prosperity is likely to persist, but the fast ascendance is clearly over.

To fully appreciate China's remarkable decades of rising to abundance, this book traces the origins of China's economic rise prior to its takeoff, follows its trajectory, and offers a new interpretation. In contrast to studies that rely on monetary measures such as income or capital investment to track and showcase economic ascendance, this book uses changes in measures of consumption as vital markers to profile improvements in the standard of living. In contrast to attributing China's abundance to its cheap labor, this book makes the argument that what China had was *good* labor, and that labor was *made cheap* in part by its unique institutional arrangements created under its socialist planned economy era, arrangements that subjected the population to different life chances. And in contrast to prevalent narratives that focus on reforms and privilege the roles of leaders, this book follows and highlights the forces at work from the bottom of society that improved living standards, the forces that made China's miraculous era possible.

Three pivotal transformations defined China's path to material abundance. They were, respectively, private farming, rural industrialization, and rural to urban migration. *None* of these three movements, as this book will document, was a state-initiative. Instead, they were all born out of the strong desires of the population, who were desperate and determined to improve their lives. Such grassroot initiatives were often resisted by the government at first, before being accepted and embraced by them.

Four arguments hence organize the core contents of this book:

1. China's material abundance was not fully anticipated. It came as a surprise to those living within and outside the country, to those

guiding the process from the top, and to those participating and experiencing it from below. The ascendance to abundance came with full of twists and turns. Historical junctures, large and small, were the critical drivers.

2. The ascendance to prosperity was built on two distinct legacies: a population that already had gained improvements in health and literacy, and a population divided into two types of citizens, who were living under increasing material scarcity thanks to decades of socialism. The notion that China's boom was due to its "cheap labor" misses the essential qualities of the Chinese population that made the abundance possible.
3. The Chinese path to prosperity was similar to those in other industrialized economies. It was essentially a process of industrialization and urbanization. It was a process, however, with Chinese characteristics. A legacy of the socialist planned economy era, China's rural population did not have the same freedom as those in other nations undergoing the industrialization process. The Chinese process consequently had two distinct but interconnected phases: first, in situ industrialization in the countryside, followed by massive migrations to cities.
4. The age of abundance has come to an inevitable end. China entered the age of abundance due to a fortunate congruence of historical factors. The most important of them were a large and divided population, the tragedy of the Cultural Revolution, and the unique leader Deng Xiaoping. These conditions, historical, are not replicable. With the increase of consumption outpacing income growth and an accelerating population aging process, the vast surplus accumulated during China's age of abundance is already shrinking.

As its age of abundance draws to a close, China faces headwinds that have gathered force over time. China's achieved prosperity is unlikely to disappear. Nor will the strong headwinds. The era of massive migration supplying exploitable labor has reached its end. China's population is aging at an accelerating and irreversible rate, exacerbated further by numerous families having only one child. Abundance also came with a sharp rise in economic inequality, which has already quickly shifted from income to wealth stratification and reset the starting lines for the next generation. Hundreds of millions of migrants in Chinese cities continue to live the life of secondary citizens, a fate unlikely to be reversed in a generation or more. The return to tightened political control, made possible in part by a complacency accompanying material prosperity, could also once again send China down a road of economic stagnation and social suffocation. China's age of abundance is therefore now largely a subject of history.

China's Under-Ambitious Leaders and Nobel Laureates

Let us begin with the surprises.

Emerging from the late 1970s and the shadows of the ten-year Cultural Revolution that devastated economic production and tore the social fabric, China's post-Mao era leaders announced an ambitious goal: to quadruple China's per capita income in twenty years, by the end of the century.

This goal was not based on any rigorous analysis of the Chinese economy at the time, nor was it new in style. Setting ambitious goals had long been a Chinese political tradition under Communist Party rule. Two decades before this latest goal was set, in 1958, China experienced a Great Leap Forward, under the then supreme leader Mao Zedong. Mao called for China to surpass Britain's steel output in fifteen years and the United States' in fifty years.[2] Then, in 1977, Mao's immediate successor Hua Guofeng called for accelerating China's economic modernization with the goal of mechanizing most of its agricultural production in three years by 1980. Given that the Great Leap Forward in the late 1950s ended with the largest famine in human history, Hua's post-Mao leap forward was soon deemed unrealistic and was scrapped.

Setting the new goal for China's age of prosperity was Deng Xiaoping, the unique leader with determination and political genius who guided China out of its socialist planned economy. Hosting Japanese Prime Minister Ohira Masayoshi in Beijing in December 1979, Deng outlined that the China he wished to see beyond his lifetime. At the age of seventy-five and returning to power after being purged twice in as many decades, Deng laid out his imagined new long-term path for China, beyond his own life span.

Deng envisioned a Chinese modernization that would unfold in two broad phases. First, in twenty years, he imagined that China's economy would reach a level of *xiaokang*, which can be translated as "somewhat comfortable" or "moderately prosperous." He proposed a goal of achieving US$1,000 per capita income by the end of the century; a level that would put China among the wealthier Third World countries, a goal that he admitted would require great effort.[3] Then, for the second phase, he envisioned that in another thirty to fifty years China would approach the per capita income level of a developed country.

Deng repeated these goals in the following years, determined, though not always fully certain. His goal for per capita annual income by the year

[2] https://zh.wikipedia.org/wiki/超英赶美 (Surpassing Britain, catching up with the United States).

[3] Zhonggong zhongyang wenxian yanjiushi 2004, 582.

2000 often wavered between $800 and $1,000. In a conversation with visiting Australian Prime Minister Malcolm Fraser on August 6, 1982, Deng explained that the estimate of $1,000 that he mentioned to Prime Minister Ohira Masayoshi in 1979 was perhaps too high. Considering population growth, he trimmed the number to $800.[4] Deng probably knew that this goal was an estimate at best, a lightning rod to rally the Chinese population into a new era, though he supposedly had consulted with those knowledgeable about the Chinese economy at the time. Carrying Deng's charge, in 1982 the Chinese Communist Party (CCP) formalized his ambitious twenty-year economic goal of quadrupling China's economy in the CCP National Congress.[5]

A decade later, in 1992, at the age of eighty-seven and after bearing the severe setback of the bloody crackdown from the massive 1989 Tiananmen protests, Deng revisited his long-term goal for China. He did so in conversations during his momentous tour to South China, a tour aimed at recouping the forces of economic reforms and reigniting the engines of economic growth. That was his last public attempt to inspire the leadership and masses again. He envisioned a China that would, when celebrating the centennial of the People's Republic in 2049, achieve the income of a middle-level developed country. That would be remarkable, he commented.[6]

The result? Deng and his comrades would be totally surprised at how severely they underestimated the performance of the Chinese economy in the two decades after the goal had been set. Deng lived to see his ambitious goal realized. Prior to the century's end, when Deng passed away at the age of ninety-three in 1997, China's per capita income had already more than quadrupled.[7]

The size of China's economy expanded vastly during those last two decades of the twentieth century. Each decade saw the size of the

[4] Zhonggong zhongyang wenxian yanjiushi 1998, 226. In April 1981, Deng elaborated on his goals for China in more concrete and numerical terms: to double the size of the economy in a decade and to double it again in the decade following to reach a per capita income level of $1,000, or $800, $900 by the year 2000. In 1987, Deng also imagined that by the end of China's march to modernization, the per capita income level would reach $4,000, a goal passed by 2010, decades ahead of time.

[5] As announced by the top nominal leader of the Chinese Communist Party, Hu Yaobang, in his address to the 12th National Congress of the Chinese Communist Party, "the overall goal of our country's economic construction in the twenty years from 1981 to the end of the current century, is to strive to quadruple the total output of industry and agriculture, from 710 billion yuan in 1980 to around 2.8 trillion by 2000." http://cpc.people.com.cn/GB/64162/64168/64565/65448/4526430.html

[6] Zhonggong zhongyang wenxian yanjiushi 2004, 1345.

[7] From $430.9 in 1980 to $1,787.3 in 1997 (constant 2015 US$). https://data.worldbank.org/indicator/NY.GDP.PCAP.KD?locations=CN

economy more than double, despite frequent and rampant price inflation.[8] The World Bank put China's gross domestic product (GDP) at $422.77 billion in 1980, $1.03 trillion in 1990, and $2.77 trillion in 2000 (constant 2015 US$), expanding by 2.4 and 2.7 times, respectively, each decade.[9] Instead of quadrupling, the size of China's economy expanded by 6.55 times in the two decades after Deng had made that audacious wish. On a per capita basis, the increase was from $431 in 1980 to $905 in 1990, and to $2,194 in 2000 (constant 2015 US$), a fivefold increase over those two decades.[10] Chinese leaders had underestimated the goal by more than 25 percent (see Figure 1.1).[11]

Not having learned the lesson, Chinese leaders succeeding Deng Xiaoping made the same mistake, again by being too conservative. After surpassing the earlier goal of quadrupling the economy in two decades, China's leaders in the new millennium renewed their ambitious push: to again double China's economic output in a decade, by 2010. This goal was declared in 1995 at the plenary session of the Central Committee of the CCP.

> The main goal for 2010 is to double the GDP of 2000, making the people's well-off life more prosperous and forming a relatively complete socialist market economic system. With fifteen years of hard work, our country's social productivity, overall national strength, and people's living standards will reach a new level.[12]

Chinese leaders set the goal too modestly again, this time underestimating by an even larger margin than in the previous decades. In the first decade of the twenty-first century, following China's entry into the World Trade Organization in 2001 and despite the worst global financial crisis in seven decades, the country grew its economy by more than 270 percent, from $2.77 trillion to $7.55 trillion.[13] Per capita income rose 2.57 times from

[8] Inflation was 69 percent in the 1980s and 58 percent in the 1990s. (Inflation numbers are based on National Bureau of Statistics, *China Statistical Yearbook* 2001 (SYB 2001), table 9–1.)

[9] https://data.worldbank.org/indicator/NY.GDP.MKTP.KD?locations=CN

[10] https://data.worldbank.org/indicator/NY.GDP.PCAP.KD?locations=CN. Chinese official statistics report the same increase. In 1980, China's GDP was at 452 billion yuan; it expanded to 1.85 trillion by 1990, then to 8.94 trillion by 2000, a fourfold increase in the first and a nearly fivefold increase in the second decade (SYB 2001, table 3–1).

[11] Official statistics gave a per capita income of 489 yuan for the year 1981 and 7,084 yuan for 2000 (current price; SYB 2002, table 3–1). Adjusting for inflation (396% over the period), the increase is close to but not above four times (3.65 times). By the goals set in US$, from $200 to $800, however, the goal is overreached. Per capita GDP rose over five times from $347 to $1,768 between 1980 to 2000 (constant 2010 US$).

[12] Communique of the CCP 5th Plenum of the 14th Party Congress, September 28, 1995, Beijing.

[13] All in constant 2015 US$. https://data.worldbank.org/indicator/NY.GDP.MKTP.KD?locations=CN

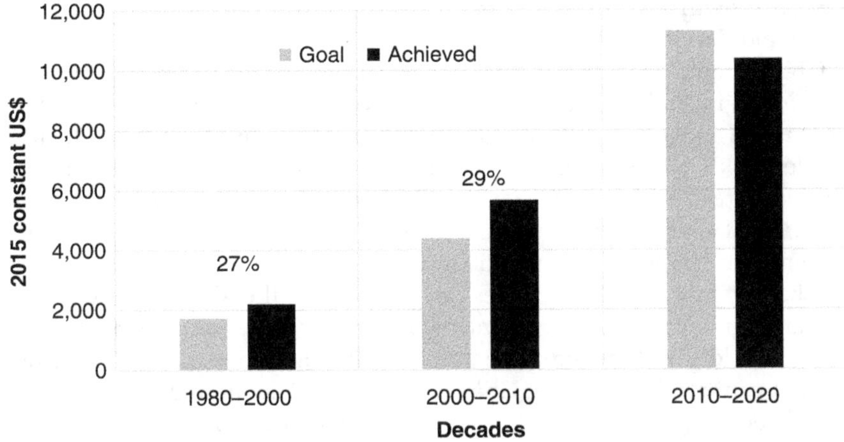

Figure 1.1 Underestimating China's growth: goals and achievements, 1980–2020 (per capita income, constant 2015 US$)
Source: World Bank, World Development Indicators (WDI)

$2,194 to $5,647 and 29 percent above the goal (Figure 1.1). With an average annual growth rate of 10 percent, the first decade of the twenty-first century also turned out to be the Chinese economy's fastest growing decade in its modern history.

Only on their third try in the forty years since China's economic ascendance had begun were China's leaders finally getting a better grasp of how fast their nation's economy might grow. In the early 2010s, a goal was renewed, to double the size of the economy within a decade, by 2020. The economic growth rate slowed down substantially during that decade. After reaching its peak in 2007, the annual rate of per capita income growth started a sustained downward trend from over 10 percent in 2010 to less than 6 percent by the decade's end.

Had it not been for the unexpected global COVID-19 pandemic in 2020 that devastated much of the world economy, China could have met but perhaps not exceeded its goal. Between 2010 and 2019, the size of China's economy increased from $7.55 trillion to $14.3 trillion, an increase of nearly 90 percent. Heading into 2020, China was still confident of reaching its goal, as a growth rate of only 5.5 percent was required, and the growth rate had not dropped to below 6 percent since 1991. At an annual growth rate of 2.2 percent in 2020, however, the unexpected global pandemic put a clear end to the era of hyper growth.[14]

China's rapid economic ascendance surprised not just its leaders but also academics, including Chinese economists who were studying the process at close range and advising leaders along the way. In the mid-1990s, citing the World Bank's numbers, three of China's best-known economists predicted in the widely read book, *The China Miracle: Development Strategy and Economic Reform*, that China's economy could surpass Japan's and the United States' to become the largest in the world by the year 2035.[15] Even adjusting for purchasing power, which triples or quadruples the Chinese economy, China was not expected to become the world's largest economy until 2015.

The world's best recognized economists had not done that much better when it came to anticipating China's unexpected economic boom. In the fall of 2004, the *Wall Street Journal* surveyed a group of the world's most prominent economists, all winners of the Nobel Memorial Prize in Economic Sciences.[16] These Nobel laureates in economics were asked to share their prediction for which of the world's economies was expected to the biggest in the world *in seventy-five years*, by *2079*: the United States, the European Union, or China. A list of the distinguished economists and their summarized predictions are in Table 1.1.

Of the twelve prominent economists gathered in this "panel," not everyone believed that China would rise to be the largest economy in the world. Not even in seventy-five years. Half of the group were certain that China would rise to be the largest economy. The other half, however, were not sure, or not quite sure, that *by 2079* China could overtake the United States and the EU as the world's largest economy:

US (Vernon L. Smith, Nobel Prize winner, 2002)

In order: US, China, EU (Clive W. J. Granger, Nobel Prize winner, 2003)

50 percent chance: China; 30 percent chance: EU; 20 percent chance: US (William Sharpe, Nobel Prize winner, 1990)

Some gave their reasons:

I think the current gap between China and the US and the EU is probably too large to make up. (George A. Akerlof, Nobel Prize winner, 2001)

Well, since the European Union is an undefined area, as of the year 2079, if it then includes Russia, it should be the largest. If not, the US would be likely, even

[14] Growth rate as reported by the World Bank: https://data.worldbank.org/indicator/NY.GDP.MKTP.KD.ZG?locations=CN

[15] Lin, Cai, and Li 1996, 11–12.

[16] "Nobel laureates offer views on the economy," *Wall Street Journal*, Sept. 3, 2004. www.wsj.com/articles/SB109415683639808339

Table 1.1 *Nobel Prize winners' predictions of world's largest economy by 2079 (from 2004)*

Nobel laureate	Prediction (overall economy size)	Prediction (per capita income)
George A. Akerlof	EU	
Kenneth J. Arrow	China	China less than half of that in the EU
Ronald H. Coase	China	
Milton Friedman	China	
Clive W. J. Granger	US, China, EU	
Lawrence R. Klein	China	US
Harry M. Markowitz	China	
John F. Nash Jr.	EU, US, China	
William F. Sharpe	China (50%), EU (30%), US (20%)	
Vernon L. Smith	US	
Robert M. Solow	China	US
Joseph E. Stiglitz	Disparity will be greatly reduced	

Source: www.wsj.com/articles/SB109415683639808339

though China and the US have similar land area. (John F. Nash Jr., Nobel Prize winner, 1994)

The most circumspect and nuanced prediction came from the person who was then perhaps the most familiar with the Chinese economy. Joseph Stiglitz, who had just stepped down from the position of chief economist of the World Bank, observed the following:

It's too difficult to make a projection 75 years from now on those issues. We don't know what other countries will be joining the European Union and how it will expand in terms of size. Secondly, the question that one has to recognize is that even if China is not the biggest, China will continue to have a lot more population. Even if growth doesn't remain at the rapid growth levels of the last 25 years, the disparity between China and the EU and the US will be greatly reduced. The result is that it is likely that there will be a different balance of economic powers. (Joseph E. Stiglitz, Nobel Prize winner, 2001)

Economists after all are not fortune tellers. At least half of this group got it wrong. But the economists cannot be faulted for not fully anticipating the magnitude of China's phenomenal economic growth, just as many of them failed to foresee the 2008 global financial crisis. And most members of the discipline are not close observers of China, even though many were frequent guests of the Chinese government, advising on China's economic reforms and development.

To some extent it is understandable that while they all recognized the global implications of China's economic rise and the enormous potential of the Chinese people, not everyone was equipped to make an informed prediction that the Chinese economy would continue to grow, and at what rate. Half of the twelve economists predicted without hesitation that China would become the largest economy by the last quarter of the twenty-first century, if not before. Still, three of those who predicted that China would be the largest economy by 2079 also believed that on a per capita basis China would not overtake the EU or the United States, not even in the long run.

China did not need to wait seventy-five years. Instead, if using the measure taking into account the purchasing power of its currency, China became the largest economy in the world in less than fifteen years, just ten years after the panel members' guesses. China was six decades ahead of schedule. As it turned out, China, even in current dollar terms, overtook Japan as the second largest economy in 2010, not 2015, ahead of predictions. By 2020, the size of China's economy was nearly three times that of Japan.[17] As of 2021, measured in current US dollars, the size of China's economy had surpassed that of the EU (including the United Kingdom, which left the EU in January 2020), but it was still 23 percent below that of the United States.[18]

Taking pricing differentials into account, however, the lineup is different. Using the World Bank's purchasing power parity 2011 price, the International Monetary Fund estimated that China overtook the United States as the world's largest economy in 2014. By 2019, China's economy was 27 percent larger than the United States'. A later price comparison by the World Bank, which inflated the price gap between China and the United States by 17 percent, suggests that it was not until 2016 that China became the largest economy in the world.[19] The same World Bank comparison, placing China and the United States with shares of 16.4 percent and 16.3 percent of the world's total, also confirmed that by the late 2010s China's economy had clearly passed that of the EU, which, with its twenty-seven member states, had a combined size of 16 percent of

[17] In current US$, China's 1,472.3 billion versus Japan's 505.8 billion in 2020. https://data.worldbank.org/indicator/NY.GDP.MKTP.CD

[18] Comparisons based on data from https://data.worldbank.org/indicator/NY.GDP.MKTP.CD

[19] "How big is China's economy? Let the Big Mac decide," *The Economist*, July 15, 2020. http://bit.ly/3ZCXt2m

world GDP.[20] The same comparison put China's economy size at four times that of Japan. On a per capita basis, China was still far behind however, at only a quarter of the United States and a third of the EU.[21] Even in constant 2015 US dollar terms, China's per capita income in 2020 reached $10,358, a level that was *more than twice* what Deng Xiaoping had hoped for China thirty to fifty years into the twenty-first century. China's spectacular economic rise was truly unexpected.

Not all economists were as reserved as some of the Nobel laureates listed above. Some were much more optimistic. One notable example is the economic historian Angus Maddison, who reconstructed data sources to track long-term world economic growth. Maddison was also a strong believer in China's return to economic prominence in the world. Largely assuming a constant high growth rate, but with little account of underlying forces, he made both accurate and inaccurate predictions about China's economy in relation to other world economies. He was correct in his estimates of 2007 about China's economic ascendancy:

> The official (Chinese) GDP measure exaggerates growth. For 1978–2003, I found average annual GDP growth of 7.9 percent compared with the official 9.6 percent. On the other hand, the size of the Chinese economy is greatly understated, if exchange rates are used to compare performance. With a purchasing power parity converter, China's GDP in 2003 was 74 percent of that in the United States and more than twice as big as Japan. By 2015, on rather conservative assumptions, China should have resumed its position as the number one economy. By 2030, it will represent 23 percent of the world economy, compared with less than 5 percent in 1978.[22]

His predictions, while rather accurate, did not differ too much from those who failed to make the correct prediction, in that he made the same conservative mistake in predicting a much slower growth rate:

> It is likely that the catch-up process will continue in the next quarter century, but it would be unrealistic to assume the future growth trajectory will be as fast as in 1978–2003. . . . The pace of Chinese progress will slacken as it gets nearer to the technological frontier. I have assumed that per capita income will grow at an average rate of 4.5 percent a year between 2003 to 2030, but that the rate of advance will taper off over the period. Specifically, I assume a rate of 5.6 percent a year to 2010, 4.6 percent between 2010 and 2020 and a little more than 3.6 percent a year between 2020 and 2030.[23]

We now know what happened between 2003 and 2010, and between 2010 and 2020. Even the optimistic and prescient Maddison missed in his

[20] Measured in Purchasing Power Standards (PPS).
[21] Eurostat News Release 84/2020, May 19, 2020. https://bit.ly/3t2m83V
[22] Maddison, 2007, 14. [23] Maddison 2007, 20.

estimates for both periods, by a very large margin. China's economy grew nearly twice as fast as he predicted in 2007 for the period between 2003 and 2010, and by more than 50 percent for the period between 2010 and 2020.[24] Unlike the Nobel laureates who were tasked with predicting China's economy in the distant future, Maddison, an economic historian specializing in long-term economic growth, made his prediction for the immediate future, right in the middle of the process, but he also got it wrong.[25]

Touching an Elephant: What Did China Do Right?

How could generations of China's leaders, as well as many of the world's most renowned economists, including the most enthusiastic, fail to anticipate fully the rapid rise of the Chinese economy?

To begin with, telling the story of China's material ascendance could be compared with the fabled parable of the blind men touching an elephant. China's economic success story resembles a gigantic elephant, one roaming through domestic and global terrains. As the parable goes, many parts of the elephant can be touched; but each story, although factual, only contains part of the whole picture. An attempt to offer a full description is likely to be futile. The size and the complexity of the Chinese economy, the variations within such a large country, and changes in the domestic and international environments over the decades deny an easy and comprehensive portrait.

Yet the size and the complexity of this elephant have not deterred the brave men and women who have tried to touch it, to make sense of this gigantic story. As the most significant economic story in the last century, and one of the few in the last millennium, there is no shortage of scholarly investigation and punditry. Models have been created and schools established. A copious body of literature already exists on this remarkable chapter of human history, a chapter that transformed the lives of more than one-fifth of humanity in a short four decades. Much more will no doubt be written. The "rise of China" is a topic that will no doubt be explored continuously for decades and beyond.

[24] Calculated based on the GDP purchasing power parity (PPP; current international $). China's economy grew by 11.51 percent and 7.13 percent annually for these two periods. https://data.worldbank.org/indicator/NY.GDP.MKTP.PP.CD?locations=CN

[25] Projecting China's economic growth was such an arbitrary exercise that in 2020 a leading economics consultancy in the UK advanced its timing for China to surpass the US economy by five years, with just a one-year time difference, attributing the change to the COVID-19 pandemic that year. Tax Axelrod, "China expected to surpass US economy in 2028: analysis," *The Hill*, Dec. 26, 2020. https://bit.ly/3ro2Wxk

With few exceptions, and understandably, interpreting China's ascendance often starts at the head of the elephant. Detailed accounts and attributions are abundant on how the reforms were designed and growth was led by the government and its advisers.[26] China's economic transformation began and unfolded under the banner of "reform and opening up." The most consequential transformation was no doubt the dismantling of the planned economy system under socialism and reestablishing a market-based economic system. Studies of China's transformation therefore have overwhelmingly centered on reforms, and in particular, on the prominent roles of two seemingly contrasting institutions: state and market.

The state-centered narratives focus on China's political leadership, on the design and implementation of reform blueprints. They credit the Chinese government with following a gradualist reform strategy, in contrast to the "shock therapy" used in many other former socialist economies, an approach that led to widespread economic misery, social discontent, and political chaos.[27] Such narratives also point to the government's role in setting up Special Economic Zones, attracting foreign capital investment, promoting an export-oriented growth model, reforming state-owned enterprises while maintaining strong state ownership, control, and regulations, and for designing explicit industrial policies. As China's economic dominance increased, such narratives, which the economist Yingyi Qian labels as "the School of Chinese Characteristics,"[28] have gained more currency.

In contrast to this "Chinese uniqueness" narrative, an alternative and common narrative favors the "universal principles" for a market economy and for economic growth.[29] Instead of government intervention and control, this narrative advocates the central role of the market, rather than that of the government. After all, the institutional goal of China's reforms was to establish a market economy. China has ascended economically simply because it followed the "universal principles" of the market: privatization of state enterprises, attracting foreign investment, deregulation, trade liberalization, protecting property rights.[30] In sum, China's successes do not depart in general from the prescriptions of the so-called Washington Consensus.

The market, however, does not exist in a political or social vacuum. Nor does state or political power. Market and state could simply be seen as two faces of the same elephant head. The market, as argued by the classic work of Karl Polanyi, is embedded in or even created and

[26] See, for instance, J. Wu 2005; Brandt and Rawski 2008; Peng and Chen 2008; and Naughton 2013; see also Gewirtz 2017.
[27] Shirk 1993; Walder 2000; Weber 2021. [28] Qian 2017, chap. 1. [29] Ibid.
[30] Williamson 2000.

protected by the state.[31] China's transformation from a socialist planned economy to a market-based economy indeed serves as a fantastic example of how the state initiated and navigated a complicated and often painful process.

Neither the state nor the market is static over time; they are embedded in each other. As markets are recreated and developed, the role of the state is also transformed. These two institutional forces therefore coevolve and coadapt. Such an interactive and balanced approach was adopted in studies of rising income inequality over two decades ago, and it is also the approach of a more recent interpretation of China's economic growth, of how China "escaped poverty."[32] Rather than focusing on design and theoretical formulations, the latter study concludes that "China escaped the poverty trap by constructing a set of underlying conditions that focused on an adaptive, bottom-up search *within* the state for localized solutions."[33]

The large body of institutional analyses focusing on reforms, while informative and important, tend to leave little space for changes experienced by the common people and forces at the basis of society that made the changes possible. China was successful in its gradualist reform approach largely because its economy continued to grow, and it eventually grew "out of the plan."[34] Growth delivered continued improvements in the population's standard of living. Improvements in living standards in turn generated support for sustained, though often painful, reform efforts.

The new and growing segment of the economy was market-based. Both in employment and in economic output, the market-based sector caught up and further surpassed the planned economy sector. A new economic system was born. "China's reforms were gradual, " notes a study of gradualist reform strategies, "not merely in the matter of pace but also in moving from the margins of the old industrial system toward its core. Unleashing a dynamic of growth and reindustrialization, gradual marketization eventually transformed the whole political economy while the state kept control over the commanding heights."[35]

As this book shall document, much of the initial growth that delivered improvements in living standards, from diet and clothing to housing, came from the non-state sector, in particular from the vast Chinese countryside. Similarly, that reindustrialization also sprung up from the Chinese countryside. Moreover, it was the massive migration of the rural

[31] Polanyi 1980. [32] Zhou 2000; Ang 2016, 17. [33] Ang 2016, 17.
[34] Naughton 1996. [35] Weber 2021, 126.

population into cities that propelled and defined the fastest economic growth decade, the 2000s.

In contrast to the vast literature that has already been devoted to reforms or institutional changes, this book focuses on growth. It is not a book about designs or reforms. Rather, it is about outcomes and processes. This book profiles China's age of abundance by documenting how its population's living standards improved. It also offers an account of the underlying forces and the process of this material ascendance. The book pays particular attention to two factors suggested as answers to the question "What did China do right?": initial historical conditions and contemporary constraints.[36] It traces China's growth to some of its origins, highlights the unique historical conditions and junctures, and offers an interpretation of the underlying forces. In doing so, this book joins studies that attempt to understand this chapter of Chinese history by showcasing "how development actually happen[ed]."[37] It is "less about why reform worked and more about how reforms worked." Just as observed by Yingyi Qian, China's success "is less about the goal of reform than the reform process itself."[38]

In doing so, this book is just another blind person's report on touching the elephant. Rather than starting from the elephant's head or its shoulders, though, this account starts from the foot: the Chinese population. It is the population who created "the China miracle" and formed the foundation of this gigantic elephant. The population defined here is not the political leaders or economists who resided in Beijing or the academics who advised the Chinese leaders from Washington DC to Geneva. It is the ordinary Chinese people, especially those in the countryside, who were the majority of the country's population at the start of China's economic ascendance.

Abundance

Tracing Abundance: From an Egg Every Other Week to One Every Other Day

China's age of abundance began with the most basic necessity in life: food.

In the spring of 1972, a four-year-old boy was running away from his grandmother with a boiled egg in hand. At that young age, the boy already knew how precious an egg was in comparison to everything else he was fed and how rare it was for such an item to show up on the writing desk, which

[36] Qian 2017, 7. [37] Ang 2016, xii. [38] Qian 2017, 7.

was also used as a dining table in their cramped apartment with three generations co-residing. He snatched it without hesitation. To stop the boy, his grandma shouted, "It is not an egg, it is not an egg, it is an egg from a dog!" No matter. The boy quickly swallowed the egg down, savoring it with mischief and great satisfaction. The egg, he later learned, was a special nutritional supplement allocation for his father, who had fallen ill with a liver disease due to poor working conditions in his lab. His father had an important job few others in the country had: he was participating in making China's first computer circuit boards, at what was then one of China's top technical universities. The egg came from the university's hospital. To make sure his father could consume the daily allowance of an egg, the boy's grandma had carefully hidden an egg away from the boy every day. She was apparently not so successful on that day.[39]

The boy's family belonged to a lucky and privileged group in Chinese society at that time. An egg for breakfast was an enviable luxury. The officially reported number of eggs consumed in 1970 was only 1.32 kg per person per year.[40] Real consumption of eggs could have been slightly higher than this – but not much higher – as some households, in particular those in the countryside, raised chickens themselves. By 1978, government-published statistics showed that annual egg consumption had increased to 1.97 kg per person. At such a level, the average Chinese consumed fewer than 1 egg *per week*.[41]

Eggs were by no means the only food items in short supply. Daily consumption of food certainly corresponded to China's low income level in the late 1970s. According to official reports, the amount of pork available to the average Chinese was less than 8 kg per year, or about 140 g *per week*. Poultry was less than half a kg per capita *per year*. Again, some rural families were allowed to raise a pig or two and some poultry, but that was only in some parts of China, and they were often subject to restrictions by the rural collective. One careful examination of official records concluded that the Chinese diet was "monotonous and barely adequate," and "saw no changes between 1957 and 1977."[42] After more than two decades into the socialist planned economy, at 195.46 kg, grain consumption per person in 1978 was even lower than the level reported for 1957.

[39] This story was retold by the boy to his own son in the year 2020 when his son refused to eat an egg. By then the boy who had run away with the egg was already a distinguished scholar and an administrator in one of China's best universities, having grown up during China's age of abundance and having studied overseas.

[40] SYB 1994, table 9–3. This amount is estimated to include rural households' self-consumed products. See Chapter 3.

[41] SYB 1994, table 9–3. [42] Smil 1986, 26.

In 1978, the nationwide per capita annual consumption of pork, the most commonly consumed meat, was only 7.67 kg, slightly over 0.5 kg per person *per month*.

By the mid-2010s, the average urban resident in China consumed nearly 11 kg of eggs per year, compared with 1.32 kg over four decades ago. Egg consumption rose to 220 eggs per person per year, more than one egg every other day. Even in rural China, at 8.5 kg per person in 2016, consumption of eggs was also nearly one egg every other day on average. These numbers do not include eggs from chickens raised by farming households as those eggs are not reported in government statistics. Rural households have more grain and other feeding materials and also more freedom to raise their own chickens than in the days of collective farming. By the end of China's four-decade economic boom, eating an egg was no longer a rarity and delicacy. The same improvements were realized in other items in people's diets: pork, poultry, cooking oil, sugar, vegetables, and fruit.

In contrast to the dazzling portrayals of China's skyrocketing economic output, this study traces China's rise to material abundance and changes in the population's standard of living by looking at consumption. This account demonstrates how their lives changed. Using measures such as egg consumption is a much more concrete and meaningful way to document changes in the standard of living than the commonly used measure of income. While abstract and simple to use for comparison across time and space, the most commonly used measure of economic growth, GDP per capita, conveys little in terms of how people live their lives.

Years from now, an average income number may mean little for those looking back to get a sense of how people lived, except for those who rely on such a measure to make the most general statements about the economy. Moreover, this monetary measure can easily underestimate or distort improvements in the standard of living. As noted by Robert Gordon, who documented US economic growth with consumption data, GDP per capita has two basic flaws in representing changes in the standard of living.[43]

First, GDP omits many dimensions important to people's living standards, as it only includes goods and services exchanged in markets. The measure does not consider the value of nonmarket activities. The standard of living improves when home production is included, when the value of leisure time increases, and the unpleasantness of work decreases. But such improvements are not captured in the quantity and quality of goods and services purchased on the market.

[43] Gordon 2016.

Second, even for the value of market-exchanged activities and services, the use of "constant price" to adjust for inflation can actually overstate the effect of price increases, therefore underrepresenting improvements in the standard of living. One way of illustrating this flaw is the increased utility of products such as: televisions, air conditioners, and automobiles. The utility of these products increases over time as the quality of these products increases and the price falls.

For China, there is a third reason. China began its ascendance to material abundance under a planned economy system. The stratospheric rise of per capita income in the past four decades, by nearly 25 times, started from a very low base of less than $450 in 1980 (constant 2015 US$). Monetary income under the planned economy regime, however, is hardly a reliable measure to reflect fully the standard of living. Prices were set administratively, affecting directly monetary national accounting of income.

The following examples illustrate how the reported income level could not be used directly to measure the standard of living in a planned economy. A national survey in 1981 of 8,715 urban households in forty-six cities, for instance, reported a per capita monthly income of 41.7 yuan, or 500 yuan per year, for urban China.[44] With the official exchange rate at the time of 2.52 yuan for each US dollar,[45] per capita income for urban Chinese was merely $16.55 per month, or slightly less than $200 per year.

Despite the material scarcity at the time, the average urban Chinese person was living far better than the low income level would suggest. The planned economy system came with virtually free healthcare and education, and a small amount of monetary income was enough to cover food and housing. The annual income of 500 yuan in 1981 could purchase about 1,500 kg of grain (enough to feed five or more people), or 240 kg of pork, or the same amount of eggs.[46] Set at about 1.5 percent of the income amount, the rent an average urban household paid in 1982 was only 0.59 yuan, or less than US$0.25 per month. Housing, in other words, was virtually free.[47] To compare with a market economy society, the share that an urban Chinese household paid out of their income for rent back in 1982 was only one-tenth the share the average US household spent on rent in 2013, or about one-ninth in 1940.[48] For industrial goods, however, the distortion was the reverse: a television set (a nine-inch black-and-white set, of uncertain quality) cost a person's entire yearly income, while a bicycle cost a third of annual per capita income.

[44] SYB 1981, table 11–13. Based on a survey of 8,716 households in forty-six Chinese cities at the time.
[45] www.ceicdata.com [46] Retail price data from SYB 1982, 417–18.
[47] SYB 1983, table 11–2. [48] Gordon 2016, 38.

To account for discrepancies between currency and its purchasing power, an alternative monetary measure is often used, known as purchasing power parity (PPP). Even this broad adjustment in currency remains problematic. For China, the earliest adjustment from the World Bank in 1990 inflated the Chinese yuan by 95 percent. This adjustment increases China's per capita income in 1990 from $729 to $1,424, and from $8,242 to $16,804 in 2019 (constant 2010 US$).[49] This adjustment from the World Bank, however, has remained fixed for three decades since 1990. A case could be easily made that the purchasing power of Chinese yuan in 1982 was more than twice the monetary income represented then, as suggested by the examples above. The purchasing power of the yuan for basic life necessities in 1982, food and shelter, could be much more than the 200 percent calculated, though less with respect to industrial goods such as a television set or a bicycle. From the standpoint of living standards, food and housing were much more important than a television. Similarly, as the Chinese economy transformed into a market economy, the gap between nominal currency and currency inflated by purchasing power would also decrease. Measures of consumption, therefore, are the most direct and more appropriate gauges for tracking changes in the standard of living.

China's "Cheap Labor"

Journalistic and scholiastic accounts often credit China's economic boom to its abundant and cheap labor. China indeed had a vast supply of labor, and the labor was cheap. The massive volume of hard-working cheap labor was a most crucial historical foundation for China's economic boom. There is no better indicator of China's prosperity than the improved living standards of this cheap labor. Yet, abundant and cheap as labor is, this simplistic account of "cheap labor" fails to appreciate the core qualities of this abundant labor, and it ignores the institutional arrangements that *made* this labor cheap.

This book shows that China had not just abundant and cheap labor, China had *good* labor, and the population were desperate and ready for change. As the following chapter (Chapter 2, Origins) documents, on the eve of China's reforms away from its socialist planned economy system in the late 1970s, the country's population had already achieved levels of health and literacy that were far higher than China income levels at the time would suggest.

With a per capita income level belonging solidly to low-income countries, by the 1970s China had already achieved health and education

[49] https://data.worldbank.org/indicator/NY.GDP.PCAP.PP.KD

levels easily rivaling the middle-income countries at the time. China had largely completed an epidemiological transition, drastically reducing deaths due to infectious diseases. In other words, China had undergone a "thermodynamic and physiological" transformation, a transformation that is the foundation for long-term economic growth, borrowing the theory from Robert Fogel, another Nobel Prize winner in economics.[50] Prior to its economic takeoff in the 1980s, China had already accumulated two crucial sources of capital: human capital, with prevalent literacy among its young population, and physiological capital, with much improved population health.[51] By the late 1970s, China had also largely completed its modern fertility decline, creating a time window for China to reap a demographic dividend later on.

This resourceful and abundant Chinese labor force was *made* cheap. It was made cheap by an institution erected during China's socialist planned economic days, prior to the economic boom, an institution that assigned the majority of the Chinese population to secondary citizenship status. Importantly, China's first socialist industrialization was designed to be built on the backs of the Chinese population, in particular, its vast rural population. That episode of the socialist experiment, while allowing China to industrialize rapidly for a short time period, created a one-country, two-systems social and economic arrangement. It sowed the seeds of China's original sin that has brought both economic prosperity and pain to Chinese society until this very day. The arrangement subjected China's vast rural population to severe economic and social disadvantages, a discriminatory system that first constrained Chinese farmers to the countryside, and then pushed them out of farming and into cities. This deep urban-rural divide, in addition to the healthy and literate population, provided the two fundamental conditions for Chinese ascendance to prosperity.

Paths to Prosperity

The path China has followed to prosperity is highly similar to that of other societies which underwent periods of rapid increase in their standard of living. Improvements in living standards begin with what people eat, wear, how they live, and what they have inside their homes

[50] Fogel 1994; 2004b.

[51] Fogel 2004b. This physiological capital differs from the so-called health capital, as noted by Fogel (645), "Although health capital presupposes physiological capital, it does not deal with it explicitly. Health capital assumes the health stock that each individual is born with and considers how investment in health care can reduce the rate of depreciation in that stock. It does not address why some people have a greater initial stock than others, and it does not recognize the relationship between the size of the initial stock and its rate of depreciation."

(Chapter 3, Abundance). As in other societies, the first decade of China's ascendance to abundance saw rapid improvements in diet and clothing. These changes were followed in its second decade, the 1990s, by purchases of household appliances. The next two decades subsequently saw a vast increase in housing ownership, followed by a rise in leisure activities such as tourism. By the late 2000s, China had become a country with among the highest home ownership in the world. When Deng Xiaoping said China could allow 10 or 15 million emigrants to the United States during his trip there in 1979, as he countered criticism that China restricted its citizens' movement,[52] he could hardly have imagined that ten years after his death 35 million Chinese traveled overseas in a single year. Even more remarkable was that twenty years after his death, over 135 million overseas trips were made each year, for tourism, business, and study. Nearly 3 million of these travelers visited the United States in a single year.[53]

Among the many forces that led to the rise as well as the end of China's age of abundance is China's population, notably China's rural population. At the start of the journey, the rural population made up 80 percent of China's total population. Tracing improvements in the standard of living in China therefore needs to focus first on what happened to their lives. No understanding of "the China miracle" is possible without first appreciating how the overwhelming majority of the population experienced it. Rural Chinese lived in a socially divided society that *made* their labor cheap. It has been through their hard work and ingenuity that the living standards of all Chinese, including their own, have improved. They were not "lifted" out of poverty. They broke out of poverty with their bare hands and under a social arrangement that discriminated against them. They made the China miracle a reality.

In two successive stages, the Chinese rural population completed China's industrialization with urbanization, achieving China's material abundance (Chapter 4, Ascendance). The first phase, leaving farming but not the land began in the late 1970s, before the start of urban reforms. Freed from the previous two decades of mandatory collective farming under the commune system, farmers in China's countryside quickly increased food supplies for all Chinese. It was with their output that per capita grain consumption for all Chinese rose by nearly 30 percent in just five years between 1978 and 1983. Also in those five years, per capita

[52] Vogel 2011, 342.
[53] www.statista.com/statistics/214813/number-of-visitors-to-the-us-from-china/. Also see Chapter 3 for more detailed discussions.

consumption of eggs increased by 50 percent, pork by 61 percent, vegetable oil by 150 percent, and poultry by more than 250 percent.

This rural labor force then quickly shifted away from farming and in turn launched China's second industrial revolution. The number of rural industrial firms, otherwise known as township and village enterprises (TVEs), rose eightfold, from 1.52 million to 12.22 million between 1978 and 1985, before doubling to 25 million a decade later. By then, these rural firms already employed more than 150 million people, one in three of the entire rural labor force. By the early 1990s, when the majority of China's state-owned firms were mired in troubles, output from these rural firms generated 40 percent of China's total industrial growth and also 40 percent of China's total export value, spearheading the country's rising export-oriented economy. These rural firms, large in number and in variety, produced not only goods but also millions of entrepreneurs for China's future capitalist growth.

Following this first phase of industrialization, characterized by industrialization in situ, came the second phase of urbanization. Beginning in the mid-1980s, China's vast rural population started to move from the countryside to the cities as hard-working laborers, contributing to and also paying for the creation of wealth, now evident in Chinese cities. Migration to cities edged up initially from less than 50 million in the early 1980s to around only 70 million in the mid-1990s. Removal of food rationing in cities, thanks to increased output produced by the rural population, and rising demand in cities for construction and manufacturing led to the boom of rural migrants in Chinese cities. After producing for domestic needs as well as for export to the world market in the Chinese countryside, China's rural labor force moved away from their places of origin to build up Chinese cities, roads, bridges, railways, and airports. In the second half of the 1990s, the number of rural migrants doubled to nearly 140 million, before jumping up again in the decade following to 221 million.

This narrative, that China's rural population drove China's ascendance to prosperity, is not the first. The rise in agricultural productivity, the importance of rural township and village industries, and rural migrants to cities have been extensively analyzed.[54] The arguments in this book are inspired in particular by the work of two scholars. One of the first and most extensive, was Jean Oi's *Rural China Takes Off: Institutional Foundations of Economic Reforms*, a book documenting the roles of local

[54] As in several general books on China's reforms and growth, such as Naughton 1996, Naughton 2006, and Brandt and Rawski 2008, as well as books that examine these processes, in particular, Oi 1999, Y. Huang 2008, Solinger 1999, and numerous scholarly articles.

governments in economic transformation in rural China.[55] The other, a seminal work that places rural China forcefully at the center of China's economic miracle, was Yasheng Huang's *Capitalism with Chinese Characteristics: Entrepreneurship and the State*.[56] Huang's book showcases the critical roles of rural industries in China's economic transformation. That book and his subsequent writing serve as essential starting points in tracing China's economic growth and transformation.[57] New materials in this book collaborate and extend his arguments.

Accelerating rural out-migration since the early 1990s and large-scale urbanization in the 2000s are among the most defining features of China's age of abundance. More than rural industries, rural to urban migration and urbanization have received continued scholarly scrutiny and media exposure. Often, however, rural industrialization and migration are treated as if they were two separate processes: one in the countryside and the other in the city, both driven by the same force, China's surplus labor.

Building on earlier analyses, this book treats rural industries and rural migration to cities as two connected phases in the same process of China's second industrialization: industrialization with urbanization. In contrast to the industrialization during China's socialist planned economy era, an industrialization that transformed the economy but kept the majority of the population in the countryside, this second industrialization thoroughly industrialized the country and urbanized the population.

The story of China's second industrialization, which led the country to its material abundance, was not just an economic one. It was social as well as political. It is far more than just a story of "surplus labor" or a "large supply of cheap labor." China's economic transformation was characterized as a process of "growing out of the plan."[58] This growth occurred first and foremost in rural China, with increased agricultural productivity, with rural industries, and eventually by the vast exodus of rural labor moving to cities. This vast rural migrant labor force built China as well as the world economy. For both phases, the socialist segregation regime served as the most important institutional framework. The regime first confined industrialization to the countryside, making rural labor "surplus." Then, with its discriminatory arrangements, the regime made rural migrant Chinese labor cheap in Chinese cities.

Ascendance to material prosperity consequently was not equally or fairly shared by all Chinese citizens. Rather the paths they took and

[55] Oi 1999. [56] Y. Huang 2008. [57] Y. Huang 2012. [58] Naughton 1996.

the dividends they shared depended upon the person's social status, specifically their location in the urban-rural designation.[59] For most Chinese of rural-origin, their path to wealth was through their hard labor, labor *made cheap* in part because of their rural status. For the more privileged urban residents, their special and protected status allowed them to benefit exclusively from a historical form of wealth creation: the privatization of urban housing. Housing reforms and real estate price increases accompanied the largest wealth creation and distribution in modern Chinese history. Yet this opportunity was mostly reserved for those with an urban household registration status, especially in large cities where real estate values shot up most rapidly. There were, in other words, two paths to prosperity (Chapter 5, Two Paths).

China's ascendance to abundance began among the masses living in the Chinese countryside. The masses who began and subsequently drove China's economic growth were at the margins of society. The history narrated in this book echoes broadly the observations of the two prescient economists, Ronald Coase and Ning Wang, the former also a Nobel Prize winner in economics. For them, China's economic success began at the margins of the socialist planned economy. Chinese leaders and many others were taken aback by the pace of change in China. As Coase and Wang wrote: "No one could possibly have foreseen such a sea-change in the Chinese economy as occurred in the first decade of reform."[60] China's transition to capitalism was an economic success, credited largely to what Coase and Wang singled out as "four marginal revolutions":

> The four marginal revolutions – enacted by actors marginalized in Mao's socialist economy – quickly gave birth to a dynamic private sector in China, freeing 800 million peasants from the state, allowing almost 20 million "returned youth" in the cities to set up their own businesses, and creating a few spots for foreign and domestic entrepreneurs to flourish and inadvertently showcase the dynamism.
>
> China would probably have stayed on the intended path to socialism were it not for the marginal revolutions that reintroduced private entrepreneurship to the economy. Initially, private farming, rural industrialization, and the return of the "individual economy" in cities were all invariably treated with open hostility and even criminalized, as in the case of private farming.[61]

[59] In the Chinese household registration system, residents are actually differentiated as "non agricultural" or "agricultural." The urban versus rural designation here corresponds to that official differentiation (see, for instance, T. Cheng and Selden 1994; Chan 1994; F.-L. Wang 2005; and Whyte 2010).

[60] Coase and Wang 2012, 67.

[61] Ibid., 65.

Organization, Research, and Data Sources

The seven chapters in this book are grouped into three sections. The first and second chapters (Chapter 1, "Surprise" and Chapter 2, "Origins") introduce and provide background to this remarkable chapter of human history. The middle section's three chapters document this age of abundance with reference to consumption changes (Chapter 3, "Abundance"), and examine the driving forces of this growth (Chapter 4, "Ascendance," Chapter 5, "Two Paths"). In the third and final section, Chapter 6 (Surplus) combines changes in both consumption and income with an economic lifecycle approach to illustrate how the age of abundance is approaching an end and the accompanying challenges this will bring.

The last chapter (Chapter 7, "Aftermath") revisits the historical conjunctures and conditions that made China's age of abundance possible. Chapter 7 also highlights several headwinds China faces as it moves beyond the historical phase of material abundance. Chief among these headwinds are the diminishing exploitable labor force, new forms of inequality, accelerating population aging with Chinese characteristics, and a rebirth of state monopoly. Decades of migration and urbanization have by and large exhausted the continued supply of cheap and exploitable labor from the Chinese countryside, while hundreds of millions of China's new urban residents are yet to receive the same social benefits as the old ones. Children of first-generation rural migrants are either unable or unwilling to continue the lives of their parents' and grandparents' generations. This, along with other historical opportunities that led to China's age of abundance, is no longer replicable. The strong headwinds are inevitable and irreversible.

Research for this book draws from multiple data sources, made possible by their broader availability over time. Over the last four decades, along with China's material boom, there has also been a boom in statistical data, which allows for a construction of China's ascendance to material prosperity. These sources include mostly, though not exclusively, China Statistical Yearbooks, specialty statistical compilations, census tabulations, and survey data.

One legacy of China's pre-abundance era was the statistical data the government collected and maintained. Such a statistical system had both its utilities and deficiencies. On the one hand, and under the centrally planned economy system, most production and consumption goods were under the state plan and subject to state pricing and procurement. The government was able to collect data via a reporting system on the main economic activities, from labor force participation to investment as well as economic output. At the same time, the very same system also bred corruption and abuse and was highly susceptible to deliberate political manipulation and distortion. Partners in the planned economy system, from factory managers to government officials, had incentives to report good news and to hide bad news and hoard goods. False reporting and statistical manipulation were rampant when political pressure was too high, as was the case during the disastrous Great Leap Forward campaign. Grain output was inflated by nearly 100 percent and such misinformation contributed to the worst famine in Chinese history.

In contrast to China's socialist years under Mao, when collected statistical information had been kept only in the hands of government planners, reporting-based statistics were made public with annual updates soon after China's economic transition from the planned economic system began. Systematic statistics over a relatively long time period, together with data from other sources, allow for cross-checking of data reliability. These systematic statistics from the annual yearbooks are used extensively throughout this book. In addition to national statistical yearbooks and census tabulations, various government ministries publish their own statistical yearbooks. These more specialized government-published statistics supplement the national statistical yearbooks. This book uses also statistics from these specialized publications, especially in health, birth control, and education.

Demographic data based on population censuses are less systematic. Unlike the regular government statistics collected and kept during the planned economy years, China did not have regular population censuses until 1990, when the census became a regular, decadal, affair. In contrast, the earlier censuses were carried out on an ad hoc basis, following major political or social upheavals. China conducted its first census under the Communist government in 1953, following a successful stabilization of the national economy and nearing the end of the Korean War. That census provided the first full account of the population for modern China. The next census followed some eleven years later, in 1964, following the disastrous Great Leap famine, which resulted in a sharp rise in mortality and fall in fertility, leading to a net population loss in 1960. That census allowed the government to have a new set of demographic information more than ten years after the previous census and after the devastating famine. Thereafter, China had to wait nearly two decades for its next census, in 1982. The decade-long Cultural Revolution from 1966 to 1976 disrupted all aspects of economic and social life, including conducting a population census. As with the two previous censuses, the census in 1982 was also conducted when the country emerged from war or domestic distress. The 1982 census was regarded as the first modern census in Chinese history because of its use of computers to compile, store, and process individual records. Beginning in 1990, China has been conducting decennial population censuses. Between censuses, an intercensal population survey of 1/100 of the population is also conducted. Data from population censuses and large-scale intercensal surveys supply basic and verifiable information on changes in such measures as residential distribution, education, employment, and even housing.

An entirely new and rich data source emerged as China's age of abundance began. This was data based on surveys. In the early 1980s, survey research methods were introduced into the data collection enterprise, utilizing probability sampling designs. Unlike the statistical reporting system during the planned economy era, both rigid and subject to political manipulation, well-designed surveys provided much more detailed and timely information. In contrast to statistics collected via the reporting system dating from the planned economy days, household income and expenditure surveys supply rich information on household consumption changes. Statistics based on those household surveys provide the bulk of materials in this book, which uses consumption data as the primary benchmark to measure changes in the population's standard of living. In addition to data from the annual household income and expenditure survey, this book also uses other sources based on government-conducted surveys: health and nutritional surveys, surveys of migrants, and survey data collected by social science researchers.

Of course, none of these data sources can be taken at face value. Limitations and problems exist in each of them. Some statistics are published sporadically, lacking consistency. Items reported differ, and so do units or measures used. Data from household surveys tend to exclude households at the very high end of the income scale as well as miss income from unofficial sources. Yet, consumption data based on household surveys, with their imperfections, are less likely to be subject to misreporting, especially when it comes to items such as household appliances, computers and automobiles, and ownership of residential property. Working through these statistics sometimes feels like walking through a maze or resembles detective work. In the end, however, the availability of such a vast amount of rich data has allowed me to document and examine China's age of abundance. Together, these materials allow a partial portrayal of the elephant, the elephant of China's transition from material scarcity to abundance and prosperity.

2 Origins

In the fall of 1982, only a few months after China conducted its first population census after Mao's death, eighteen long years since the previous one, a World Bank study team arrived in Beijing for a four-week study. The team produced a comprehensive report, *The Health Sector in China*. The first of its kind, the team's report was shared with the World Health Organization (WHO) in a seminar chaired by no other than the then director-general, Dr. Halfdan Mahler. Earlier versions of the report were also shared with the Chinese government, revised, and made public in April 1984.[1]

The report confirmed what the Chinese government and the outside world already knew, that China had undergone a period of unusually rapid population growth. Between 1953 – when China had conducted its first population census after the founding of the People's Republic in 1949 – and 1982, China's population grew by 73 percent, from 588 million to slightly over 1 billion, an annual rate of 1.9 percent for the 29-year interval. At such a rate, the size of the population would double again, to over 2 billion people, by the early twenty-first century.

The World Bank's report on China's population and health also brought other news, much of it encouraging and even to be admired. Most important was how, in just three decades, even with a large segment of the population still living at subsistence level, and with notable regional disparities, overall health had improved markedly for all Chinese people. Between 1950 and 1982, life expectancy at birth increased from 32 years to 69 years, making China's overall health level nearly comparable to that of the richest countries at the time. By the early 1980s, life expectancy at birth in China was "only about six years less than in the industrialized market economies."[2] Later studies with more abundant demographic sources would report that life expectancy at the start of the period was likely to be higher than 32 years, but the rapid increase between 1949 and 1982 was not in dispute. The rapid pace of life expectancy extension,

[1] World Bank 1984. [2] Ibid., viii.

rising by about 1.5 years per annum, was unmatched by any comparably sized population in world history, as assessed at about the same time by two distinguished demographers.[3]

This rapid health improvement was not to be found in low-income societies elsewhere. Five years prior to the World Bank's report, with virtually no data available, a twenty-three-year-old Harvard graduate student undertook an ambitious examination of living standards in China. After reviewing the available sources on population, food supply, literacy, women's status, and economic inequality, Nicholas Eberstadt, later a prolific and preeminent scholar of population and political economy, concluded that:

> "Mao did not eliminate what we might think of as poverty in China; even if income were distributed virtually evenly, China's people would be comparatively poor by international standards. But Mao did try to set a floor below which no Chinese would sink, and to his eternal credit, within a generation he dramatically reduced the incidence of destitution in a land where wretched poverty had been the accepted lot of the lower classes for three thousand years."[4]

In the same monograph on China's poverty, Eberstadt also observed that "Mao's 'social experiment' was a limited, though I believe an important, success, but it was not a solution. Mao did not bequeath the world a faultless 'model' for the eradication of poverty; what he left behind was a wealth of clever policies and embarrassing mistakes from which his nation and others can learn, if they choose to."[5]

While acknowledging the impressive improvements in health, the same World Bank report also noted ongoing substantial undernutrition, especially among China's large rural population. As the report summarizes, "In urban areas, malnutrition has been substantially reduced and can no longer be considered an important problem. Many children in rural areas, by contrast, continue to suffer moderate-to-serious malnutrition." The report cites a 1979 survey of sixteen provinces that showed an estimated 12.7 percent of seven-year-old rural boys having stunted growth, a share that was as high as 37 percent in the province of Sichuan. The urban-rural divide was vast and glaring: in urban areas only 2.6 percent of children were found to be stunted.[6]

These mixed legacies on the eve of China's age of abundance – reduced but still prevalent poverty, improved health, and extended literacy – laid the foundation for China's economic takeoff in the years to follow. China already had a population that had grown rapidly and was young, and a population that was in general healthy and literate. Narratives of

[3] Banister and Preston 1981; Banister 1987. [4] Eberstadt 1979, 27. [5] Ibid., 31.
[6] World Bank 1984, viii.

China's economic growth often attributes it to China's cheap labor. China's young and vast labor pool, however, was not just cheap. It was quality labor: healthy, literate, and eager to work hard to improve living standards. China had *good* labor.

Moreover, this labor was *made* cheap. Population health and literacy improved at the same time when a new form of social division was created. As China pursued its industrialization strategy under the socialist planned economy order that prioritized the development of heavy industry at all costs, China's vast rural population shouldered much of the cost. An outlier in the world's history of economic development, China was able to engineer a rapid industrialization without the attendant urbanization. China's population was divided and segregated by residential status: urban (non-agricultural) and rural (agricultural). The separation led to a "one-country, two systems" institutional arrangement,[7] an arrangement that has continued to plague China socially.

The combined legacies of a healthy and largely literate population, with the overall majority designated as second-class citizens in their own country, and a population desperate to improve its livelihood, are the very origins of China's historical economic boom and material prosperity. Striving to improve their own lives, China's people, in particular, the rural population who accounted for 80 percent of the total population at the start of China's economic takeoff, were the force that propelled China to its age of abundance. This population produced for itself and manufactured for the world. This good labor built China into prosperity. In the absence of this good labor, the boom would never have occurred.

A Healthy Nation

China's rapid improvement in its population health level was unprecedented both in China and around the world. Within a mere three decades, over one-fifth of humanity transformed from a poverty- and illness-stricken people to a healthy population, creating the health conditions for the great wealth generation that would be realized.

The pace of health improvement in China was unparalleled among the world's large countries. A comparison with a select group of countries proves this point (Figure 2.1). It took nearly a century, from 1860 to 1960, for the three leading high-income countries of the world, England, France, and the United States, to realize an increase in live expectancy from around 40 years to 70 years. For Japan, a latecomer but a leader in Asia, it took less time, only about 55 years, from 1910 to 1965. For China,

[7] Whyte 2010.

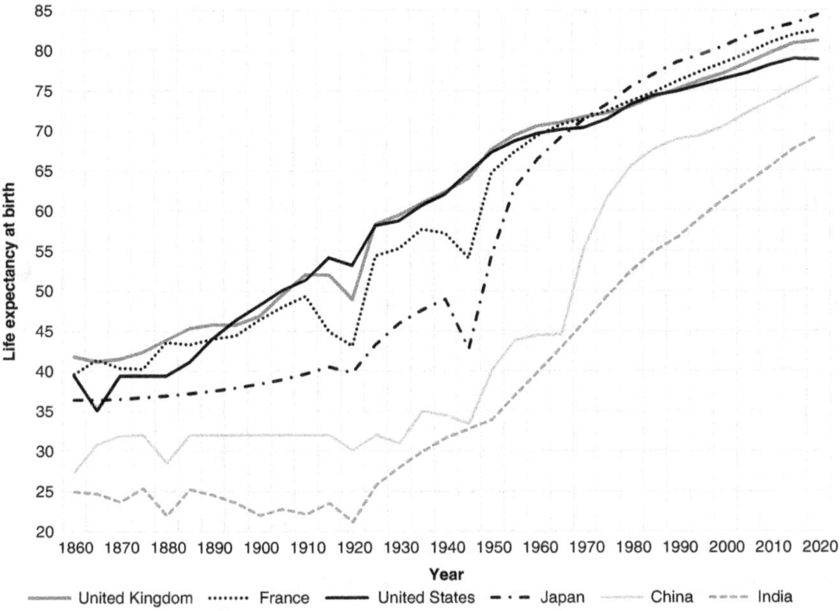

Figure 2.1 Comparison of life expectancy improvements, China and selected countries
Source: www.statista.com/statistics/

the journey took only about 50 years, from 1950 to 2000. Moreover, most of the improvement in China took place in just 15 years, between 1965 and 1980, when life expectancy at birth increased more than 20 years, from 44.5 to 65.5 years. China's largest neighboring country, India, which also saw fast mortality decline after 1950, took 30 years to gain 18.5 years in life expectancy. In 1980, life expectancy in India was 12 years below that in China (Figure 2.1).

Rapid mortality decline has profound economic and social implications. Lower infant and child mortality reduces physiological waste for women. Reduced childhood illness enhances children's cognitive abilities to learn, as well as leading to better health status later in life. Mortality decline in China prior to 1980 also had another important consequence: rapid population growth for the world's largest nation. In contrast to a popular myth that China's rapid population growth was the outcome of its high birth rate, it was *not* the long-claimed high fecundity and high fertility of the Chinese population but its world record-setting speed of rapid mortality decline that was chiefly and directly responsible for the rapid population growth.[8] In other words, rapid mortality decline led to both a healthier as well as a larger population, two critical factors in China's dawning economic transformation.

Public Health on the Margins of Subsistence

What drove the rapid improvement in population health during the period preceding China's economic boom was, however, not increased food supply or nutritional intake. Increased food supply did play an indispensable role in feeding a population that almost doubled in size. But its role was mostly through more equitable distribution than increased supply per person. As the next chapter will show, calculated on a per capita basis, food supply and nutritional intake for the population barely improved for nearly three decades, until the early 1980s.

Nevertheless, to the extent that a more equitable distribution of food contributed to lower mortality, a mortality-reducing role was achieved in part by relieving the pressures on poor families to kill or to neglect their female offspring. For instance, the incidence of excess female mortality declined precipitously. Such an excess mortality was estimated, based on Chinese census data, to be at over 15 percent for birth cohorts of the 1930s and the early 1940s, and over 10 percent in the late 1940s. By the 1970s, it dropped to not far above 2 percent.[9]

Rather than increased food supply, it was largely organized public health efforts that led to the rapid improvements in population health. This was noted in the World Bank report:

> The rapid improvement in population health, instead, can be easily traced and credited mostly to the massive public health efforts, chiefly immunization, infectious disease prevention and control, and environmental sanitation. Although China's overall living standards have substantially improved during the period since 1949 – indeed, they have improved somewhat more rapidly than have living standards in developing countries generally – it is important to emphasize that general improvements in living standards alone can account for only a fraction of China's achievements in health.[10]

Data made available since the World Bank study nearly four decades ago now offer a fuller picture of the process of China's historical mortality decline. Public health programs in China did not begin with the socialist era.[11] Yet it was not until the 1950s when wars had ended and a socialist government was in place that public health could be implemented

[8] J. Lee, Campbell, and Wang 2002.

[9] Coale and Banister 1996; J. Lee and Wang 1999.

[10] World Bank 1984, 4.

[11] Campbell 1997; Rogaski 2014; Baum 2020.

nationwide. China's socialist government launched public health campaigns and began establishing a public health infrastructure soon after it came to power in 1949. In 1951, the first patriotic health campaign was launched. Such campaigns were carried out on average four to five times per year for the next three decades. One memorable episode was the 1956 campaign to eradicate pests that included rats, flies, mosquitos, and sparrows. Later campaigns replaced sparrows as pests with bedbugs.

With the vast rural population organized into people's communes and the urban population into work organizations by the late 1950s, the planned economy system enabled direct control and implementation of public projects, of which health was a top priority. A national system of public health monitoring was established. The nationwide public health monitoring stations, which in 1953 numbered only 313, shot up to 1,464 by 1956. The number of public health monitoring stations further expanded to 2,513 by 1966 and to over 3,000 by the late 1970s.[12] In 1981, prior to the dissolution of the people's communes in China's countryside, 1.4 million rural health care personnel had been trained and counted as "barefoot" doctors, with an additional 2 million part-time rural health care aides and 585,000 rural midwives.[13]

Containing Infectious Diseases

Infant and child mortality was the first to fall, contributing most significantly to the increase in life expectancy. Infant mortality, mortality during the first year of life, was in the range of 150 per 1,000 births, or 15 percent, in the early 1930s when relatively large-scale population data first became available.[14] Child mortality, defined as mortality between the ages of one and four, was around 100 per 1,000. These combined rates suggest that about a quarter of all births did not survive beyond the age of five. By the mid-1970s, China's large-scale epidemiological survey estimated that infant and child mortality had been reduced by two-thirds to three-quarters from the 1930s levels. This swift decline was confirmed by China's 1982 population census, which reported a mortality under age five of 70 per 1,000.[15]

Of all diseases affecting population health, especially among infants and children, infectious diseases transmitted due to unhealthy environments, water, waste, and air play a prominent role. Public health efforts are the most effective means in combatting infectious diseases. Overall infectious occurrence rates in the mid-1950s exceeded 2,000 per 100,000

[12] SYB 1983, 541. [13] Ibid., 545. [14] J. Lee and Wang 1999, 56.
[15] Banister and Hill 2004.

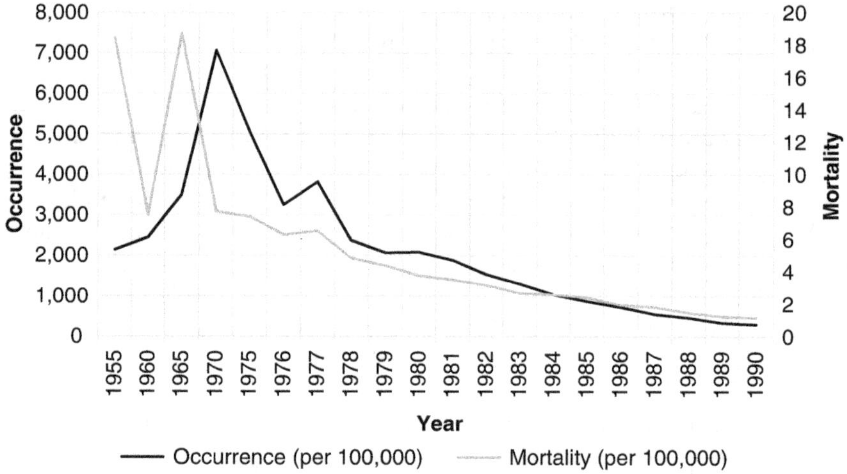

Figure 2.2 Decline in infectious diseases, China, 1955–90
Source: National Commission of Health, *China Health Statistical Yearbook* 2016 (HSYB 2016), table 10–1–3

or 2 percent of the population (Figure 2.2, left axis). This low occurrence rate appears to be doubtful, nevertheless, in part due to the absence of a fully established national monitoring and reporting system at the time. The more trustworthy occurrence rates numbers should be those after 1970. For the years 1970 and 1975, the occurrence rate was reported to be as high as 7,000 and 5,000 per 100,000 population, or 7 and 5 percent, respectively, driven up by spikes of seasonal flu (which infected over 3 and 2.7 percent of the population). By 1980, it returned to 1950s levels, about 2,000 per 100,000. Subsequently, occurrence rates dropped to 297 per 100,000 by 1990, nearly a magnitude lower in just a decade.

In contrast to occurrence rates, mortality due to infectious diseases serves as a better measure to track changes in population health. Whereas incidences of such things as influenza could hardly be fully captured, deaths and causes of deaths are more accurately recorded. Mortality due to infectious diseases, also plotted in Figure 2.2, shows more convincingly the lessening role of infectious diseases in affecting population health. Reported mortality due to infectious diseases stood at 7.73 per 100,000 in 1970 (Figure 2.2, right axis). This mortality rate was halved in a decade, to 3.76 in 1980, and more than halved again in the decade after, to 1.17 per 100,000 population. By the mid-1970s, deaths due to infectious, parasitic, and respiratory diseases accounted for 25.5 percent of all deaths. While such a share was still considerably higher than that in the high-income countries at the time (10.8 percent), it was vastly lower than other low-income countries (43.7 percent).[16]

A highly contagious type of infectious disease, measles, affects young children especially. Aside from neonatal infection, measles along with pneumonia and diarrhea is among the top causes of infant and childhood illness and mortality. They accounted for more than 40 percent of all children's deaths worldwide at the turn of the twenty-first century.[17] The decline or disappearance of measles is attributable to vaccination. The official health statistics of the Chinese government clearly indicate both the magnitude and the effect of measles immunization. The declining trend of measles is shown in Figure 2.3. The number of measles occurrences in this figure are plotted in log form (2 is 10 times 1, and 3 is 10 times 2 . . .), given the massive magnitude of the reductions.

It is worth noting the timing of the decline in measles occurrences and mortality. Between the mid-1950s and the early 1980s, the recorded occurrence rate of measles in the population dropped by almost

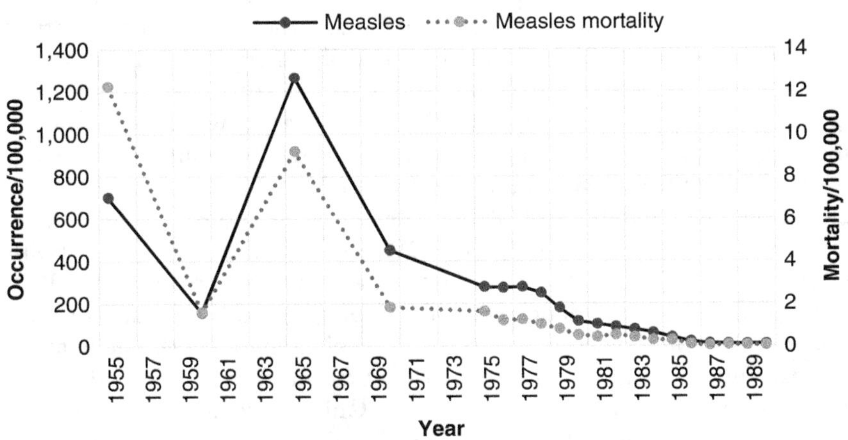

Figure 2.3 Reduction in measles and measles mortality, China, 1955–90
Source: HSYB 2016, table 10–1–3

[16] World Bank 1984, 13, table 2.3.

[17] According to the WHO, even at the turn of the twenty-first century, 70 percent of all children's deaths can be accounted for by these sources: acute lower respiratory infections, mostly pneumonia (19%), diarrhea (18%), malaria (8%), measles (4%), HIV/AIDS (3%), and neonatal conditions, mainly pre-term birth, birth asphyxia, and infections (37%). www.who.int

a degree of magnitude, from around 700 per 100,000 to less than 90 (Figure 2.3, left axis). This massive reduction was already underway prior to China's ascending prosperity. As early as the mid-1970s, the occurrence rate had already been cut by more than half that in the 1950s, no doubt due to immunization. Mortality directly attributed to measles (right axis Figure 2.3) dropped correspondingly. The 1960 numbers should not be taken at face value as these rates were based on reports during China's worst famine, when health statistics collection was likely to be unreliable. Instead, the numbers in the mid-1950s and mid-1960s are preferable reference points for the pre-immunization era. Up to the mid-1960s, around 10 in 100,000 deaths were attributed to measles. By the end of the 1960s, this number was reduced to below 2. By the end of the 1980s, measles had virtually disappeared from the Chinese population and was no longer a health risk, with a recorded occurrence rate of merely less than 8 per 100,000 and a mortality rate of 0.02 per 100,000 in 1990.

The most direct evidence of the reach of public health programs comes from vaccination and immunization records. Immunizations against infectious diseases are directly responsible for reducing morbidity and mortality among infants and children. Immunization is also a direct outcome of public health efforts. One general indicator for immunization is the percentage of children receiving the diphtheria, tetanus, and pertussis (DPT) vaccine. DPT1, the first dose given to children, was already prevalent at the 80 percent level in 1983, and so was MCV1, a vaccine for measles (Table 2.1). Global levels at the time, by comparison, were 30 percent for DPT1 and merely 16 for MCV1. China far exceeded the global average. By the end of the 1980s, vaccinations for diphtheria, tetanus, and pertussis (DPT1, DPT3), measles (MCV1), polio (POL3), and tuberculosis (BCG) all reached near universal levels.[18] Smallpox, with an incidence rate of 200 per 100,000 population at the start of the People's Republic, had been eradicated by 1960. Vaccination against tuberculosis, a leading cause of adult deaths prior to 1949, reached 500 million by 1978, given China's capacity to produce 50 million doses of vaccine per year. Deaths due to tuberculosis had dropped to ninth in the main causes of death by that year.[19]

Changes in two other forms of infectious diseases, bacterial dysentery and malaria, reveal the effectiveness of public health interventions other than immunization. Unlike measles, which was eradicated with mass vaccination, reduction in these two other infectious diseases depended upon environmental sanitation and disease prevention. As

[18] https://data.unicef.org/topic/child-health/immunization/ [19] World Bank 1984, 16.

Table 2.1 *Immunization rates (%), China, 1983–2010*

	DTP1	DTP3	POL3	MCV1	BCG
1983	80	58	81	78	34
1984	90	73	84	84	59
1985	92	78	87	88	64
1986	92	78	68	63	70
1987	91	75	78	77	85
1988	98	95	96	95	98
1989	98	95	96	95	98
1990	98	97	98	98	99
1991	97	94	95	92	97
1992	97	91	93	87	94
1993	96	88	90	81	92
1994	95	85	87	75	89
1995	93	80	82	80	79
1996	94	83	84	84	84
1997	94	84	85	83	83
1998	94	84	85	83	83
1999	94	85	86	84	84
2000	94	85	86	84	84
2001	95	86	86	85	85
2002	95	86	86	85	85
2003	95	86	87	85	85
2004	95	87	87	86	86
2005	95	87	87	86	86
2006	99	93	94	93	92
2007	99	93	94	94	94
2008	99	97	99	97	97
2009	99	99	99	99	99
2010	99	99	99	99	99

Source: https://data.unicef.org/topic/child-health/immunization/

seen in the case of measles, recorded cases of bacterial dysentery and malaria both began their declines before 1980. By the end of the 1980s, the recorded occurrence rate of dysentery was less than one-fifth of the level in the mid-1970s.[20] Reduction of occurrences of malaria, impressively, was only 3 percent of the level of the mid-1970s, declining from 455 per 100,000 in the population in 1975 to merely 12.6 by 1989 (Figure 2.4). Again, the most notable downward trends began in the mid-1970s.

[20] From 732 per 100,000 in 1976 to 132 in 1989. The published statistics show a spike of 1,000.7 for the year 1975. Used 1976 instead.

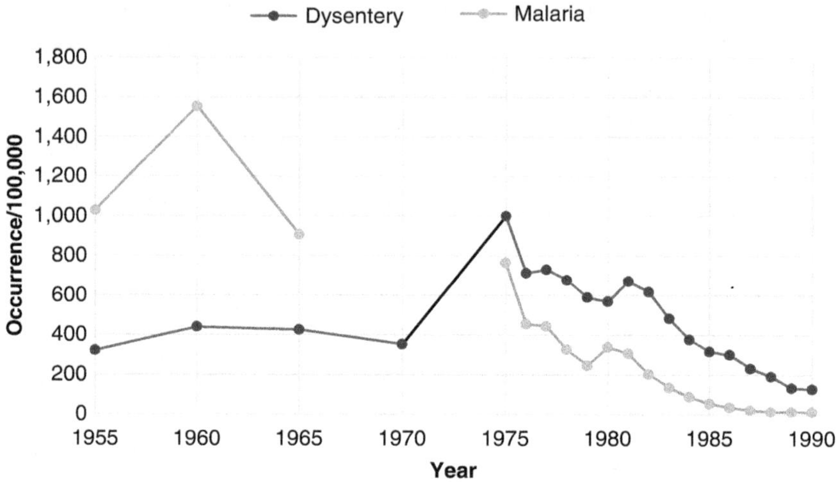

Figure 2.4 Reduction in dysentery and malaria occurrences, China, 1955–90
Source: HSYB 2016, table 10–1–3

A Global Outlier

On the eve of China's economic takeoff in the 1980s, China was a global outlier when income and health measures are considered together. Figure 2.5 plots mortality rates under age five, a commonly used measure of population health level, and measured income level (GDP per capita, log transformation) in the world in 1976. On the eve of China's economic takeoff and in the year Mao died, China's location was well below the "fitted line," a line that summarizes the negative relationship between income and mortality levels. With a very low measured income level (less than $200) and with over 80 percent of the population residing in the countryside, the health level of the Chinese population (under-five mortality of 79.8 per 1,000) had already reached that of populations living in upper-middle-income countries at the time (under-five mortality rate of 90.9 per 1,000, average income level of $574), and much below the level of middle-income countries (under-five mortality rate of 134.1 per 1,000, average income level of $400).

These improvements in population health, especially health among the young population, had profound implications, both at the societal level and for individual lives. For the country as a whole, increased survival of children led to a rapid, albeit temporary, growth in population. Under a planned economy system, rapidly increased population exerted

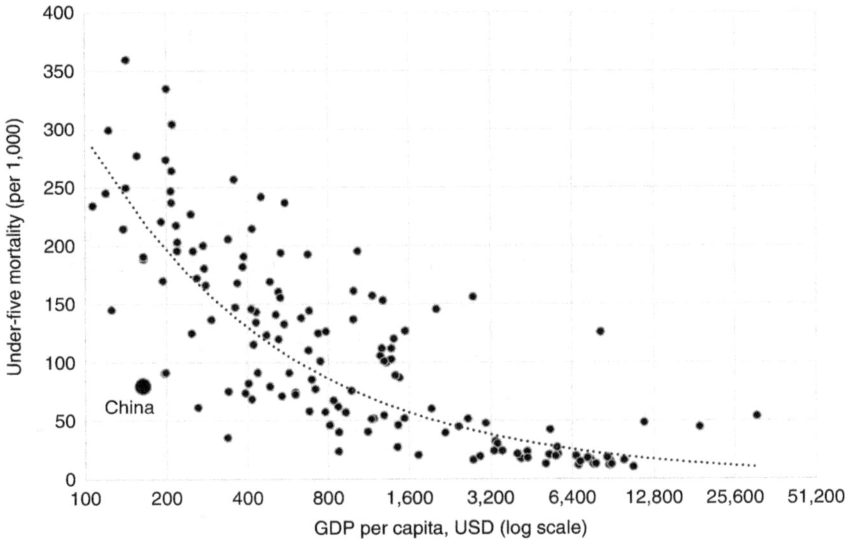

Figure 2.5 Global comparison, per capita income level (log transformed) and mortality under age five, 1976
Source: WDI

mounting pressures for planners to provide food, employment opportunities, income, and social benefits. A rapid increase in the young population also led to the increased pressure of out-migration, especially from rural to urban areas, as China's rural population was growing at a faster rate than urban areas, in part due to a lag in fertility decline.

For families and individuals, sharp reductions in infant and child mortality greatly improved reproductive efficiency and contributed to improvements in women's health as well. Combined with reduced childbearing and childrearing, health improvement resulted in increased resources available for each of the surviving children.[21] Increased child survival contributed directly to the other main feature the Chinese population: education. While the large number of surviving children initially strained school resources, healthier children could learn better and faster. It is well understood that illness undermines both school attendance as well as children's cognitive capacity.[22] With China's significant achievement in improving population health via public health efforts, a much higher share of the large number of births in the 1960s and afterward survived to adulthood. Births after the early 1960s also grew up with fewer

[21] Reher 2011. [22] Bloom, Canning, and Sevilla 2003.

health-related infirmities. These large cohorts of people grew up to be the main labor force for China's economic ascendance in the decades that followed.

Eradicating Illiteracy

By the early 1980s, the vast population of China was not only much healthier than two decades previously but also much more educated. China's 1982 census collected information on literacy and educational attainment levels of all Chinese citizens for the first time.[23] Census results reported the overall literacy level in the population for those aged 12 and above, the age of primary school completion. Data collected from this census could also be used to gauge improvement in the literacy level of the population over the three decades under socialist rule, an achievement accomplished through school expansion and illiteracy-reducing campaign classes.

By the start of its new era of economic transformation, China's young population was mostly a literate one, with the basic abilities of reading and writing. Among the youngest group at the time (15 to 19 years), who were born in the 1960s and would soon enter the labor force when China's economic boom took off, over 96 percent of males and 85 percent of females had at least basic literacy. For all persons over the age of 12, the census counted 69 percent as literate. The gender differential, however, was considerable: 81 percent of males but only 55 percent of females aged 12 and over were enumerated as literate. Among those who had completed primary school recently, aged 15 to 19 in 1982, the literacy rate was close to universal for males, at 96 percent. Females had made rapid gains but remained behind males, at 85 percent (Figure 2.6).

Eradicating illiteracy was a remarkable feat going into China's age of abundance. One approach to appreciate the change is to compare shares of population enumerated as literate by their age in 1982. Among those aged 60 and above, 60 percent of males could neither read nor write. Among women in that age group, illiteracy was nearly universal: only less than 5 percent were literate. As these are national numbers, in rural areas the shares of illiterate people were even higher. By comparison, among those who reached school age after the founding of the People's Republic,

[23] A person was counted as being semi-illiterate or illiterate in the census if the person could not read up to 1,500 Chinese characters, could not read at all, or could not write a simple note. Those who had not attended school but could read more than 1,500 Chinese characters, could read newspapers and popular books, and could write a simple note were classified as having a primary school-level educational attainment.

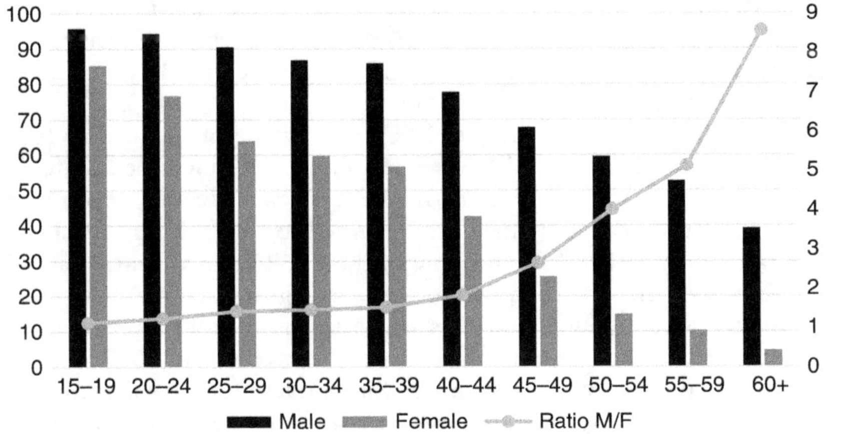

Figure 2.6 Improving literacy: share of literate population by age and gender, China, 1982
Source: National Bureau of Statistics of China, *Tabulation of the Chinese Population Census* 1982 (China Population Census 1982), vol. 5

or persons aged 39 and younger in 1982, over 85 percent of males and more than half of all females became literate (Figure 2.6).

A notable change along with improved literacy was the narrowing gender gap. A gender gap in literacy was still notable in 1982, with the ratio of male and females among the youngest group (aged 15 to 19) at 1.12 to 1. The reduction in the literacy gap, however, was vast over the years. As also shown in Figure 2.6, the gender literacy gap among the oldest age group (aged 60 and over) was enormous, at a ratio of 8.56 to 1, with 39 percent of males but only less than 5 percent of females counted as literate (Figure 2.6, left axis). For those aged 40 to 44 in 1982, or people in their teens in the 1950s, the gender ratio dropped massively, to below 2 to 1, with 77 percent of males and 43 percent of females counted as literate. For those in the 35–39 age group and younger in 1982, who had reached school age after the founding of the People's Republic, the majority of women were literate.

Eradicating illiteracy was clearly a result of the efforts of expanding public education, starting at the primary school level. During the first decade of the People's Republic, between 1949 and 1959, the number of students enrolled in primary schools increased nearly fourfold, from 24.39 million to 91.18 million, far exceeding the growth of the primary school-aged population at the time. Two decades later, by 1979, the enrollment numbers further rose to 146.62 million, again far exceeding the growth of the population.[24] Eradication of illiteracy was most evident in the early decades of the People's Republic, as seen in the shares of illiterate people being reduced consecutively by more than 10 percent for every five years in the 1950s and 1960s.[25]

Educational expansion at higher levels was even more swift. For secondary schools, enrollments between 1949 and 1959 increased tenfold, from 1.27 million to 12.9 million. In the next two decades, secondary school education capacity further expanded by 4.7 times, reaching 60.25 million by 1979.[26] By the time of the 1982 census, nearly half of all school-aged children (46.69 percent, age group 15–19) also had a secondary school education. This was a nearly fivefold increase over three decades, as the share for those aged 45 and older in 1982 was no more than 10 percent of the population. Similarly, though at a lower level, the share of the population with a senior high school education reached 28.27 percent for those aged 20 to 24, increasing from 2.38 percent or lower three decades earlier (those aged 50 and over).[27]

In contrast to the vast improvement in basic literacy, expansion of college-level education was abysmal in the first decades of the People's Republic. China's supreme leader Mao was forever distrustful of what people with an advanced education could do; an open mind was considered a threat to a totalitarian rule. College education was instead reserved mostly for training elite engineers and other experts to meet the needs of a planned economy. College education not only remained extremely limited and selective but was also disrupted by almost incessant political campaigns and purges.

For a country with a population of 500 million in 1949, a mere 117,000 students were enrolled in higher educational institutions. A decade later, with substantial expansion, the number grew quickly but was still below 1 million, at 812,000, in 1962. The subsequent political campaigns and turmoil did not do much to help China's college-bound aspirants as enrollments had been almost wiped out during China's Cultural Revolution. In 1966, the number of university enrollments dropped to only half a million. In 1970, enrollments bottomed out with fewer than 50,000 students on campuses across China.[28]

It was not until 1978, with the reinstatement of the college-entrance exams and reopening of the universities, that college enrollments

[24] SYB 1981.

[25] The share of illiterate or semi-illiterate population dropped from 52.12 percent for the 45–49 age group to 38.71 percent for the 40–45 age group, and to 28 percent for the 35–39 age group (calculated from China Population Census 1982, vol. 5, table 47).

[26] SYB 1981. [27] Calculated from China Population Census 1982, vol. 5.

[28] SYB 1985, 582.

returned to the level achieved two decades earlier, at around 800,000 students nationwide. In 1977, the year the college-entrance exam was first reinstated, fewer than 5 percent of exam takers were admitted. At the end of China's socialist planned economy era, fewer than 2 percent of the population of prime working age had a college education, a deficiency that would be made up quickly in the years to come.[29]

As with its population health level, China was a world outlier in achieving literacy on the eve of its ascendance to economic prosperity despite its low per capita income level. One good measure of literacy is female middle school education, which captures both schooling above the most elementary level and gender equality in a society. Figure 2.7 makes this comparison by plotting the level of female middle school education (female secondary school gross enrollment ratio) against income level in 1976 (log transformation of GDP per capita) with data assembled by the World Bank. With its income level (less than $200), China clearly stood out from other countries with an enrollment ratio of 45.74 percent.

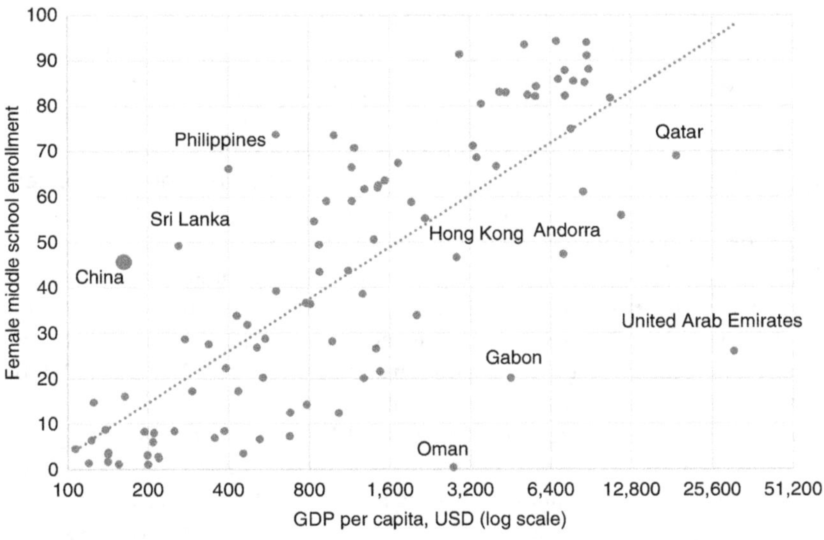

Figure 2.7 Global comparison, per capita income and female middle school enrollment, 1976
Source: WDI

[29] The highest share is among those aged 40–44 at 2 percent. It was 1.33 percent and 0.69 percent for those aged 35–39 and 30–34, respectively (calculated from China Population Census 1982, vol. 5, table 47).

This level was nearly three times higher than that in India (16.11 percent). It was on par with South Korea and Malaysia, for which the female enrollment ratio stood at 49.53 percent and 43.52 percent, respectively. Both countries had an income level more than four times China's at the time. China's female education at the secondary school level was not only high by its measured income level but significantly higher than the average of middle-income countries (with a ratio of 33.82 and an income level more than twice China's at the time). China's young population then was not only healthy but also relatively well-schooled. The labor force China had in the late 1970s, on the eve of China's economic takeoff, was not just cheap but well-endowed in both health and literacy. Again, it was not just cheap labor but *good* labor.

One Country, Two Peoples

Improving population health and reducing illiteracy were parts of a national agenda to turn China into a twentieth-century modern society. Another objective, perhaps more daunting and urgent, was to transform China's weak and agrarian economy into a strong and industrialized one. Developing a heavy industrial base was the main strategy to achieve such an objective.[30] Mao's sense of this urgency partially contributed to China's Great Leap Forward in the late 1950s. An ambitious goal, to surpass iron and steel production in Britain within fifteen years, was used to mobilize the whole country. Backyard furnace steelmaking and collective farming under the newly formed people's commune system plunged the country into the worst famine in human history.

Industrialization did arrive in China prior to its age of abundance; but it was a highly distorted industrialization, one without the accompanying urbanization. Over two-and-a-half decades under the socialist planned economy system, China quickly industrialized. Between 1952 and 1978, the total volume of economic output, as measured by national income, rose by 4.5 times.[31] Industrial output increased by over 15 times during the same period, with the share of heavy industries rising from about a third of the total value of industrial output to nearly 60 percent. The total value of agricultural production also increased, although not as impressively, increasing by 2.3 times over this period. As a result, the share of industrial output in the overall economic output (combining industrial and agricultural output) rose from 41.5 percent in 1952 to 74.3 percent in 1978. The share of economic output in the heavy industries rose sharply, from 35.6 percent to 57.3 percent of all industrial output.[32]

[30] World Bank 1983. [31] SYB 1982, 5. [32] Ibid., 17.

This heavy-industry led developmental strategy came with severe and enduring costs. One of the costs was the continued worsening shortage of all daily necessities, including: food grain, meat, and eggs, soap, matches, sewing machines, and bicycles. Near the end of the planned economy era, consumer goods shortages grew increasingly prevalent and acute. This chronic and worsening shortage, endemic to the planned economy system around the world, drove citizens' desire for change and served as a basis for their support to abandon the socialist planned economy system.

A deeper and more latent cost of this industrialization model was the creation of a "one-country, two-systems" society. In just two decades, from the late 1950s to the late 1970s, urban and rural parts of China were segregated into two societies, creating two classes of citizens. This legacy, a society in which the majority of the population was subjected to secondary-citizen status, became a most crucial force in propelling China to its age of abundance.

Once released by economic reforms, the ingenuity and energy of China's rural population produced enough food and other materials to improve the living standards of all the Chinese population. Their transformation from farming to manufacturing, long before the success of industrial reforms in cities, converted China into a world factory and produced many of China's first generation of capitalist entrepreneurs. Their massive migration to cities built up China and produced for the world. This secondary-citizen status of China's vast rural population *made* their labor cheap. Far beyond its economic consequences, the institutional divide also sowed deep seeds of social injustice and inequality, forging an "original sin" of China's socialist era, a sin that has plagued China for over four decades, a sin with continued repercussions to be reckoned with. The diminishing availability of this cheap labor force decades later would also spell the end of China's age of abundance.

Of all the countries that underwent an industrialization transformation, China was unique in doing so without the accompanying urbanization.[33] Figure 2.8 portrays China's unique trajectory of industrialization without urbanization, by contrasting the changes in these two processes. At the start of the socialist planned economy era in the early 1950s, China's share of urban population was largely commensurate with its share of industrial output in the economy. China was decidedly an agrarian society, with industrialization and urbanization levels both remaining low; about 20 percent of economic output came from the industrial sector and less than 15 percent of the population was classified as urban. Less than one decade into the socialist planned economy era, the share of economic

[33] Lavely, Lee, and Wang 1990.

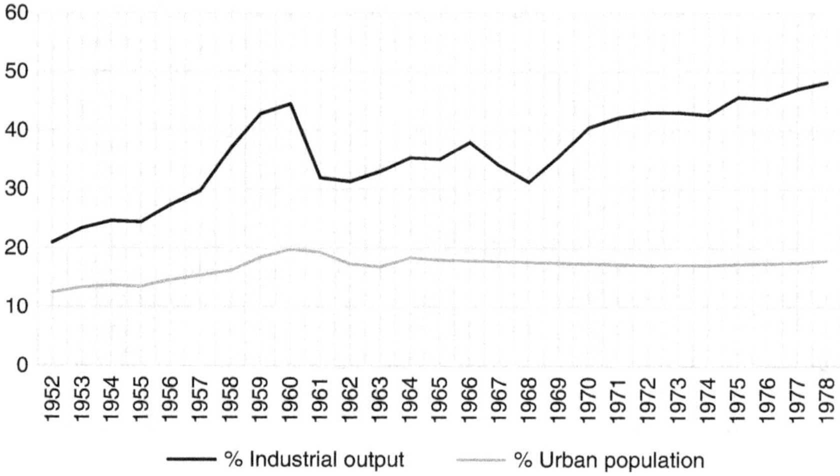

Figure 2.8 Industrialization without urbanization, China, 1952–78
Sources: SYB 1990, 89; SYB 2001, table 3–2.

output from industrial sectors more than doubled, from 20 percent in 1952 to 43 percent in 1959 (Figure 2.8). A main source of this surge came from the push during the Great Leap Forward campaign (1958–62). Between 1952 and 1959, when economic output from the first sector of the economy (agriculture) increased 12 percent, the value from the second sector (industry) rose 334 percent.[34] The share of industrial output in the economy shot up from about 30 percent in 1957 to 44.5 percent in 1960.

For a brief period, China's compressed industrialization drew a large number of people into cities. Between 1952 and 1960, China saw its first and only urbanization wave in its history prior to the 1980s. In that first decade of the planned economy, nearly 60 million people were added to the urban population, doubling the total from 71.6 million in 1952 to 130.7 million in 1960. The disastrous Great Leap Forward led to a sharp contraction in China's industrial output and a reversal of China's bourgeoning urbanization. The share of industrial output plunged 25 percent in one year, from 44.5 percent in 1960 to 31.9 percent in 1961. The same contraction also sent over 14 million urban residents back to the countryside in just three years, between 1960 and 1963, reducing the share of the urban population by 3 percent.[35] For the next two decades, economic

[34] Current price. Calculated from SYB 2002, table 3–1.
[35] Calculated from data in SYB 1990, 89.

output from the industrial sectors resumed its increase, reaching 50 percent of the total output value on the eve of China's reform era. In contrast to the brief surge in urbanization in the 1950s, however, China's urban population share remained at under 20 percent; at one point it was as low as 15 percent.

This peculiar pattern of industrialization without urbanization was enabled by two institutional pillars: government control over the price and supply of agricultural products via a uniform procurement system, and a draconian urban-rural divide via residential control that precluded migration from rural to urban areas. With these two institutional arrangements, two societies within one country or one country with two types of citizenship were created.[36]

The first pillar was erected soon after the founding of the People's Republic out of concerns over grain supply and food security. The government implemented a procurement system in late 1953, which lasted until the early 1990s. Starting with food grain, pork, eggs, sugar, cotton, silk, linen, tobacco, aquatic products and extending to others, the government eventually put 180 types of agricultural products under its procurement regime. [37] Farmers were not allowed to sell these products themselves; they could only sell to the state for government-dictated prices. To guarantee supply to urban residents, the government issued rationing coupons. These coupons became "second currencies"; their types and numbers increased from a dozen to too many to count by the end of the planned economy era. Rationing coupons enveloped the daily lives of urban residents (rural residents were on their own), ranging from food grain (even by type, such as rice, wheat, and others), meat (by type, such as pork, beef, and mutton), poultry, eggs, sugar, and cooking oil, to consumer goods from watches, bicycles, furniture, and clothes to soap and even matches.

Retooling the population registration system as needed for a planned economy, in the late 1950s the Chinese government designated all members of society as one of two household types: "agricultural" or "non-agricultural."[38] Those classified as "non-agricultural," or urban, were entitled to government provisions of food, housing, employment, education, and health care; the majority of the Chinese population, classified as "agricultural" or rural, were self-reliant in providing for themselves under the people's commune system. The household registration institution, known as *hukou*, prevented rural to urban migration and strictly controlled migration across geographic areas. It effectively served as an

[36] Whyte 2010; F.-L. Wang 2005. [37] www.1921china.com
[38] T. Cheng and Selden 1994; F.-L. Wang 2005.

internal passport, segregating the two populations within the same country.[39] The two societies within the same country were so tightly sealed, that migration from rural to urban China was extremely rare, if it occurred at all.[40]

Beginning in November 1953, urban Chinese residents started to live under a food-rationing system, with food supply guaranteed by the state. State food subsidies alone, not counting numerous other types of direct and indirect subsidies, were equivalent to about one-fifth of the total consumption by urban residents in 1982, a considerable privilege.[41] In 1981, China devoted 4.2 percent of its gross national product (GNP) for urban food subsidies alone, 1.3 times the total government spending on health care for the whole country, of which the urban population also received a disproportionate share. Moreover, urban residents had guaranteed employment and income, and urban employees received up to 20 percent of their income as work-related welfare subsidies from the state.[42] With state-subsidized public housing, urban residents spent only 1.5 percent of their disposable income on rent.[43]

In comparison, a person born in rural China had an entirely different set of life chances. There was no guaranteed or steady food supply, and the rural population had much poorer access to clean water, basic health care, schools, or employment. They were tied to the land by their rural *hukou* with no escape. The significance of *hukou* was best summarized by a popular 1990 book exposing the urban-rural divide: "to have an urban *hukou* canceled is equivalent to being condemned to prison; to transfer one's *hukou* from rural to urban is to have gotten a ticket to heaven."[44]

Exact estimates are hard to come by, but attempts to quantify the "implicit tax" due to the price scissors, a term to symbolize the price-setting practice of underpricing agricultural while overpricing industrial goods, suggest staggering numbers. Studies by China's National Bureau of Pricing in the late 1970s estimated that agricultural goods were undervalued by 25 to 30 percent, while prices for industrial goods were overvalued by 15 to 20 percent.[45] Another estimate put a price tag for the differential prices in agricultural and industrial products over the period of 28 years after 1950 between 448 and 700 billion yuan.[46] This amount was between 1.24 and 1.9 times the total economic output for the country in 1978, which was 362.4 billion yuan. By forcing the rural population to

[39] Chan 1994; F.-L. Wang 2005. [40] X. Wu and Treiman 2004.

[41] Food subsidies per person were reported to be 96.1 yuan per person per year (World Bank 1984, 93) and total expenditure per urban resident was 501 yuan in 1982. Rural per capita expenditure was only 212 yuan (SYB 1983, 484).

[42] SYB 1983, 491. [43] Ibid., 494. [44] Guo and Liu 1990. [45] Peng and Chen 2008.

[46] https://baike.baidu.com/item/粮食统购统销

remain on their land and sell their products exclusively to the state with prices that were set artificially low, resources were extracted from the rural population for the benefit of industrialization. Over this period, even by conservative estimates, the number would have amounted to 1.4 times the total capital stock of the state-owned industrial sector in 1978.[47] China built its unique industrialization off the backs of its vast rural population, and rural Chinese paid more than farmers in other socialist countries. Despite a significantly lower per capita grain output level, for instance, Chinese farmers shouldered a heavier burden of extraction than those in the former Soviet Union.[48]

Urban and rural differences were also ostensibly apparent in two other legacies under socialism: health and education. In 1981, for instance, per capita public health expenditure for urban Chinese was 3.4 times that of the rural population. State subsidies covered 80 percent of urban residents' costs but only 29 percent of the rural population's. State subsidies for per capita health expenditures for urban residents were nearly 10 times more than those for rural residents.[49] In the mid-1970s, a person born in rural China had a life expectancy of 57 years; an urban person's was 72 years, a stunning 15-year difference.[50] A large-scale survey in 1979 reported that among seven-year-old boys, one in eight in the countryside versus one in 40 in cities were stunted due to malnutrition, a difference of five times.[51] Improvement in rural health in the 1970s, as shown earlier in this chapter, contributed to narrowing the health gap. But even in 1981, a newly born urban girl still had a five-year advantage in life expectancy over her rural counterpart: 73 versus 68 years, as estimated from the 1982 population census data.

The rural population also lagged far behind in educational attainment. Even after more than two decades of improving literacy, about 5 percent of rural youth aged 15 to 19 in 1982 were still reported to be illiterate and 16 percent were semi-illiterate. This is compared with 1.4 and 3.2 percent of urban youth of the same age. Among the 25 to 29 years old in 1990, who went through most of their schooling during China's socialist years, only 11 percent of females and 19 percent of males in the countryside had an education beyond junior high school. The comparable numbers for urban youth were 47 and 48 percent respectively. Whereas among urban residents, 8 percent of females and 12 percent of males in this age group had a college education,

47 Yang 1998, 183. 48 Ash 2006, 971. 49 Calculated from World Bank 1984, 65.
50 Ibid., 93.
51 Ibid., 32. Stunting is defined as less than 90 percent of the median height of the same age group compiled by the US National Center for Health Statistics at the time.

a number still rather low, there were virtually no college-educated rural residents.[52]

In only one generation, one country-two systems became by far the most consequential legacy of modern Chinese socialist history. At the end of the planned economy era, China had become an isolated, static, and immobile society. By the 1970s, only two decades after the urban-rural distinction by *hukou* status, though sharing similar skin color and linguistic traits, the two types of Chinese were dissimilar in almost all other aspects, more than just where they lived and worked. The urban-rural divide became a legacy that left a country deeply divided socially; a legacy that created a particular kind of migration and urbanization, propelling China to the age of abundance. A rapidly growing population due to improvements in health, combined with a strict migration control policy, created a huge and untapped labor force pool in China's countryside; a labor force that was eager and ready to leave farming and to seek better economic opportunities elsewhere, in non-farming activities, and eventually, by moving to cities.

From Demographic Curse to Dividend

As discussed previously, the immediate demographic effect of improved health, with a delayed fertility decline, was rapid population growth. Within only three decades, by 1981 China's total population size had nearly doubled, from 552 million in 1950 to over 1 billion. As China's public as well as its leaders started to look for the causes of China's failure to improve living standards under the planned economy system, their eyes focused on China's large and fast-growing population. A dark cloud of Malthusian worries replaced Marxist teachings. China's swelling population was blamed not only for consuming what was produced but also for depriving China of the potential for investment and economic growth. Blaming overpopulation as the root of all evil not only dominated public discourse and became an academic fashion, it also led to the disastrous public policy known as the one-child policy.[53] The pending coming-of-age of the large cohorts born in the 1960s and 1970s generated extra anxieties for policymakers in Beijing in the late 1970s, who were tasked to provide education, employment, and housing for the large number of young people soon to arrive. Such concerns served as a further impetus

[52] Calculated from data from China Population Census 1990, vol. 2, tables 5–6 and 5–8. The urban population is those counted as living in a city (*shi*) and rural in a county (*xian*).
[53] J. Lee and Wang 1999.

for the leadership to implement in haste the disastrous and harmful one-child policy.[54]

Yet, little did one know that China was favorably primed for an economic takeoff. Not only was the share of the elderly population still extremely small, with less than 5 percent of the population aged 65 and over, China's fast fertility decline in the 1970s already started to pay off. China's share of the population aged 0 to 19 at the time of the 1982 census still accounted for nearly 40 percent of the total population, but it was to drop continuously, to 32.9 percent by 1990 and to only about a quarter, 27.9 percent, by 2000. What was truly opportune was that the share of the population around the working age of 20 to 64 would increase by more than 10 percent in the ensuing three decades, from 48.7 percent in 1982 to 60.1 percent in 2000 and to 65.5 percent by 2010 (Table 2.2). What matters is not just the overall size of the population but also the composition of that population. In 1982, the population dependency ratio – defined here as the number of persons in the dependency age

Table 2.2 *Population age composition and dependency ratio, China, 1982–2050*

	Age composition (% of total)			
Year	0–19	20–64	65+	Ratio
1982	39.20	48.65	4.56	89.96
1985	36.44	51.69	4.82	79.82
1990	32.86	55.13	5.30	69.20
1995	30.74	58.53	5.98	62.74
2000	27.93	60.07	6.92	58.01
2005	24.15	62.39	7.83	51.25
2010	21.17	65.51	8.62	45.47
2015	20.67	65.68	10.02	46.73
2020	20.26	63.81	12.60	51.50
2025	18.26	63.34	14.88	52.33
2030	15.62	62.33	18.23	54.30
2035	13.00	60.74	22.52	58.48
2040	12.45	59.03	26.15	65.40
2045	12.71	57.20	27.84	70.88
2050	12.95	54.71	30.09	78.68

Source: United Nations Population Division: World Population Prospect 2022
Note: The dependency ratio is calculated as the number of people aged below 20 and above 64 as the share of those aged 20 to 64.

[54] F. Wang, Cai, and Gu 2013; F. Wang, Gu, and Cai 2016; F. Wang et al. 2018.

(0–19 plus 65 and over) per working age (20–64) person, multiplied by 100 – was close to 90, or slightly more than one working age person supporting one person of the dependency age. By 2000, that ratio was reduced to 58, and in 2010 only half of the level in 1982.

What China had on the eve of its economic takeoff was not just a favorable age structure, with the bulk of its population at prime working age; but, as documented earlier in this chapter, China's young population was largely healthy and literate, and more than eager to take risks to abandon a life of subsistence at the margins. They were ready to escape the sterile social environment, an environment created under socialism that had become increasingly more insufferable toward the end of the Cultural Revolution. Without these fundamental characteristics, and in the absence of the economic opportunities made possible by the reforms later on, China's large working-age population could have been indeed a demographic curse, as feared by many. Instead of a curse, however, reforms brought economic opportunities, and China's population turned into a demographic dividend that was crucial in creating the country's economic boom.

The term "demographic dividend" is among the least understood and most abused terms in assessing the role of population in economic changes. It is not an uncommon argument, and an entirely understandable one, that a large and increasing number of young people does not translate readily into a dividend for a country. More young people could increase the potential for more unemployment and poverty, even social unrest.

To understand the term demographic dividend, however, two clarifications are essential: one conceptual and the another computational. Conceptually, the demographic dividend is broadly understood as the benefits brought about by the unprecedented demographic changes in human history – declines in mortality followed by fertility, and changes in population age structure.[55] Mortality reduction and improvements in health lead to a population with enhanced physical and cognitive capabilities for learning and working. Reduced childbearing and childrearing cut down drastic reproductive waste, in particular, on women's bodies. They liberate women to engage in other types of activities, including but by no means only limited to economic activities. One estimation that best summarizes the significance of reduced pregnancies due to increased infant and child survival is that by reducing the number of pregnancies from five to two, the share of a woman's adult life spent on childbearing and rearing is reduced from 70 to 14 percent.[56] With increased certainty in life and an extended life span, the human

[55] Bloom and Williamson 1998; A. Mason 2003; Bloom, Canning, and Sevilla 2003.
[56] R. Lee 2003.

calculus for life and social engagements has also changed in many fundamental ways.[57]

To achieve the demographic dividend, it is necessary for the working population to be productive. This is where the computational part of the demographic dividend comes in. An appropriate approach would need to take into account labor income and consumption when calculating the dependency.[58] By weighting age-specific population groups with their corresponding labor income and consumption levels, this method calculates an effective support ratio. It corrects the caveat in the generally seen dependency ratio, where a large number of young people may not be gainfully employed and therefore not generate economic output.

China's demographic dividend in its post-socialist economic takeoff is evident. Using the computational method that considers income and consumption, the growth rate of effective producers was above that of the effective consumers in China, until 2013. The growth rate of this support ratio, which is the measure of the demographic dividend, increased in the 1980s. In the case of the number of effective producers per effective consumers, the support ratio rose continuously for three decades after 1982, coinciding with and contributing to the economic boom. The demographic dividend, expressed as the growth rate of the support ratio, remained in positive territory throughout this time period. For the first two decades, this demographic dividend accounted for at least 15 percent of the increase in per capita income.[59]

The turning point of change in the demographic dividend for China came in 2013. This calculation of the demographic dividend, made in 2005, suggested that China's demographic dividend would cease to be positive by the year 2013.[60] The estimate was that by 2013 the support ratio would have stopped increasing and the growth rate of the support ratio, which is the demographic dividend, would drop to below zero. Starting in 2013, the demographic dividend entered negative territory for China. It is no coincidence that beginning in 2010 economic growth entered a sustained period of slowing down. The annual growth rate was never able to return to double-digits, as had been the case in the previous decade when in five out of the ten years the annual growth rate was at 10 percent or higher. In 2013, the annual growth rate of GNP dropped to 7.1 percent, almost 30 percent lower than the level in 2010 (10.3 percent).[61]

57 Reher 2011. 58 F. Wang and Mason 2008. 59 Ibid.

60 These calculations were first presented at a research conference held in 2006 that led to the publication of Brandt and Rawski 2008.

61 SYB 2021, table 3.4.

Health, Education, and Fertility Decline

The unprecedented opportunity of the demographic dividend, which contributed significantly to China's economic boom, resulted largely from China's rapid fertility decline. As with its mortality decline, China's fertility decline was a compressed process. Moreover, the reduction in mortality, especially in infant and child mortality, and improvements in illiteracy under socialism all contributed to China's fertility decline. Improved child health and reduced fertility and illiteracy opened an entirely new social sphere – improvements in gender equality. Driven by a state ideology that gender equality is to be found in the workplace and encouragement for universal employment, female employment in the formal economic sectors also reached historically high levels, rivaling the highest female labor force participation in the world. The combined effects of these important demographic and social changes on China's rapid fertility decline, however, were often underappreciated, in part because of the strong government birth control policies that existed at the same time.

Contrary to the myth about China's high fertility resulting in rapid population growth in China's modern history,[62] fertility in China began to decline not only early but much more rapidly. Rapid population growth, resulting from a time lag between mortality and fertility decline, is now a well-recognized universal experience known as a phase of the demographic transition. China's unusually rapid mortality decline only accelerated this phase of rapid population growth. China was not only an overachiever in its mortality decline in world history (as shown in Figure 2.1) but also a super achiever in fertility decline. Fertility decline from about five births per woman to about two births per woman, the replacement level, took roughly 75 years in the three large European populations: England and Wales, France, and Italy. China achieved that in only 20 years, less than a third of the time.[63] Had fertility in China not declined as early and quickly, population growth would have been more extensive. The near doubling of the Chinese population between 1950 and 1980 was therefore a consequence of mortality decline, not because of fertility increase.

Another common myth about China's population is attributing the rapid fertility decline almost entirely to China's coercive birth control programs, especially the extreme one-child-per-couple policy. Launched at the start of China's age of abundance, the policy was implemented a full 35 years out of the 40 years after 1980. As with other public programs, the

[62] J. Lee, Campbell, and Wang 2002; Tsuya et al. 2010. [63] F. Wang 2011a.

policy was enforced as a political campaign, with coercion a common feature. Coercive practices and abuses became more widespread and intensified in the early 1980s, following the announcement of the one-child policy in 1980. The coercive enforcement, however, especially the extreme one-child policy, masks the underlying conditions and need for birth control, a need that followed reduced infant and child mortality.

Fertility decline among China's more affluent population, urban dwellers, started long before the coercive birth control programs. The fertility level for urban women was at 3.75 in 1965. It began to drop continuously and precipitously after 1968, after a small fluctuation associated with the Cultural Revolution. By 1973, the fertility level had already dropped to 2.39, not much above replacement level, which is normally set at 2.1 births per woman. In the following year, fertility among urban couples was already lower than the replacement level, at 1.98, and it has not increased since.[64] China's nationwide birth control program began in the early 1970s, characterized by later marriage, longer birth intervals, and fewer births. Nationwide, the fertility level was more than halved in the 1970s, reducing from 5.8 births per woman in 1970 to 2.79 in 1979. At the advent of the one-child policy, fertility had already dropped to just above replacement level.

Reduced infant and child mortality is a commonly recognized precondition for fertility decline worldwide.[65] Based on preconditions for modern fertility decline such as reduced early life mortality, China was certainly not that different from other populations around the world. With its radically reduced infant and child mortality, China joined other populations in the world in reducing fertility rates. As shown in Figure 2.9, China's fertility level would have been predicted almost perfectly by its mortality level in 1976, prior to the one-child policy.[66] China tracks only slightly below the predicted linear line of associations between under-five child mortality and fertility for all countries globally, where data are available. Government birth control programs certainly facilitated, and even accelerated, China's fertility decline with the availability of free contraceptives and services. China's mass campaign mode and its coercive birth control approach, however, helped reinforce a misconception that fertility declined only because of coercion. Such a misconception neglects other fundamental forces driving China's fertility decline. Improved infant and child health was no doubt the most important force and precondition.

One glaring example of such a misconception is the fraudulent claim that China's one-child policy reduced its population by a whopping

[64] Whyte, Wang, and Cai 2015. [65] K. O. Mason 1997. [66] F. Wang et al. 2018.

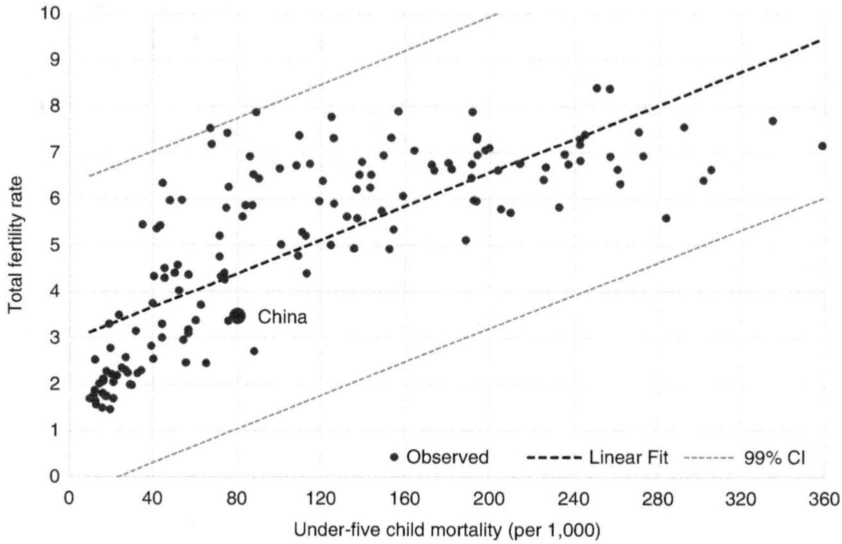

Figure 2.9 Correlations between under-five child mortality and fertility, 1976
Source: F. Wang et al. 2018

400 million, or even a billion. Oblivious of the heavy human cost endured by hundreds of millions of Chinese families and the prolonged dire consequences, this myth of "400 million averted births" dismisses the underlying preference already existing in Chinese society to reduce fertility. It gives undue credit to a policy that should be remembered as a textbook example of bad science combined with bad politics. Fertility would have declined without the coercive government programs, as is the case for almost every other society on earth. For China, over 75 percent of all its fertility decline took place in the 1970s, prior to the one-child policy. The policy, by forcefully creating over 100 million single-child families over its three-and-a-half-decade existence, only created more turmoil in society and inflicted misery upon the population.[67]

As China was covered by a dark Malthusian cloud, with an extreme birth control policy allowing only one child per couple, ordinary Chinese people, especially farmers who were living on the margins of subsistence under the planned economy system, knew better than policymakers in Beijing. They understood that by simply reducing births, their lives would

[67] Ibid.; Y. Cai and Wang 2021.

not instantly improve but could get worse in the long term, with fewer or no laborers in the family to support them in their old age. In desperation, these poor farmers managed their way out of their material misery otherwise by applying their energy and ingenuity to increase agricultural output. That was the only way out. To do so, however, required them to break the shackles of the state; to do so required both their common sense and their courage. A new era was about to begin.

3 Abundance

On a chilly autumn night in November 1978, eighteen men in an East China village gathered in a dilapidated thatched house under a kerosene lamp. They were there to mull over a heretical move at the time in China: to farm as individual households.

Leaving collective farming was never their lot to choose, but they were forced to risk this step out of desperation. The village, Xiaogang, and the region where the village was located were known to suffer from poor harvests and poverty. The collective farming system made it worse. Over a decade and a half previously, in the early 1960s during the Great Leap famine, over a third of the village's 176 residents starved to death. Six out of the 34 households in the village went into extinction. The severe drought in 1978 left them with little choice but to seek an alternative to increase farming output in order to avoid starvation and begging for food in other villages.

The risk they contemplated was so high, that the eighteen villagers representing twenty households made a vow. They each pressed their thumbs on a hastily written note to cement their commitment. They promised to fulfill the state procurement obligation and to raise the children of the group's leader until the age of eighteen if he were imprisoned and executed due to his defiance. That very note with the red thumb stamps is now archived in the National Museum of China (Guojia bowuguan) in Beijing as a testament to the beginning of China's rural reforms and de-collectivization.[1]

The balance between people and food was precarious nationwide. And it was worsening in much of the country. At the end of the 1970s, China reached a health and literacy level few other nations with a comparable income level in the world could rival. Yet, while China had largely escaped from severe starvation, its population, accounting for more than one-fifth of humanity at the time, was still mostly living on the margins of subsistence. The first World Bank study team to arrive in

[1] Much has been written about this village. See, for example, Chen and Wu 2009.

China, while praising China's improved population health, also noted a grown population that was subsisting on the margins of basic nutritional intake. Official statistics confirm the abysmal record of income increase. In 1976, the year Mao died, the average Chinese person had an annual income level barely higher than it had been twenty years prior when China began its planned-economy experiment. Even for employees in China's state-owned enterprises, the most privileged, their annual income increase after adjusting for cost-of-living inflation amounted to less than 1 percent over nearly three decades of socialism.[2]

The predicament of the Xiaogang villagers is just one extreme and well-documented example. Daily necessities, from food grain, vegetables, meat, and eggs to matches and soap, were in serious short supply nationwide. Such was the case for the vast rural population, who were confined to their land and denied access to many goods not produced locally. And it was also the case for those in the more privileged segment of Chinese society, in the cities. For them, rationing was a way of life, and the scope of goods rationed was widening as time went by.

Scarcity of consumer goods was endemic in all societies that adopted the planned-economy system in the twentieth century. The socialist planned-economy, which at its peak encompassed over a third of the world's population, earned the nickname "the shortage economy."[3] In China, with up to 80 percent of its labor engaged in farming, food supply still could hardly keep up with population growth; food quality also continued to decline. Nutritional intake per capita stagnated for the two decades up to the late 1970s, slightly higher than the level when the collectivization began in the 1950s, and by some studies no better than in the 1930s. Only due to the more equitable distribution through collective farming in the countryside and rationing in cities was large-scale and frequent starvation prevented. The notable exception was the massive famine following the Great Leap Forward between 1959 and 1961.

The main staple grains were becoming ever scarcer and of deteriorating quality. Cooking oil, vegetables, eggs, and meat were all in extremely short supply. Whereas rural families lived in mostly decades-old farmhouses, newly constructed public housing in cities could hardly meet the increasing demand. People crowded in tight spaces, with only the most privileged few having a private toilet or bathing facilities. As lumber and furniture production fell under state planning, most urban residents only had a few basic pieces of furniture in their

[2] The annual income was 605 yuan in 1976. Even in 1981, after an increase to 812 yuan, the level was only 29.4 percent higher than 1952. Calculated based on data in SYB 1982, 426.

[3] Kornai 1980.

homes, often rented from the government. Home appliances existed in science fiction. A new set of clothes or a new pair of shoes was often reserved for annual replacement bestowed during the Chinese New Year's holiday. It was not unheard of in parts of rural China for family members to take turns leaving the house because they did not have enough clothes to cover every member of the household at once. In cities, the lucky ones had bicycles as a modern means of transportation. For those living in the countryside, and some in the cities, a bus or train ride was a rare experience not to be had until well into their adulthood, if they were lucky enough to have that experience.

A mere four decades after the farmers in Xiaogang village pressed their thumbs on their note of promise, an entirely different China has emerged. Leaving behind a life of scarcity and deprivation, one-fifth of humanity on earth now lives in a land of material abundance. The road to prosperity and abundance began with meeting people's most basic needs, then moved on in stages: what they ate, what they wore, where and how they lived, how they got around, and how they connected with one another in the country and beyond. Improvements in the standard of living continued in phases and, not surprisingly, depended upon a person's social status, most notably their status assigned to them during the years of socialism. It all began, however, with the people who made up the majority of the Chinese population, those in the countryside. They were the ones directly responsible for producing the most basic necessities in life. The ascendance to abundance began with nourishing the body.

From Starvation to Gluttony

A Diet on the Margins

Feeding the population dogged the country's leaders during the entire period of China's planned economy practice. A vast and rapidly growing population often teetered precariously on the margins of subsistence. For nearly two decades after the mid-1950s, there was virtually no improvement in the most basic food supply items such as grain and vegetable oil (Figure 3.1). Per capita grain supply, the most important of all plant-based sources, remained virtually unchanged at below 200 kg per year between the mid-1950s and the mid-1970s. In 1970, the average Chinese consumed less cooking oil, poultry, fish, and red meat than they did in 1957, at the peak of communization in the Chinese countryside. For some of these food items, the level was even below that in

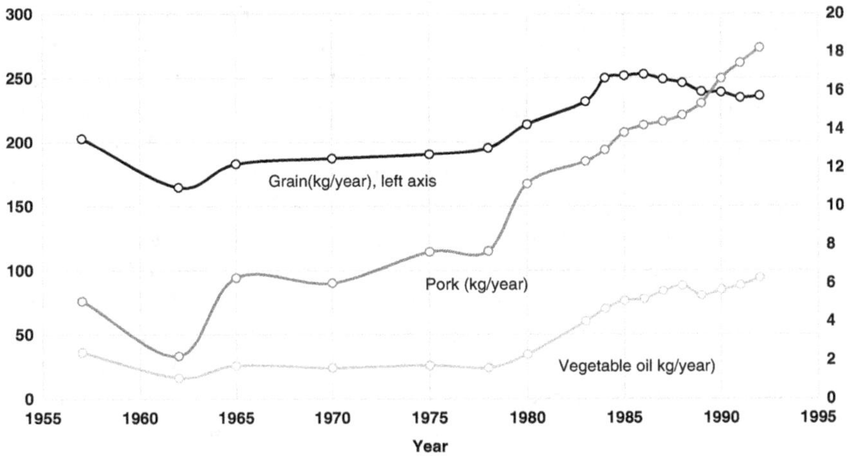

Figure 3.1 Per capita food consumption, selected food items, China, 1957–92
Source: SYB 1994, table 9–3

1952. For over a decade and a half after the mid-1960s, there was little increase in per capita pork availability (Figure 3.1).[4]

Such a food supply level, translated into nutritional measures, was hardly above the minimum required to maintain normal physical activities for the population. Pork consumption was at less than 1 kg (640 g) per person per month and cooking oil was at only 130 g. These quantities translate to a daily consumption of 20 g of meat and 4 g of vegetable oil per person. In the countryside, many farmers would not see any meat or high protein foods for months. At times of crises and poor harvests, food supply levels dropped far below the minimum required to sustain daily survival. This was the case during the Great Leap famine when food supplies decreased sharply. Per capita grain supply in 1962 was only 80 percent of the level of 1957, vegetable oil supply was only 45 percent, and pork was only 44 percent (Figure 3.1). The population drew their nutritional intake predominantly from plant-based sources. In 1970, over 80 percent of the estimated daily energy came from carbohydrates, only 9.6 percent came from protein, and 7.4 percent came from fat.[5] This diet, once converted to energy units of kcal, suggests a population living on the margins of subsistence, punctured by intermittent starvation.

[4] These per capita consumption amounts include both market-purchased and self-produced and consumed, and they include processed goods using these materials (SYB 1994, table 9.3).

[5] Chinese government statistics, cited in Du et al. 2014.

Moreover, analysis of food consumption suggests that in the late 1970s per capita food availability was no higher than it had been over four decades earlier, in the early 1930s. The first large-scale land utilization survey in Chinese history, headed by US agricultural economist John L. Buck, produced the first estimate of food intake available to Chinese farmers at the time.[6] At the time of the survey, between 1929 and 1933, the estimated per capita food availability was calculated at 2,130 kcal, after adjustment of population by age and sex.[7] This level, as assessed by Vaclav Smil, corresponded closely to the nutritional needs of an "overwhelmingly rural population engaged in moderate-to-heavy unmechanized fieldwork," which is about 2,200 kcal/day.[8] During the Great Leap famine, however, the food supply collapsed to 1,462 kcal/day, only two-thirds of the needed intake level.[9] Tens of millions of people died from starvation.[10] Food production increased in the 1960s and 1970s, as did the population. By the mid- to late 1970s, per capita food availability returned to pre-famine levels, about 2,200 kcal/day.[11] For most of the years during China's four Five-Year-Plans (between 1953 and 1975), the average energy intake for the rural population was less than the per capita energy requirements.[12]

For the average person living in China in the 1970s, the difference between the 1930s and 1970s was a much more equal distribution of food. As noted by Smil, "It was evident that the typical Chinese diet, while not implying chronic massive malnutrition, did not provide any safety margin either."[13] And "only a highly equitable distribution of food could have prevented massive malnutrition."[14] But for a country the size of China, any fine-tuned and perfectly equal distribution was an untenable social-engineering exercise. Local variations in food production resulted in vast variations in food availability and in incidences of hunger and malnutrition. The reality faced by the farming households in Xiaogang village was just one example. While some households had more food grains and other food products available to them, the rest had less. The average resident in urban China, for instance, had 22 percent more nutritional intake available in 1978 than a person residing in

[6] The first of its kind in Chinese history, the survey included 17,351 individuals in 2,727 households across 21 provinces.

[7] Smil 2003, table 3.1. [8] Ibid. [9] World Bank 1984, table 4.1.

[10] Estimates of excess deaths vary. One study by a demographic expert, for example, put it at over 20 million (Peng 1987).

[11] Smil gives estimates of 2,045 for 1974 and 2,130 for 1977–1978 (2003, table 3.1). The World Bank reported a number of 2,226 for 1975 (World Bank 1984, table 4.1). Official Chinese statistics give a number of 2,311 for 1978 (SYB 1983, 509).

[12] Ash 2006, table 6. [13] Smil 1986, 25. [14] Smil 2003.

rural China (urban 2,715 kcal versus rural 2,224 kcal), despite a greater physical labor demand for the rural person.[15]

Over the decades, while on average the Chinese population did not seem to eat less in terms of grain, they certainly ate worse. Per capita grain production in 1975 was reported at 310 kg, the same as in 1956. An increasing share of that grain output, however, turned out to be those grains less liked for consumption by the population, such as corn and sorghum, grains for the most part used as animal feed or for making alcohol. Toward the last years of China's planned economy, more farmland was allocated to produce higher-yield but considerably less preferable grain for consumption. Between 1970 and 1978, for instance, land devoted to corn cultivation increased by 26 percent, compared with the 6.4 percent increase for rice. During the same period, corn output rose by 69.38 percent while overall grain production increased by only 27 percent and rice output increased by only 24.5 percent.[16] In 1978, the "fine grains" – the preferred wheat and rice – accounted for less than half of the grains consumed by rural households. It was not until the mid-1980s, when rural reforms led to much increased output, that there was an increase in grains favored by rural households. The share of wheat and rice in daily diets went up to over 80 percent.[17]

Other sources of nutritional intake show similar or even more severe scarcity. Output statistics confirm those illustrated by consumption data above. Per capita output for vegetable oil seeds dropped by nearly half over two decades, from 8.2 kg in 1956 to 4.3 kg in 1976. Per capita vegetable oil consumption did not see any improvement. Per capita pork production increased only 30 percent over the two decades of 1957 to 1977 from 6.3 kg per person per year to 8.25 kg.[18] Were this distribution to be equal, it would amount to a pork supply of about 0.6 kg per person per month, less than 100 g (86 g) per week, and about 10 g (12 g) per day. Given that some yield was wasted and that distribution was not equitable, much of the population was unable to procure any meat for months on end. In the late 1970s, meat rationing dropped to 0.25 kg per month per person for most urban residents. In 1978, per capita cooking oil available to the rural population was only 1.97 kg per year, meat at 5.76 kg, and eggs at 0.8 kg, translating to fewer than one egg *per month*, much below the national average.[19] Although animals, particularly chickens, raised privately by farmers were not accounted for, the overall numbers portray a picture of a diet that was both precariously low in quantity and poor in nutrition.

[15] SYB 1983, 509. [16] Ibid., 162. [17] Calculated from SYB 1994, table 9–25.
[18] SYB 1983, 184. [19] SYB 1994, table 9–25.

Eating Better

The first signs of abundance began with food and diet change. Returning farming to the household injected new incentive and energy into agricultural production. The change began with a household responsibility system as first ventured by Xiaogang village in late 1978, culminating in the full dissolution of the people's commune system in 1984. In 1978, nearly two-thirds (66.3 percent) of rural households' incomes was from collective farming, and 26.8 percent was from household economic activities. By 1984, the share of income from the collective was reduced to 10 percent, while the share from individual farming and household economic activities rose to 80 percent. Per capita rural income rose 166 percent in six years, from 133.57 to 355.33 yuan.[20]

The turnaround in agricultural output was swift and broad. In just five years, between 1978 and 1983, total grain output rose by 27 percent. The state procurement system, enforced over thirty years, started to fade out in the early 1980s: the types of agricultural products under state procurement dropped swiftly, from a long list of 183 items in 1980 to 38 in 1984.[21] In 1985, state procurement quotas were eliminated; by 1992, the state procurement of agricultural products had faded into history.

It was not just that the total output increased but also that the outputs of what people wanted to eat also increased. Soy bean output rose by 29 percent, wheat by 52.17 percent, and corn by comparison only 21.91 percent. Vegetable oil seed yields rose even more, 202 percent in five years. Fruit, a rarity under the planned economy, saw a production increase of 44.38 percent in five years.[22] In the five years from 1978 to 1983, per capita nutritional intake rose by 24.5 percent, from 2,311 to 2,877 kcal, with 3,183 in cities and 2,806 in the countryside. The share of nutritional intake from animal-based sources rose from 6 percent to 7.85 percent.[23]

The first decade of China's age of abundance, between 1978 and 1988, was also the most revolutionary decade in Chinese history. In no other decade had an entire nation experienced this kind of improvement in both the quantity and quality of their daily diet. Official data on food consumption document how this transformation took place. Table 3.1 summarizes per capita consumption of selected major food items between 1957 and 1992.

[20] SYB 1985, table 11–22, based on household surveys. 6.9 percent of the income in 1978 was from loans and borrowing.

[21] These include Chinese medicinal materials. Yang 1998, 207.

[22] SYB 1994.

[23] SYB 1984, 480.

Table 3.1 *Per capita consumption of food items (kg), China, 1957–92*

Year	Grain	Cooking oil	Pork	Beef & mutton	Poultry	Fresh eggs	Aquatic products	Sugar	Liquor
1957	203.06	2.42	5.08	1.11	0.50	1.26	4.34	1.51	1.37
1962	164.63	1.09	2.22	0.79	0.38	0.77	2.96	1.60	1.14
1965	182.84	1.72	6.29	1.02	0.36	1.42	3.33	1.68	1.30
1970	187.22	1.61	6.02	0.82	0.32	1.32	2.94	2.06	1.51
1975	190.52	1.73	7.63	0.72	0.35	1.63	3.26	2.26	2.18
1978	195.46	1.60	7.67	0.75	0.44	1.97	3.50	3.42	2.57
1980	213.81	2.30	11.16	0.83	0.80	2.27	3.41	3.83	3.41
1983	231.52	4.01	12.31	1.10	1.18	2.95	4.00	4.46	5.79
1984	249.65	4.66	12.93	1.23	1.35	3.88	4.32	4.85	6.55
1985	251.69	5.08	13.84	1.31	1.56	4.93	4.84	5.57	7.61
1986	252.67	5.17	14.22	1.32	1.72	5.20	5.33	6.04	8.97
1987	248.88	5.60	14.39	1.43	1.71	5.50	5.49	6.59	10.39
1988	246.10	5.87	14.73	1.58	1.75	5.74	5.66	6.17	11.42
1989	239.12	5.35	15.36	1.58	1.79	5.88	6.17	4.92	11.33
1990	238.80	5.67	16.64	1.73	1.73	6.27	6.53	4.98	11.63
1991	234.50	5.89	17.44	1.79	1.98	7.10	6.79	4.98	11.93
1992	235.91	6.29	18.22	2.05	2.31	7.75	7.29	5.42	12.94

Source: SYB 1994, table 9–3

To better visualize these rapid improvements, Figure 3.2 shows the changes in per capita consumption of select food items in the first one-and-a-half decades of the economic reform era. Grain consumption increased by as much as 30 percent between 1978 (the reference year) and the mid-1980s, before starting to decline. But grain consumption increase was the least among the items included on this chart. As soon as people had enough grain for consumption, they started to eat better. Between 1978 and 1983, per capita egg consumption rose 50 percent, pork 61 percent, vegetable oil 151 percent, and poultry 268 percent. By 1988, diet had greatly improved; the average consumption rose 25 percent for grain, but it rose by twice as much for pork and other meats, over three-and-a-half times for vegetable oil, nearly three times as much for eggs, and nearly four times for poultry (Figure 3.2). By 1992, following a decade of food production increases, the share of energy intake from carbohydrates dropped to 65.8 percent, from 83 percent in 1970, while protein increased to 10.7 percent and fat to 22.5 percent.[24] By 2002, the energy intake from animal sources increased to 25 percent compared with 8 percent in 1982.[25]

[24] Chinese government statistics, cited in Du et al. 2014. [25] Y. Wu et al. 2005.

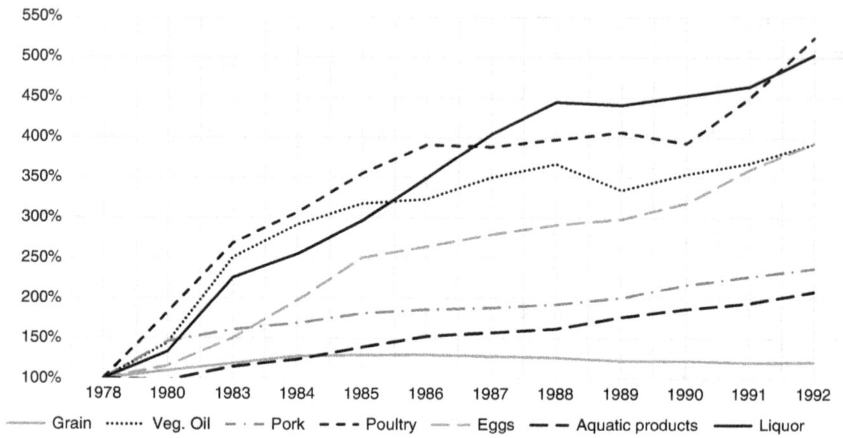

Figure 3.2 Changes in per capita food consumption, selected items, China, 1978–92 (1978=100)
Source: SYB 1994

Pleasure and vice consumption soon followed. The decade of China's diet revolution registered sharp increases in the consumption of tobacco, alcohol, and sugar. Compared with the 60 percent increase in per capita pork consumption and 151 percent increase in vegetable oil consumption in the decade after 1978, per capita liquor consumption rose 344 percent, from 2.57 kg in 1978 to 11.42 kg in 1988, per capita sugar consumption rose by 180 percent, from 3.42 kg to 6.17 kg.[26] Cigarette consumption doubled from 31 to 69 packs per person annually. This consumption level translates to more than one pack per person every week, for every person in the country. Given that most smokers were males over the age of fourteen, the average smoker could have puffed on average 192 packs of cigarettes a year.[27]

Eating New

Until its closing in 1994, to give up its space for more important functions, the first Kentucky Fried Chicken restaurant in China was the largest KFC anywhere in the world. Opening in November 1987 with 500 seats, this first-ever Western fast-food operation to enter China was an instant sensation. It quickly became a favored venue for special

[26] SYB 1994, table 9–3.
[27] In 1988, 28 percent of the population were under the age of fifteen.

occasions, such as dates or special celebrations. In 1988, the restaurant fried 2,200 chickens per day.[28]

For a population that had experienced extreme food deprivation just a decade earlier, and in a city where special rationing coupons were still used, chicken deeply fried to a golden color and served in a spotlessly clean and aromatic environment was exotic and alluring beyond imagination. Not long after the first KFC, Pizza Hut opened its first store in China in 1990. Then, in April 1992, another Western fast-food chain entered the Chinese market: The first McDonald's in Beijing was located at the entrance of the capital city's most venerable shopping district, Wangfujing. Not to be outdone by KFC, this store was built with 700 seats and 29 cash registers, and it sold 40,000 hamburgers on its opening day. Food, no longer a nutritional necessity, became a social and cultural symbol. Other Western fast-food chains soon followed. By 2019, there were close to 6,000 KFCs and 3,383 McDonald's across China.[29]

Next came Starbucks. Gourmet coffee, totally foreign to most Chinese tea drinkers, became the fastest growing and the most exotic taste entering China. Starbucks opened its first shop in 1999 in Beijing's central business district. Offerings with names of cappuccino, Frappuccino, and Americano saw a sustained explosive increase in the following two decades. Five years after setting its foot in China, Starbucks posted an impressive expansion of stores: from 209 in 2005 to 470 by 2010. The number of stores more than tripled in the next five years, to 1,811 in 2015, then more than doubled again, to 4,400 by 2020, in over 180 cities in mainland China. The number of Starbucks in China alone accounted for one in seven of the company's stores worldwide in 2020 and one in four of those outside of the United States.[30] China became another caffeinated country.

Along with the rapid increase in the availability of basic and traditional food items was the emergence of new and highly nutritious food consumption. Particularly striking was the availability of milk and other dairy products to the general population, not just the elite. For a population in which over 90 percent are lactose intolerant,[31] milk consumption was largely absent in most people's diet prior to the recent boom. Per capita milk production was at only 1.2 kg per person per year in 1980; while it doubled to 2.4 kg per person by 1985, it was still at a very low level. In 2000, per capita milk production rose again, but to only 6.6 kg per person.

[28] https://en.wikipedia.org/wiki/Fast_food_in_China#KFC%E2%80%99s_success_in_China
[29] https://en.wikipedia.org/wiki/KFC_in_China; www.statista.com/statistics/256049/mcdonalds-restaurants-in-the-emea-region/-in-the-emea-region/
[30] www.statista.com/statistics/277795/number-of-starbucks-stores-in-china/
[31] www.omicsonline.org/china/lactose-intolerance-peer-reviewed-pdf-ppt-articles/

After the turn of the century, however, milk production more than tripled between 2000 and 2005, exceeding 20 kg per person per year. Consumption of dairy products has since stabilized at this high level.[32] This threefold increase in domestic production of dairy products in just five years does not include the massive increase of imported dairy goods (the majority as whole milk powder). In the decade after 2008, the total value of dairy imports increased by sixfold, from less than $1.8 billion to around $12 billion. Imports boomed in the five-year period between 2009 and 2014, when dairy imports grew at an annual rate of about 40 percent.

China has been by far the largest dairy importer in the world since 2010, accounting for over one-fifth of global dairy product imports. Raised incomes, demographic change, and particularly lifestyle changes all contributed to the boom in dairy consumption. Bakeries turned up on every other city street corner. From the young to the elderly, milk along with eggs became a routine breakfast option. Notably, the breastfeeding of infants under six months of age dropped from 50.8 to only 20.8 percent between 2003 and 2013. The Chinese, living in the land of tofu for millennia, started to become cheese eaters. Chinese cheese imports grew at an annual rate of 25 percent for the decade following 2008. As with whole milk powder imports, China is expected to become the world's largest cheese importer in the 2020s.[33]

Unlike the new and exotic food items introduced, consumption of grains and even other traditional food items such as pork slowed down after the initial rise up to the late 1980s. The boost in consumption of vegetable oil and pork was almost entirely pushed up by rural consumers catching up to urban consumption levels. In both rural and urban households, consumption of food grain dropped, the faster decline being among rural households. For them, per capita grain consumption dropped to 157 kg per year among rural residents by the mid-2010s, down 40 percent from the level in the late 1980s. Up until 2010, however, the urban-rural gap in per capita pork and cooking oil consumption persisted, although the gap in pork consumption narrowed significantly by the year 2000. In contrast to a ratio of more than two to one between urban and rural residents in meat consumption in 1980, the gap was reduced to only slightly above 25 percent by the year 2000 (Figure 3.3). By the mid-2010s, these urban-rural consumption gaps were largely closed, as these two consumption levels converged.

32 SYB 2018, table 12–16.

33 Brad Gehrke and Lesley Ahmed, "Agricultural Trade with China: Dairy Import Giant," US International Trade Commission Executive Briefings on Trade, Sept. 2019, www.usitc.gov/publications/332/executive_briefings/ebot_brad_gehrke_lesley_ahmed_china_dairy_pdf.pdf

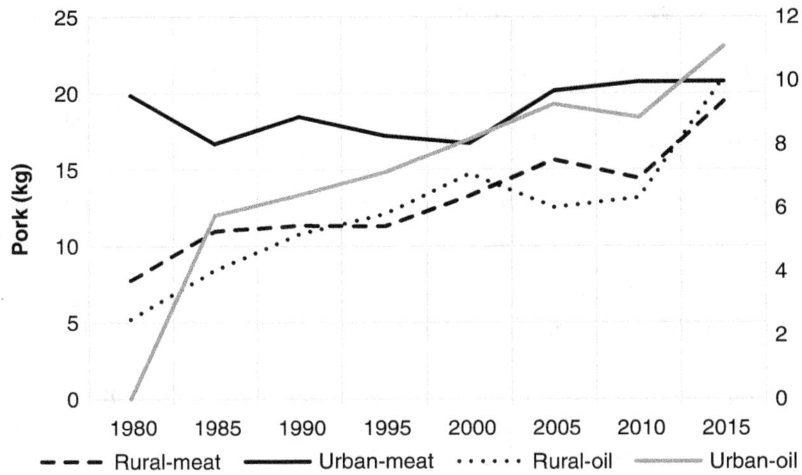

Figure 3.3 Closing urban–rural food consumption gap: pork and vegetable oil, China, 1980–2015
Source: SYB, various years

Eating Out Once food supply became sufficient, a new pleasure in food consumption returned, and at an accelerating pace. This was dining out in restaurants, appreciating food prepared and served by others, and tasting cuisines from different regions of the country. During the planned economy era, institutional food services in work organizations (cafeterias and canteens), combined with the increasingly severe food shortage, effectively drove restaurants out of existence. By the late 1970s, restaurants were few and far between in Chinese cities. For those still operating, they were open only a few hours a day and required both money and food rationing coupons for their scant offerings. The planned economy also decimated other retail businesses. In 1978, for every 10,000 people there were only 13 retail stores, restaurants, and service stalls, down from 96 in 1952 and 42 in 1957.[34]

Consumption outside the home rose substantially into the 1980s. The number of retail stores, restaurants, and service stalls shot up from 13 per 10,000 people in 1978 to 102 by 1985 and then 116 by 1988. The share of individuals engaged in these services also rose quickly from 63 per 10,000 people to 240 and further to 276.[35] In 2016, China's restaurants and institutional food services posted $461 billion

[34] SYB 1990, table 8–1. [35] Ibid.

in sales, an amount equivalent to 63 percent of food that the food-service sector supplied in the United States, approximately $731 billion. For a country where the per capita income level was still about one-fifth of the United States' in 2014 and where only about 55 percent of the population lived in urban areas, this level of spending on food services was very high.[36]

Consumption in hotels and restaurants began to rise sharply and at a rate consistently faster than that in general wholesale and retail sales. Between 1990 and 2008, wholesale and retail sales rose 15-fold, unadjusted for inflation. Spending on hotels and restaurants by comparison rose 36-fold (left axis, Figure 3.4). Whereas eating out in restaurants was initially largely for business customers, starting in the mid-1990s ordinary urban residents became the majority of customers. In the latter half of the 1990s, urban per capita income (adjusted for inflation) rose 43 percent and per capita food expenditure increased 17 percent, yet per capita expenditure on food consumed away from home shot up 88 percent. Eating out as the share of total food expenditure increased from 10 to 16 percent.[37]

That was only the beginning. Between 1997 and 2007, the share of expenditure on hotels and restaurants in total retail sales doubled from 7 to 14 percent (right axis, Figure 3.4). Among the reported hotel and

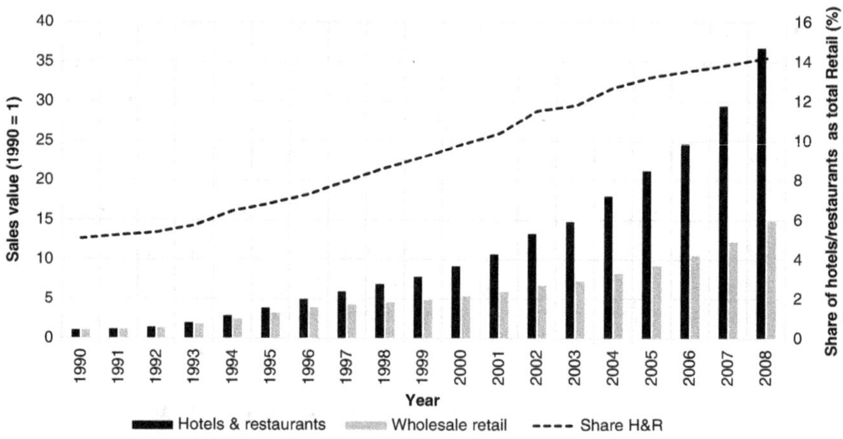

Figure 3.4 Consumption away from home, China, 1990–2008
Source: SYB 2009, table 16–3

[36] USDA Foreign Agricultural Service, *GAIN Report*, March 5, 2018. https://bit.ly/3LRRIYQ

[37] Ma et al. 2006.

restaurant spending, the lion's share, 70 percent, went on dining.[38] In 2005, only 9,748 restaurants were part of franchise chains nationwide. A decade later, the number rose by nearly 2.5 times, to 23,721. Revenue from these restaurants rose by 3.36 times during the same decade.[39] With the arrival of e-commerce, a new dining option became available: food prepared away from home for delivery. A report by management consulting firm Bain & Company in 2017 reported that among inhabitants of top-tiered Chinese cities between 2013 and 2016 food purchased for in-home meal preparation increased by only 3 percent, while dining out grew by 10 percent and food delivery by 44 percent.[40]

Getting Taller

The stature of a population is arguably the best measure to capture the effect of improved diet and nutrition. Elsewhere in the world, studies have shown how nutritional and health improvements have led to the increased height of the population.[41] The average height of human beings increased worldwide after the Industrial Revolution, largely due to better nutrition. Over two centuries, the estimated average heights for men in five European populations increased by 10 cm or more. In Britain, heights increased from 165.9 cm to 175 cm between 1750 and 1975. In Norway, where the largest increase was reported, it increased by more than 14 cm, from 163.9 cm to 178.3 cm. Nutritional improvement was estimated to account for about 30 percent of the per capita income increase in Britain for the two centuries between 1790 and 1980, in what Robert Fogel calls in his 1994 Nobel laureate lecture the thermodynamic factor or the physiological factor of modern economic growth.[42]

For much of the eighteenth and nineteenth centuries, "Europeans were severely stunted by modern standards."[43] Most of the gains in height therefore were after the late nineteenth century. In the first half of the twentieth century, the average height recorded for adult American men, who achieved near-modern stature, increased from 171 to 175 cm. The

[38] In 2017, total reported revenue for hotels was 39.64 billion yuan, of which 14.03 billion was spent on food in hotel restaurants. In addition, 53.05 billion was reported to have been spent in food establishments not inside hotels (SYB 2018, table 17–1).

[39] SYB 2018, table 17–8.

[40] Bain & Company, "'Out of home' consumption market in China thrives as country's FMCG Market continues along two different trajectories," June 20, 2017, https://bit.ly/3MgdW6O

[41] Steckel 1995; Fogel 2004b. [42] Fogel 1994, 383.

[43] Fogel 2004a, 13, table 1.4. Of the six European populations, one, Hungary, was an exception not included here. The estimated final height increased by less than 2 cm, from 169.1 cm in 1750 to 170.9 cm in 1975.

increase was faster in Europe, from 165 cm to 170 cm in France, 167 cm to 175 cm in Britain, and 169 cm to 178 cm for adult males in the Netherlands.[44] These improvements in adult height, between 1 cm and 2 cm per decade, are largely consistent with those observed at younger ages.[45] In Britain, for instance, the long-term changes in height show an increase of about 15 cm among 15-year-old adolescents over a six-decade period, between those born in 1900 and in 1960, averaging about 2.5 cm per decade.[46] Similarly, in Japan, over an eight-decade period between the birth cohorts born in 1894 and 1974, the average height for a 14-year-old schoolboy increased by slightly less than 20 cm and about 15 cm for a girl.[47] That is less than 2.5 cm per decade.

For China, the age of abundance witnessed a stunning increase of population height. In just 20 years, children in China grew at a historic pace. At age 7, upon entering primary school, a boy in urban China was 5.2 cm taller in 2002 than in 1992, and a girl was 5.7 cm taller. Height increases among the less well-off rural children were even more notable: a 7-year-old boy gained 7.8 cm in height between 1992 and 2012, and a 7-year-old girl, who was previously more underprivileged, also gained the most, 7.9 cm (Figure 3.5A). Height increases for young Chinese were nearly twice as fast as in Europe and faster than in Japan as well. In the decade following 1992, height increases ranged from 3.2 cm for an urban boy to 3.9 cm for a 7-year-old rural girl. These increases were followed by another 2 cm to 4.4 cm in the decade after 2002. Such rapid increases in stature rank among the most impressive measures of China's ascendance to its age of abundance; they are virtually unprecedented in the history of human physical development.

Moreover, better nutrition shows improved outcomes later in life. At age 15, when an adolescent approaches the height of an adult, the average height for boys in urban China reached 167.7 cm in 2012, up 3.6 cm over a two-decade period. A girl in urban China would reach the height of 158.8 cm, up 2.3 cm (Figure 3.5B). Again, height increases were twice as rapid for the rural population: for a 15-year-boy in rural China in 2012, who had been born in the late 1990s, that increase was a stunning 7.1 cm compared with a boy born in the late 1970s, and for a girl of the same age, there was a full 5 cm improvement.

At least by one measure, the distinct physical difference over China's urban-rural divide is no longer as visible as it was two decades ago. Prior

[44] Steckel 1995, 1919, table 6.

[45] In nearly all European countries, "from about 1900 to the present, children in average economic circumstances have increased in height at ages 5 to 7 years by about 1–2 cm per decade" (Tanner 1990, 150).

[46] Floud, Wachter, and Gregory 1990, 289.

[47] Gail Honda 1997, figures 7.4 and 7.5, in Steckel and Floud 1997.

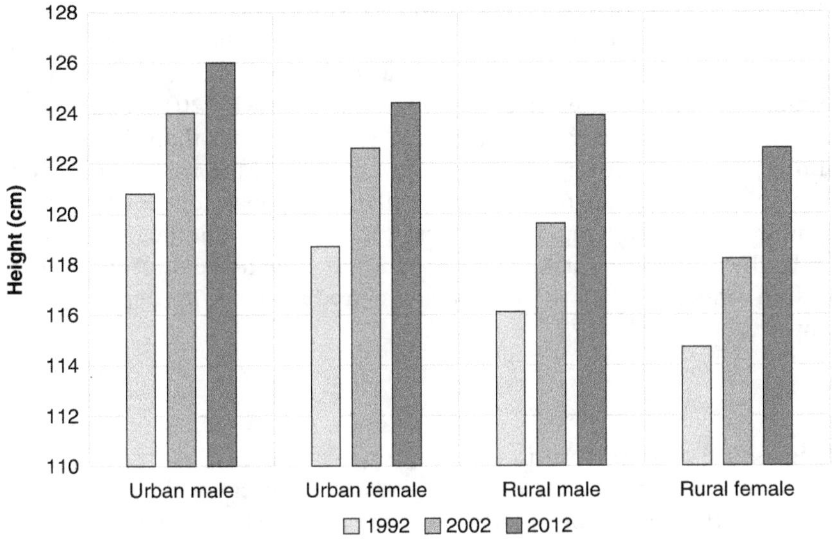

Figure 3.5A Average height at seven years of age (cm), urban and rural China, 1992–2012

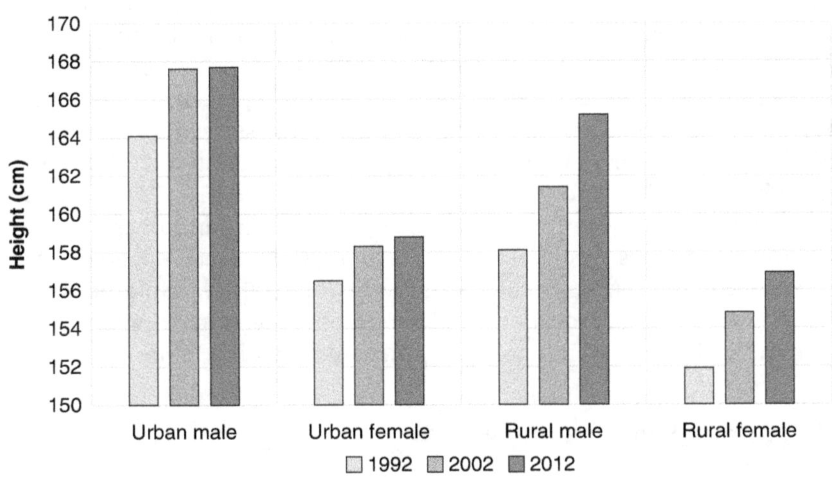

Figure 3.5B Average height at fifteen years of age (cm), urban and rural China, 1992–2012

Sources: HSYB 2013; 2015; based on China National Nutrition Survey 1992, 2002, and 2012

to the 1990s, a person from rural China was substantially shorter than one raised in urban China. In 1992, a 15-year-old urban boy was a full 6 cm taller than a rural boy; an urban girl was 4.6 cm taller than her rural counterpart. Those differences have shrunk sharply. By 2012, a rural boy was only 2.5 cm shorter and a girl only 1.9 cm shorter than their urban counterparts. As diet improvements have benefited the rural population more profoundly than the urban population, at least one of the most apparent urban-rural gaps, in physical appearance and in health, is closing. In the 1990s, as nutrition improved, the prevalence of underweight children under the age of five was also reduced by 74 percent, and stunting by 70 percent.[48]

A New Malnutrition

Along with the abundance in food supply, malnutrition has taken a new form, from undernutrition to excessive and unhealthy eating. With the rapid increase in the consumption of meat, dairy products, and sugar, and the rapid and massive influx of fast-food chains, a new scene of malnutrition has arrived. While the overall level of overweight persons and obesity in China is still relatively low compared to that in some Western countries, such as the United States, the rate of increase is stunning. Between 1985 and 2000, the share of overweight schoolchildren (aged 7 to 18) in the population increased by 28 times and the number of obese children increased fourfold, with the increases particularly pronounced among boys. Based on national surveys in 1985, only 0.2 percent of boys and 0.1 percent of girls were obese, and between 1 and 2 percent of them were assessed as overweight and obese. By the early 2000s, the obesity rate had shot up to 12.9 percent among boys aged 7–9 and 9.1 percent among those aged 10–12 in Chinese cities. Combined, the prevalence for being overweight and obese rose to 25.4 percent for boys aged 7–9 and 17 percent for girls aged 7–9, and it rose to 17 percent and 14.3 percent, respectively, for 10–12-year old boys and girls.[49] Within four decades, over the period of rising material abundance, the term "malnutrition" has acquired a new meaning in China.

From Clothing to Fashion

In a country where people hardly had enough to fill their stomachs, there was also not much to cover their bodies. In 1977, not far from Xiaogang

[48] Zong and Li 2014, 557.

[49] Ji, Sun, and Chen 2004. A body mass index (BMI) over 25 is considered overweight and over 30 is obese.

village, and a year before the farmers' defiance of collective farming, a provincial Communist Party secretary was inspecting poor rural villages. In one of the villages, an old man and two young girls were scolded by the Party boss's entourage for not showing respect. Instead of standing up to welcome the most important Party official in the province, they sat in a pile of straw next to the stove in their dilapidated hut. When the old man finally stood up, the Party officials suddenly realized the reason for the seeming disrespect: neither the old man nor his two young daughters had pants. They were too embarrassed to stand up, even in front of the highest-ranked official in the province in their humble hut. They did not have enough clothes to cover their bodies.[50]

Not all Chinese in those days were as destitute. But the signs of scarcity, in clothing, as with food, were everywhere. While residents in cities were guaranteed a minimal supply of clothing materials and footwear with rationing, many rural households lacked the income to pay for new clothes and shoes. Photos taken by the occasional foreign visitor depicted scenes of "blue and grey ants." Adults, males and females alike, mostly wore homogenously designed clothes in blue and grey.

In the twilight days of the planned economy era, the average resident spent the majority of their meager income on food, with little left for anything else. Not surprisingly, the share of the disposable income spent on food, known as the Engel's coefficient, was very high: 68 percent for rural households and 57 percent for urban households in 1978 (those numbers dropped 41 percent and 36 percent, respectively, by 2010, see Figure 3.6). In 1981, urban households spent about 15 percent and rural households 12 percent of their money on clothing. Income levels at the time were low, less than $200 per capita for the country as a whole. The share of people's income spent on clothing then translates to about $25 per person *for the whole year.*[51] The average spending on clothing for a person living in the countryside was much less, less than $10 per person per year.[52]

As prices were distorted under the planned economy system, however, clothing conditions could be better captured by the various items individuals purchased and used, not just the yuan or the dollar amount spent. Short of cash income and excluded from urban rationing, many rural residents could only afford locally available materials and tailors. It was not uncommon for

[50] Chen and Wu 2009, 7.

[51] Per capita income was 496.8 yuan, or $197.14, and annual expenditure was 456.72 yuan, of which 67.56 yuan ($26.81) was spent on clothing (at the official exchange rate that year). SYB 1981, table 11–19, based on sample survey data of urban households in forty-six cities nationwide.

[52] 23.57 yuan ($9.35). SYB 1981, table 11–16.

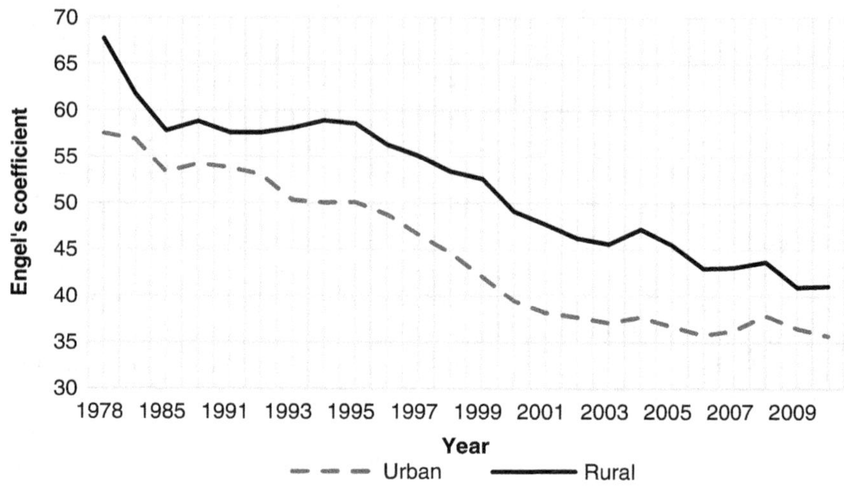

Figure 3.6 Engel's coefficient, urban and rural China, 1978–2010
Source: SYB 2011, table 10–2

urban children to have a new set of clothes made for them once a year, as a special treat upon the Chinese New Year.

Items purchased at the time depict an impoverished life in a developing country, where clothing was limited to keeping bodies covered and warm. The first statistics from the Chinese government reported that in 1981 the average urban dweller purchased *for the entire year* about 6.5 m of material for clothing, 5 m of which was cotton. This amount is barely sufficient to make two adult shirts.[53] For rural residents, the total was a meter less at 5.44 m. Urban residents, unlike their rural compatriots who made virtually all their clothes by themselves, could buy ready-made clothes in department stores. In 1981, urban residents also bought on average 1.2 sets of machine-made outfits for the entire year, in addition to a set of knitwear. In total, with roughly three sets of new clothes each year, urban residents were better clothed than those in the countryside; a minimal amount of clothing nonetheless.[54]

Machine-made shoes were expensive and a luxury, especially for those living in the countryside. For the whole country in 1981, each resident bought for the entire year one pair of shoes, 1.3 pairs of socks, and only one pair of underwear. These numbers were a substantial increase from

[53] It is estimated that making an adult shirt takes 2.5 yards (2.86 m) of cloth. https://sewingiscool.com/how-much-fabric-do-i-need-for-a-shirt-t/
[54] SYB 1981.

the previous year when the average number of socks purchased was only 0.73 pairs per person. The country had only one brand of sport sneakers, Huili, made in Shanghai. Owning a pair of Huili sneakers was a dream for youngsters in Chinese cities but something never heard of by the hundreds of millions tilling the soil in the countryside. Priced at more than 10 yuan a pair, an urban employee's entire monthly income could afford barely more than four pairs of such fancy shoes.[55] Given the urban-rural differential in consumption and habits, less than one pair of machine-made shoes, socks, or underwear were affordable for each person in rural China. In 1978, on a per capita basis, rural Chinese only bought 0.32 pairs of shoes, or one pair for every three persons.[56] Again, as with clothes, people living in the countryside made their own shoes and socks, and southerners (in the warmer weather) got by with straw shoes; all of which were not included in purchased goods tallies.

Unlike food consumption increases, improvements in how people clothed themselves transformed the Chinese social scene, from a sea of blue and grey ants to one of abundant colors and styles. The change was not just in quantity but more in quality and variety. As people started to buy more ready-made clothes, textile purchases declined. Still, as seen especially in rural China, people had more food to eat and more income. They started to buy more clothing materials and shoes. Between 1978 – the first year data were available – and 1988, the amount of clothing material purchased per capita stayed largely unchanged and even declined slightly as farmers started to buy ready-made clothes. Yet what people did purchase more were synthetic materials, which are more durable than the low-quality cotton cloth of the time (Table 3.2). By the late 1990s, urban and rural families bought very little textiles from the market as they no longer relied on making their own clothes. Per capita purchases of commercially made shoes doubled in quantity. For urban residents, the shoes they bought were no longer only those made of rubber and cotton but those made of leather.

The world's largest country soon also became the world's largest textile producer and exporter, meeting the needs of not just its own people but also the whole world. Unlike growth and diversification in food supply, where the focus was not for export but to feed the Chinese population itself, textiles and footwear industries quickly became China's first entry into the global market. In 1980, textile exports were valued at $4.25 billion. A decade later, in 1990, exports almost quadrupled to

[55] The average monthly wage for urban Chinese employees in 1978 was 51.25 yuan (calculated from SYB 1990, table 4–20).
[56] SYB 1981, table 11–18.

Table 3.2 *Changes in per capita consumption of apparel, China, 1978–99*

	Rural			Urban		
	Cotton cloth (m)	Chemical fiber cloth (m)	Shoes (pair)	Cotton cloth (m)	Chemical fiber cloth (m)	Leather shoes (pair)
1979	5.20	0.73	0.44			
1980	4.30	0.94	0.51			
1981	4.21	1.23	0.49	4.64	1.67	0.46
1982	3.94	1.53	0.48	4.24	2.00	0.48
1983	3.18	2.34	0.49	5.21	2.26	0.51
1984	2.82	2.48	0.57	8.99	1.95	0.62
1985	2.54	2.50	0.55	2.61	1.47	0.55
1986	1.98	2.53	0.66	2.54	1.79	0.59
1987	1.57	2.28	0.68	2.15	1.64	0.61
1988	1.50	2.14	0.69	2.69	1.72	0.61
1989	1.06	1.90	0.67	1.54	1.45	0.55
1990	0.90	1.83	0.74	1.33	1.46	0.61
1991	0.90	1.74	0.67	0.97	1.53	0.69
1992	0.80	1.88	0.73	0.69	1.32	0.69
1993	0.69	1.75	0.64	0.66	1.18	0.75
1994	0.56	1.78	0.65	0.49	1.07	0.77
1995	0.47	1.70	0.69	0.47	1.04	0.82
1996	0.47	1.83	0.74	0.41	1.02	0.82
1997	0.38	1.79	0.70	0.36	0.85	0.77
1998	0.32	1.57	0.66	0.34	0.73	0.74
1999	0.30	1.52	0.66	0.32	0.55	0.79

Source: SYB, various years. Some urban numbers are not reported.

$16.89 billion. This number tripled to $53.04 billion in 2000, to $212 billion in 2010, and $291.15 billion in 2015. China's share of the total value of global textile and clothing exports rose from 4.6 percent in 1980 to 14.8 percent in 2000. After China's entry into the World Trade Organization (WTO) in 2001, along with the country's accelerating economic boom, the share more than doubled within a decade to 34.3 percent by 2010, then to 37.4 percent by 2014.[57]

With increased earnings and being situated in the largest textile producer and exporter country in the world, the Chinese population directly benefited from the growth in these industries, with abundant and inexpensive supplies of raw materials as well as easily accessible and affordable

[57] Chen Yifang 陈义方, "Fangzhi daguo jueqi licheng: Zhongguo fangzhi gongye de 70 nian" 纺织大国崛起历程: 中国纺织工业的70年 (Rise of a giant textile production country: 70 years of China's textile industry) www.taweekly.com/xhdt/201612/t20161213_2332667.html.

made-to-sell textile and footwear products. By 2000, domestic per capita consumption of textiles reached 7.8 kg, approaching the global average of 8 kg. By 2015, Chinese consumption rose to 18.25 kg per capita, far exceeding the global average and closing in on the level of developed nations.[58] During the first five years of the twenty-first century, per capita income grew by 52 percent for urban residents and 38 percent for rural residents.[59] Growth of spending on clothing far outpaced that of income, rising by 225 and 431 percent, for urban and rural residents, respectively.[60]

The growth in textile industries also served as the first and foremost source of rising income and wealth amongst the vast rural Chinese population, in particular, those in the coastal Eastern and Southeastern provinces of Zhejiang, Jiangsu, Guangdong, and Fujian. As will be considered in the next chapter, most of the booming textile and footwear industries were born out of entrepreneurship of rural township and village enterprises (TVEs), a legacy of the urban-rural divide that created a large untapped labor pool in the Chinese countryside. Combined with bustling local entrepreneurship and small capital investment requirements in production equipment, this local pool, itself a product of the strict migration control policy, was an essential factor in China's rising dominance in the global textile and clothing industries.

The textiles and clothing sectors were matched in the shoe production line. At the turn of the twenty-first century, just two decades after the scarcity of shoe ownership, Chinese workers not only made enough shoes and socks to put on their own feet but also outfitted people worldwide. Chinese workers went from buying only one pair of shoes for themselves in 1981 to the scenario in 2000, when China entered the WTO and its shoe production exploded in the export market. By 2000, each Chinese person made an extra pair of shoes for people living outside of China: China exported 1.56 billion pairs of shoes (including 894.4 million leather and 744.84 million rubber-soled and other types) that year.[61] In 2005, shoe exports from China reached 2.48 billion pairs, 1.36 billion of which were leather.[62] According to Chinese statistics, the total number of shoe exports increased to 2.79 billion pairs by 2010[63] and to 3.5 billion pairs by 2015.[64] Besides satisfying a growing domestic demand for shoes of all kinds, China was producing and exporting more than enough shoes to supply over half the world's population outside of China with a pair each.[65]

[58] Chen, "Fangzhi daguo jueqi licheng." [59] Calculated from SYB 2006, table 10–2.
[60] Calculated from SYB for these years. [61] SYB 2001, table 17–8.
[62] SYB 2006, table 18–9. [63] SYB 2011, table 6–8. [64] SYB 2016, table 11–7.
[65] The world's population was 7.3 billion and China's 1.37 billion. The population outside of China was 5.93 billion.

"Made in China" appeared as the three-word label on billions and billions of clothing items sold worldwide. The labels were also sewn inside the billions of shoes worn by half of the residents on the planet around the turn of the twenty-first century. Starting in the mid-1990s, with the phasing out of the Multi Fibre Arrangement (MFA, a system of quotas that limited bilateral imports of specific types of textiles and apparel), global manufacturing of textiles and apparel shifted to low-cost regions. China was uniquely positioned to benefit from this global shift, with its abundant low-cost and hard-working labor and fast turnaround times, the two chief criteria sought after by labels and retailers selling low-margin items. In 1995, the United States was still the world's leading apparel maker, with 13 percent of the world's textile output, ahead of China's 12 percent. By 2017, China's share had expanded to 47 percent, while the United States' share had shrunk to only 3 percent.[66]

As China manufactured for the world, it also manufactured for itself. China was no longer just the factory to the world: it became the world's fastest growing consumer market. Most of those goods are now sold inside China. In 2005, China exported 71 percent of the finished apparel goods it produced. By 2017, the export share dropped to 47 percent; Chinese consumers accounted for more than 18 percent of all finished goods consumed. Moreover, Chinese laborers and consumers were not the only beneficiaries. Over a two-decade period since 1995, the real price for apparel fell by an estimated 44 percent.[67]

Clothing soon turned to fashion, and it was not just fashion but high fashion. Into the 2010s, Chinese consumers became the lead consumers of luxury goods. At the turn of the twenty-first century, Chinese consumers' spending made up a miniscule share of global luxury sales (including cars, hospitality, and personal luxury goods). That changed quickly. By 2010, Chinese consumers caught up with Japan's global share of luxury personal goods spending. It only took five more years, by 2015, for Chinese consumers' spending to triple to that of the Japanese and to surpass Europe and the United States to become the top shoppers in the world. By 2018, Chinese consumers' spending on luxury personal goods made up 33 percent of the global share, a share far greater than its share of the global population (18.34 percent), or its global ranking in per capita income (78th), at a level still below the global average.[68]

[66] McKinsey & Company, "The state of fashion 2019," https://cdn.businessoffashion.com/reports/The_State_of_Fashion_2019_v3.pdf

[67] Ibid.

[68] World Bank ranking of per capita income, with PPP, current international dollar. Global level in 2018 at $17,025 and China at $15,603.

Luxury spending is led by China's young generation, especially those born in the 1980s, who were responsible for 56 percent of all luxury spending in 2018.[69] Due to high Chinese tariffs on imported luxury goods, Chinese consumers' luxury spending mainly occurred during overseas shopping trips in the earlier years. With rising incomes and tariff reductions, luxury spending began to shift to spending within China, in the numerous high-end boutique shops in Chinese cities and online. In one year alone, between 2017 and 2018, luxury spending in mainland China grew 20 percent. Chinese consumers' appetite for luxury goods, as observed by a Bain & Company report on global luxury spending, was "unrivaled."[70]

A Roof over One's Head

Improvements in housing conditions soon followed. Housing, and its contents, represents a far larger share of household budget than food and clothing, and more importantly it constitutes a primary source of wealth creation and accumulation for most people in the country. Unlike food and clothing, for which individuals could make consumption decisions, housing during the socialist planned economy years was under tight state control in the cities. Designated as public property, housing was allotted by status. Consumption was not just the living space but also what went into it, including furniture: beds, chests, desks, and chairs. Lacking income and access to materials, the vast population living in the countryside built little to meet the need of their growing family members. After decades of neglect and disrepair, many of their old shelters also deteriorated to be barely livable.

Improving basic housing needs was clearly on Chinese leaders' minds. Deng Xiaoping himself made a highly publicized visit to a construction site of Beijing's first residential high-rises in October 1978, a year after his return to power. With twelve-stories, the apartment buildings were the highest of their type in the capital city. Prized as the best residential compound in Beijing, a two-bedroom apartment in that compound had

[69] McKinsey & Company, "China Luxury Report 2019," https://bit.ly/3Qu8TlP.

[70] Bain & Company, "Luxury goods worldwide market study, Fall–Winter 2018," https://bit.ly/3QcN490. The same report predicts that by 2025 China will account for nearly half (46 percent) of the global market. A different report, by the US financial services group Jefferies, claims that in one year, from 2019 to 2020, the Chinese share of global personal luxury goods expenditure shot up from 38–39 percent to 80–85 percent, due to China's early recovery from the COVID-19 pandemic in 2020. The report expects the Chinese market to account for 55 to 60 percent of the global market. Dominique Muret, "China to account for over 60% of world luxury market in short term," *Fashion Network*, Dec. 3, 2020, https://bit.ly/3tOdgzu.

a hallway but no separate living room, and the two bedrooms were sized at only 14 m^2 and 9 m^2 respectively. The larger model apartment had three bedrooms, at only 14 m^2, 12 m^2, and 9 m^2 each, with no additional living space. Even Deng commented that they were on the small side. But that was the best at the time in the country's capital city.

As soon as people had enough to eat and more to wear, they began to repair and to build their homes, to make them more livable and comfortable. To many, building a new home or acquiring an apartment was not just about the physical environment. It was also becoming a social expectation and requirement, and the only economic route for wealth accumulation and security. Starting in the countryside and later spreading to cities, for many Chinese parents, having a house or an apartment was a means for getting their son a bride, if they had one or more sons. For all, especially those living in the cities with skyrocketing real estate prices and few alternatives for investment, buying and selling an apartment became a guaranteed source of wealth accumulation. In 2018, 77.7 percent of urban Chinese households' wealth was in their residential housing, a share more than twice that in the United States, at 34.6 percent.[71]

Chinese official housing statistics report two separate series, one provided only after the year 2000, presumably by the Ministry of Construction, and another from the annual household income and expenditure surveys published by China's National Bureau of Statistics annually. Both are shown in Table 3.3. The main difference between the two series are the numbers used for urban housing, wherein household surveys reported both "usable" and "living" space, the other series lists only "usable" space. After the year 2000, the two series converged with only usable space reported.

Prior to China's age of abundance, both urban and rural residents were living in increasingly crowded and tight spaces, with little furniture, and lacking indoor plumbing and a private kitchen. The number of usable rooms per rural household actually decreased between 1957 and 1978, from 3.89 to 3.64; per capita usable living space reduced from 11.30 m^2 to 10.17 m^2.[72] In 1978, the government reported 8.1 m^2 and 6.7 m^2 of housing space per rural and urban resident (see Table 3.3). The government reported that it had built a total 1.1 billion m^2 of housing space for the entire period of three-and-a-half decades from 1950 to 1985.[73] These government-built housing units were exclusively provided for urban residents, whose numbers reached 251 million by 1985. On a per

[71] "Property accounts for excessive share of Chinese household wealth, investments lack diversification," China Banking News, Jan. 21, 2019, http://bit.ly/3FtxGjA

[72] SYB 1983, table 11–18. [73] SYB 1986.

Table 3.3 *Housing space and construction, China, 1978–2010*

	Available living space (m^2/person)		Construction (m^2/person)	
Year	Rural	Urban	Rural	Urban
1978	8.1	6.70	0.02	0.01
1980	9.4	7.18	0.05	0.06
1985	14.7	10.02	0.07	0.09
1986	15.3	12.44	0.08	0.12
1987	16.0	12.74	0.08	0.11
1988	16.6	13.00	0.08	0.10
1989	17.2	13.45	0.07	0.08
1990	17.8	13.65	0.06	0.08
1991	18.5	14.17	0.06	0.09
1992	18.9	14.79	0.07	0.07
1993	20.7	15.23	0.09	0.06
1994	20.2	15.69	0.10	0.07
1995	21.0	16.29	0.11	0.08
1996	21.7	17.03	0.11	0.10
1997	22.4	17.78	0.10	0.10
1998	23.3	18.66	0.11	0.10
1999	24.2	19.42	0.13	0.10
2000	24.80	20.25	0.12	0.10
2001	25.70	20.80	0.12	0.09
2002	26.50	22.79	0.12	0.09
2003	27.20	23.70	0.11	0.10
2004	27.90	25.00	0.10	0.09
2005	29.70	27.80	0.12	0.09
2006	30.65	28.50	0.11	0.09
2007	31.63	30.10	0.11	0.11
2008	32.40	30.60	0.12	0.12
2009	33.58	31.30	0.13	0.15
2010	34.08	31.60	0.13	0.14

Sources: SYB 2000, table 10–26; SYB 2011, table 10–35. Per capita construction space calculated by the author.

capita basis, the total housing space added over the three-and-half decades was about 4.4 m^2 per person. If one uses the 189.3 million urban residents added during the same period as the basis of calculation, on a per capita basis the newly built housing amounted to only 5.8 m^2 for every new urban dweller.

For a household of four in urban China (the number was 4.24 from a 1981 household survey), this number translates into less than 30 m^2 for the entire household. This number included all usable space, such as hallways and other common spaces inside a building. For net living space, the government reported per capita available space of 4.2 m^2 for urban dwellers in 1978, thus suggesting that a four-person household basically had 16 m^2, about one large room or two very small ones to live in.

Housing improvements followed two separate paths for rural and urban households. As for food production, housing improvements took off first in rural China. For urban dwellers, the change came later and more slowly. In the early post-reform years, most urban housing remained in public hands, with major improvements under state control through work organization investment and construction. It was not until the late 1990s, when urban housing reforms were fully implemented and commercial housing became widely available, that urban households saw rapid improvement. Government household surveys show that in the early 1980s, as farming families had more income with their increased yields, they started to put money and labor into building new homes or improving existing homes. Depending on the measure used, there was about a 25 to 30 percent improvement in just four years: the average farming household in 1978 had 3.64 rooms, and it increased to 4.56 by 1982; about one room added per household. The average per person living space increased from 10.17 m^2 to 13.41 m^2.[74] A decade later, per capita living space for rural Chinese doubled to 17.2 m^2 per person (Table 3.3).[75] By 2000, per capita living space for rural Chinese rose further to 24.2 m^2 and to 34.1 m^2 in 2010. Whereas in the early years rural housing quality and facilities lagged those in urban areas, such gaps were also closed in later years, as will be shown in the next section of this chapter.

Up until the year 2000, improvements in the rural Chinese population's housing far outpaced that in the cities, by either measure of urban housing conditions: living space per person or construction. The faster pace of new construction in rural China was most evident after the early 1990s when non-farming work in the countryside and remittances of rural migrants generated cash incomes. China's 2010 census, which collected information on the year when the residential housing was built, reported that over 85 percent of the houses resided in by rural Chinese were built after 1980, with over half (54.8 percent) built in the two decades of the 1980s and 1990s.[76] At the turn of the twenty-first century, per capita housing space reached almost 25 m^2 per person in rural China, compared

[74] SYB various years; SYB 1983, table 11–8.

[75] The difference in per capita use between the official number for 1978 in Table 3.3 (8.1 m^2) and reported from the survey (10.17 m^2), is likely due to the definition, with the latter being "usable space" and the former "living space," excluding space used for raising animals or storage.

[76] Calculated from China Population Census 2010, table 9–2c.

with urban Chinese residents' 20 m^2 of usable space but only about 10 m^2 of living space. This comparison actually underestimates rural improvements, as unlike housing construction in cities for which the government kept good accounting, not all housing construction in rural areas was included in these construction statistics.

For urban China, housing improvements were an entirely different story. Private and commercial residential housing returned after the late 1970s, albeit slowly and cautiously. In 1985, an urban household survey reported 84 percent of all survey households were renting from the public. In 1990, more than three quarters (77.5 percent) were still renting from a public source (Table 3.5). Explosive growth did not occur until about a full two decades later, in the late 1990s. In the early 1990s, commercial real estate development still only contributed a tiny portion of China's urban housing. On a per capita basis, the square footage sold as commercial housing was about one-tenth of a square meter per urban resident in 1991 (Table 3.4). This number at best only accounted for one-fifth of the increase in personal housing space, which was a 0.5 m^2 overall increase between 1990 and 1991 (Table 3.3). By 2000, over 70 percent of urban households owned their residential units (Table 3.5).

Just as the decade after 1978 during which the diet of the Chinese population was transformed, the decade after 1997 was an era of vast change in urban Chinese housing. Sales of urban commercial residential housing took off after 1998 when urban housing reforms began to be fully implemented nationwide.[77] Total sales rose by nearly 40 percent between 1997 and 1998. In 1998, sales amounted to 165 million m^2, only about 0.25 m^2 per urban resident (Table 3.4). In 2007, the number rose to over 700 million m^2, more than 1 m^2 for each resident counted as urban. In the next decade, the sales numbers doubled to more than 1.4 billion in 2017, nearly 2 m^2 for each urban resident.

This improvement took place while China's urban population also expanded vastly: the share of population counted as urban increased from 33 percent in 1998 to 46 percent in 2007 and to 59 percent in 2017. Between 1998 and 2007, residential housing sales continued to grow at a brisk double-digit rate, most years above 20 percent. In the one year between 2004 and 2005, sales increased by nearly 50 percent. It was not until in 2009, following a compensatory boom after the negative growth caused by the global financial crisis in 2008, that urban real estate began to cool down. Except for 2013 and 2016, when government policies caused temporary sales booms, the growth rate slowed down to single digits. By the early 2010s, China rose to be one of the highest

[77] For urban housing reforms, see, for instance, Man 2011.

Table 3.4 *Residential housing sales, China, 1991–2017*

Year	Space (10,000 m²)	Rate	Space (m²/person)	Cost (m²/yuan)	Price (m²/yuan)	Price/Cost
1991	2745.17		0.09		756.23	
1992	3812.21	0.39	0.12		996.40	
1993	6035.19	0.58	0.18		1208.23	
1994	6118.03	0.01	0.18		1194.05	
1995	6787.03	0.11	0.19		1508.86	
1996	6898.46	0.02	0.18	1111.00	1604.56	
1997	7864.30	0.14	0.20	1175.00	1789.80	1.52
1998	10827.10	0.38	0.26	1218.00	1853.56	1.52
1999	12997.87	0.20	0.30	1152.49	1857.02	1.61
2000	16570.28	0.27	0.36	1138.96	1948.43	1.71
2001	19938.75	0.20	0.41	1128.14	2016.75	1.79
2002	23702.31	0.19	0.47	1184.16	2091.72	1.77
2003	29778.85	0.26	0.57	1273.38	2197.00	1.73
2004	33819.89	0.14	0.62	1401.74	2549.00	1.82
2005	49587.83	0.47	0.88	1451.27	2936.96	2.02
2006	55422.95	0.12	0.95	1563.53	3119.25	2.00
2007	70135.88	0.27	1.16	1656.57	3645.18	2.20
2008	59280.35	−0.15	0.95	1795.00	3576.00	1.99
2009	86184.89	0.45	1.34	2021.00	4459.00	2.21
2010	93376.60	0.08	1.39	2228.00	4725.00	2.12
2011	96528.41	0.03	1.40	2372.70	4993.17	2.10
2012	98467.51	0.02	1.38	2498.03	5429.93	2.17
2013	115722.69	0.18	1.58	2642.62	5850.00	2.21
2014	105187.79	−0.09	1.40	2816.14	5933.00	2.11
2015	112412.29	0.07	1.46	3054.00	6473.00	2.12
2016	137539.93	0.22	1.73	3039.00	7203.00	2.37
2017	144788.77	0.05	1.78	3105.00	7614.00	2.45
2017 vs 1998	13.37%		6.84%	2.55%	4.11%	1.61%

Source: SYB, various years. Space per person calculated by the author.

home ownership countries in the world. More than 95 percent of all rural households, who made up more than half of all households, owned their homes as reported by the 2000 population census. With an estimated ownership share of 90 percent, it was higher than that of many high-income societies with a high home ownership rate: Japan (80.5 percent), Spain (78.2), Italy (72.9), Canada (66.3), and the United States (65).[78]

[78] https://en.wikipedia.org/wiki/List_of_countries_by_home_ownership_rate and https://en.wikipedia.org/wiki/Home-ownership_in_the_United_States

Table 3.5 *Housing ownership and facilities (%), urban China*

	1985	1990	2000	2010	2020
Ownership					
Own/private	13.05	20.13	71.98	69.78	74.24
Rent/public	84.24	77.53	16.33	2.66	3.76
Rent/private	2.51	1.87	6.89	23.11	21.99
Other	0.20	0.19	4.80	4.46	0.05
Access to piped water supply					
Private	65.11	82.13	87.46	93.18	97.79
Public	33.14	13.76	12.54	6.82	
None	1.75	3.82			2.20
Kitchen					
Private	63.20	86.50	85.37	88.75	95.54
Public	13.52	4.72	2.86	3.05	1.39
None	23.28	8.49	11.77	8.20	3.06
Fuel					
LPG	26.50	23.51			
Piped gas	17.52	16.02	69.93	80.69	85.70
Electricity					11.61
Coal	54.85	55.87	20.54	6.23	0.69
Other	1.30	4.32	9.53	13.08	2.00
Sanitary facilities					
Toilet and bathroom	6.19	12.24			
Toilet only	29.14	34.38			
Public	22.50	16.59			
None	42.17	36.38			
Toilet					
Private/flush			50.54	69.29	95.20
Public/flush			1.90	2.75	0.90
Private/other			20.72	13.74	1.03
Public/other			4.30	3.30	0.95
None			22.53	10.92	1.78
Bathing					
Private heating			40.57	68.12	90.28
Central heating			2.44	3.05	3.17
Other			7.41	6.38	1.75
None			49.58	22.45	4.80

Sources and notes: 1985 and 1990: China Urban Household Income and Expenditure Surveys; 2000, 2010, 2020: calculations based on China Population Census 2000 and 2010, tables 8–3a and 9–3a; China Population Census 2020, tables 9-3a and 9–7a. The censuses asked questions about drinking water, cooking fuel, and sanitary facilities, different from the household surveys.

Urban housing construction consequently followed the economic growth and rapid income increase. This sector also served as a pillar of China's economic boom, creating production demand as well as consumer demands for: construction, interior design and renovation, furniture, and appliances. Real estate development until the late 2010s was also a remarkably good business. Between 1998 and 2017, construction costs, as measured in current prices as reported in the official statistics, increased 155 percent, while average sales prices rose 311 percent. The average sales price to cost ratio consequently rose from 1.52 to 2.45 (Table 3.4). In the most exclusive cities, Beijing and Shanghai, the average housing cost was high: about four and three times the nation's average, respectively, by 2017.[79] Yet, these most expensive cities were also the most profitable for real estate developers. In 2017, the price to cost ratio was 7.85 in Beijing and 3.93 in Shanghai (compared to the 2.45 national average). Whereas the growth in sales slowed down substantially into the 2010s, this was not the case for price increases, as the price to cost ratio remained high and even increased further nationwide.

From House to Home

Housing improvements were more than just an expansion in space. Within three decades or so, the living environments inside Chinese homes were thoroughly transformed. Most notably, the majority of Chinese households now have their own cooking and sanitary facilities. For urban families, in 1985 nearly 40 percent did not have their own kitchen and more than 40 percent did not have access to a toilet at all. An additional 20 percent of urban households reported using a public toilet in the streets or the neighborhood. Coal was the main source of cooking fuel, with more than 50 percent of families reporting it as their main fuel source for cooking, a source both unhealthy and unsafe indoors, especially in winter time when windows were closed (Table 3.5). By 2020, 95 percent of all urban households could cook in their private kitchens, and the share using coal as cooking fuel dropped to less than one percent. Over 95 percent were cooking with a clean and safe energy source: natural gas connected with a gas pipeline or electricity.

Houses were also much cleaner inside. By 2020, 95 percent of urban households had a flush toilet inside their homes. And, for the first time, many Chinese could take a bath or shower inside their residential units. The share of households with bathing facilities (private and central heating

[79] Calculated from SYB 2018, tables 19–8 and 19–12.

combined) rose to 43 percent in 2000, 71 percent in 2010, and 95 percent in 2020 (Table 3.5).

On the eve of China's age of abundance, the accoutrements inside the tight living space of the Chinese household were even more sparse. A large share of rural residents in North China slept on a mud bed (*kang*). Those in the south made do with locally available bamboo or rattan to make their own furniture. Lumber was mostly out of reach for ordinary people as it belonged to the list of goods under the state's control. In many areas, deforestation during the Great Leap Forward for steel production largely depleted local wood supplies. Whatever remained was owned by the collective.

In urban China, with few exceptions, such as inherited furniture, residents in newly formed households borrowed or rented furniture from the government through their work organizations. Such rented furniture was highly restricted in quantity and poor in quality. In 1981, for instance, as reported by the earliest household survey data, 10 percent of all urban households had not a single sofa chair to sit on, 14 percent had no tall dresser, and 45 percent had no writing desk.[80] Even among higher income households (top 25 percent in per capita income), 25 to 30 percent did not even have a single desk at home in 1982.[81] One measure of household wealth and status in the early 1980s was how many "legs" a prospective family could offer when a marriage proposal was entertained. These legs represented how many pieces of furniture could furnish the room for the newlyweds. The other indicator of household wealth was the ownership of the "four big items." In the early 1980s, the big items were: a radio, a bicycle, a sewing machine, and a wristwatch.

In the early 1980s, home appliances such as washing machines, refrigerators, and color televisions were novelties that had only been heard of recently but had not yet been seen. Fewer than 1 in 100 urban households in 1981 had a color television or a refrigerator. A private shower stall with an in-house water heater and air conditioners to make homes comfortable were far beyond Chinese imaginations. As income grew, the new "four big items" to be acquired in the 1980s and 1990s became: a color television set, a refrigerator, a washing machine, and an air conditioner.

In contrast to their slower improvement in living space, urban Chinese residents utilized their higher income more than rural residents to make their tight living space more livable and comfortable. Their lifestyle upgrade, made possible by new household appliances, was a whole

80 SYB 1984, table 11–9.
81 SYB 1983, table 11–16. Survey based on 9,020 households in 47 cities across China.

decade ahead of those living in the countryside, who focused on building their new houses. By the early 1990s, while only about 1 percent of rural households had a refrigerator, 5 percent a color television, and less than 10 percent a washing machine; the majority of urban households already had a color television or a washing machine, and 40 percent had a refrigerator. By the end of the 1990s, color televisions and washing machines were ubiquitous urban household items, reaching saturation point. More than two-thirds of the households (77.74 percent) had a refrigerator by 1999 (Table 3.6). Not until 2010 did rural households reach comparable ownership of color televisions, and it took almost another decade and a half for refrigerators.[82]

Urban and rural households also made different choices in purchasing their household appliances. The fact that the washing machine was the first appliance that populated urban households is noteworthy. Whereas a washing machine was less expensive than a color television or a refrigerator, it was also the social characteristic of urban families that created this phenomenon. In Chinese households, women shouldered the overwhelming majority of household chores. Laundry was a major chore, often taking up a whole weekend day and requiring hard labor. Married urban Chinese women also assumed the double-burden of being full-time employees and housewives. When the modern appliance of a washing machine became available, it was the first to be acquired. It was also more affordable for an ordinary household, costing considerably less than a color television. Washing machine ownership rose sharply in the 1980s, from 6 per 100 households in 1981 to 76 per 100 by 1989, in contrast with 51 per 100 households for color televisions and only 36 per 100 households for refrigerators by 1989. It was not until 1995 that the ownership level for color televisions reached that of washing machines for urban households. It took another 15 years, to 2010, for household ownership of refrigerators to reach the same level as washing machines.

For the rural population, household appliance acquisition lagged a full decade and followed a different path. Rural households had a preference for color televisions. In the 1990s, the ownership level (number of color television sets per 100 households) rose nearly tenfold, from 4.72 in 1990 to 38.24 in 1999 (and to 48.74 the following year, 2000; Table 3.6). By 2010, ownership reached over 100 per 100 households. Ownership of washing machines and refrigerators in rural China rose much more slowly than that of color televisions, reaching only a 24 and 11 per 100 rural

[82] Note these ownership levels are ownership per 100 households. As some households could have more than one of a particular item, such as multiple color televisions or refrigerators, a level of 100 does not mean every household has one.

Table 3.6 *Ownership of consumer durables (per 100 households), China, 1981–2017*

	Color television		Washing machine		Refrigerator		Water heater		Air conditioning	
Year	Urban	Rural	Urban	Rural	Urban	Rural	Urban	Rural	Urban	Rural
1981	0.59		6.31		0.22					
1982	1.10		16.09		0.67					
1983	2.57		29.08		1.65					
1984	5.38		40.13		3.22					
1985	17.21	0.80	48.29	1.90	6.58	0.06				
1986	27.41	1.52	59.00	3.22	12.71	0.20				
1987	34.63	2.34	66.77	4.78	19.91	0.31				
1988	43.93	2.80	73.42	6.79	28.07	0.63				
1989	51.47	3.63	76.21	8.15	36.47	0.89				
1990	59.04	4.72	78.41	9.12	42.33	1.22			0.34	
1991	68.41	6.44	80.58	10.99	48.70	1.64				
1992	74.87	8.08	83.41	12.23	52.60	2.17				
1993	79.46	10.86	86.36	13.82	56.68	3.05				
1994	86.21	13.52	87.29	15.30	62.10	4.00				
1995	89.79	16.92	88.97	16.90	66.22	5.15	30.05		8.09	0.18
1996	93.50	22.91	90.06	20.54	69.67	7.27				
1997	100.48	27.32	89.12	21.87	72.98	8.49				
1998	105.43	32.59	90.57	22.81	76.08	9.25				
1999	111.57	38.24	91.44	24.32	77.74	10.64	45.49		24.48	0.74
2000	116.60	48.74	90.52	28.58	80.10	12.31	49.10		30.80	1.32
2001	120.50	54.41	92.20	29.94	81.90	13.59	52.00		35.80	1.70
2002	126.38	60.45	92.90	31.80	87.38	14.83	62.42		51.10	2.29
2003	130.50	67.80	94.41	34.27	88.73	15.89	66.61		61.79	3.45
2004	133.44	75.09	95.90	37.32	90.15	17.75	69.40		69.81	4.70
2005	134.80	84.08	95.51	40.20	90.72	20.10	72.65		80.67	6.40
2006	137.43	89.43	96.77	42.98	91.75	22.48	75.13		87.79	7.28
2007	137.79	94.38	96.77	45.94	95.03	26.12	79.52		95.08	8.54
2008	132.89	99.22	94.65	49.11	93.63	30.19	80.65		100.28	9.82
2009	135.65	108.94	96.01	53.14	95.35	37.11	83.39		106.84	12.23
2010	137.43	111.79	96.92	57.32	96.61	45.19	84.82		112.07	16.00
2011	135.15	115.46	97.05	62.57	97.23	61.54	89.14		122.00	22.58
2012	136.07	116.90	98.02	67.22	98.48	67.32	91.02		126.81	25.36
2013	118.59	112.88	88.35	71.21	89.21	72.85	80.34	43.63	102.20	29.80
2014	121.97	115.61	90.71	74.82	91.69	77.58	82.98	48.23	107.42	34.22
2015	122.29	116.89	92.28	78.82	93.97	82.55	85.58	52.52	114.58	38.77
2016	122.32	118.76	94.21	84.03	96.44	89.55	88.67	59.67	123.70	47.58
2017	123.78	120.03	95.67	86.28	98.05	91.70	90.68	62.48	128.61	52.63

Source: SYB, various years (based on household income and expenditure surveys)

households by 1999. The fastest growth in washing machine and refrigerator ownership came after 2007, in part propelled by a government program to incentivize rural residents to buy household appliances in the wake of the global financial crisis in 2008. The main driver, of course, was the greater affluence of rural Chinese and the shift in their lifestyles and preferences. By the late 2010s, rural and urban households converged in their ownership of these three consumer durable items: color televisions, washing machines, and refrigerators (Figure 3.7). As rural and urban households began to live in comparably sized living spaces, they also started to enjoy the same level of modern conveniences inside their homes.

By the late 2010s, urban and rural homes differed mostly only in two other types of appliances: in-house water heaters for taking showers and air conditioners to regulate room temperatures. Among urban households, 90 percent had a water heater by 2017, and on average a household had more than one air conditioner (128.6 per 100 households). Rural homes lagged in these items, with only 62.48 and 52.63 percent of households having a water heater or one or more air conditioners, respectively.

Over four decades, with these rapid improvements in housing conditions, seen in both the vastly expanded living space and in the prevalence of

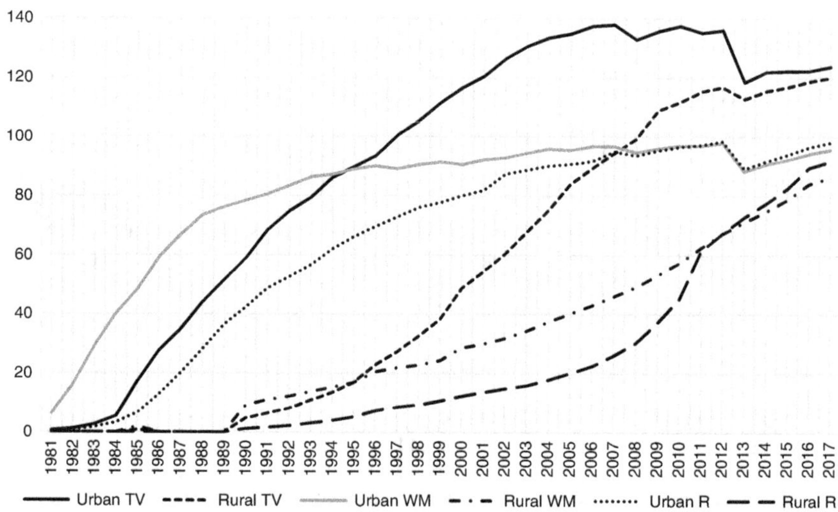

Figure 3.7 Convergence of home appliance ownership (per 100 households), urban and rural China
Source: SYB, various years

modern appliances in their homes, most Chinese had begun living the lifestyle and enjoying comfort commensurate with that in an upper-middle income society. These are the best indicators to gauge the improvement in housing conditions, heralding the final arrival of abundance in China.

Moving around and Beyond

With houses built and bought and made into comfortable homes, a vastly increased number of people began to move around and beyond. As roads, highways, railways, and airports were built, people started to travel for work and increasingly for leisure. Tourists not only flooded popular sites in China but also became the largest group of international travelers.

There is perhaps no other aspect that showcases China's transformation than the changes in transportation infrastructure. Within four decades, between 1980 and 2020, the total length of railway in China nearly tripled from 53,300 km nationwide to 146,300 km (Table 3.7, Figure 3.8, left axis). Road construction increased more than fivefold from less than 1 million km in 1980 to over 5 million km in 2017 (Figure 3.8, left axis). Air transportation, measured by the distance covered by regular flights, shot up by nearly 50 times (Figure 3.8, right axis) from about 0.2 million km to about 9.4 million km. In 1985, China had 82 airports nationwide. A decade later, the number rose to 139. By 2020, the number of airports further increased to 240. In 1990, China had only 503 civilian jet planes in use. The number nearly doubled to 982 by the year 2000, nearly tripled to 2,405 by 2010, and saw a further boom after that, almost tripling again, to 6,795 in 2020.[83]

More significant than the doubled railway length is the increased train speed. In the early 1980s, less than 5 percent of China's railroad was electrified; by the turn of the twenty-first century, that share increased to nearly 20 percent. Electrification and high-speed rail transportation accelerated in the twenty-first century. In 20 years, nearly three quarters of all railways were electrified (Table 3.7). High-speed trains now connect virtually all urban centers in China, shrinking travel time between cities such as Beijing to Shanghai from a whole day in the 1980s to less than five hours in the late 2010s. Rail travel person-trips also rose. Annual person-trip numbers first edged up slowly from 922 million in 1980 to 957 million in 1990 and to 1.05 billion in 2000. The number rose sharply in the first decade of the twenty-first century to 1.68 billion, a 60 percent increase in one decade. In 2019, rail travel person-trip numbers reached

[83] Author's calculations based on SYB, various years.

Table 3.7 *Expansion of means of transportation, China, 1978–2020*

Year	Rail (10,000 km)	Electrified (%)	Road (10,000 km)	Highway (%)	Flight (10,000 km)	International (%)
1978	5.17	1.93%	89.02		0.15	37.14%
1980	5.33	3.19%	88.83		0.20	41.58%
1981	5.39	3.15%	89.75		0.22	37.95%
1982	5.33	3.38%	90.70		0.23	42.93%
1983	5.46	4.21%	91.51		0.23	43.61%
1984	5.48	5.48%	92.67		0.26	41.28%
1985	5.52	7.50%	94.24		0.28	38.24%
1986	5.58	7.88%	96.28		0.32	33.30%
1987	5.60	8.22%	98.22		0.39	38.27%
1988	5.62	10.14%	99.96	0.01%	0.37	34.32%
1989	5.70	11.23%	101.43	0.03%	0.47	35.26%
1990	5.79	11.92%	102.83	0.05%	0.51	32.83%
1991	5.78	13.49%	104.11	0.06%	0.56	31.73%
1992	5.81	14.46%	105.67	0.07%	0.84	36.22%
1993	5.86	15.19%	108.35	0.10%	0.96	29.01%
1994	5.90	15.25%	111.78	0.14%	1.05	33.66%
1995	6.24	15.55%	115.70	0.18%	1.13	30.84%
1996	6.49	15.56%	118.58	0.29%	1.17	33.12%
1997	6.60	18.18%	122.64	0.39%	1.43	35.40%
1998	6.64	19.58%	127.85	0.68%	1.51	33.50%
1999	6.74	20.77%	135.17	0.86%	1.52	34.38%
2000	6.87	21.63%	167.98	0.97%	1.50	33.83%
2001	7.01	24.09%	169.80	1.14%	1.55	33.27%
2002	7.19	24.20%	176.52	1.42%	1.64	35.08%
2003	7.30	24.79%	180.98	1.64%	1.75	40.89%
2004	7.44	25.00%	187.07	1.83%	2.05	43.63%
2005	7.54	25.72%	334.52	1.23%	2.00	42.83%
2006	7.71	30.40%	345.70	1.31%	2.11	45.71%
2007	7.80	30.84%	358.37	1.50%	2.34	44.70%
2008	7.97	31.38%	373.02	1.62%	2.46	45.50%
2009	8.55	35.36%	386.08	1.69%	2.35	39.23%
2010	9.12	35.88%	400.82	1.85%	2.77	38.70%
2011	9.32	36.82%	410.64	2.07%	3.49	42.81%
2012	9.76	36.35%	423.75	2.27%	3.28	39.17%
2013	10.31	34.88%	435.62	2.40%	4.11	36.61%
2014	11.18	32.96%	446.39	2.51%	4.64	38.11%
2015	12.10	61.79%	457.73	2.70%	5.32	45.03%
2016	12.40	64.77%	469.63	2.79%	6.35	44.55%
2017	12.70	68.17%	477.35	2.86%	7.48	43.38%
2018	13.17	70.02%	484.65	2.94%	8.38	42.95%
2019	13.99	71.79%	501.25	2.98%	9.48	42.34%
2020	14.63	72.63%	519.81	3.10%	9.43	40.62%

Source: SYB, various years. Author's calculations.

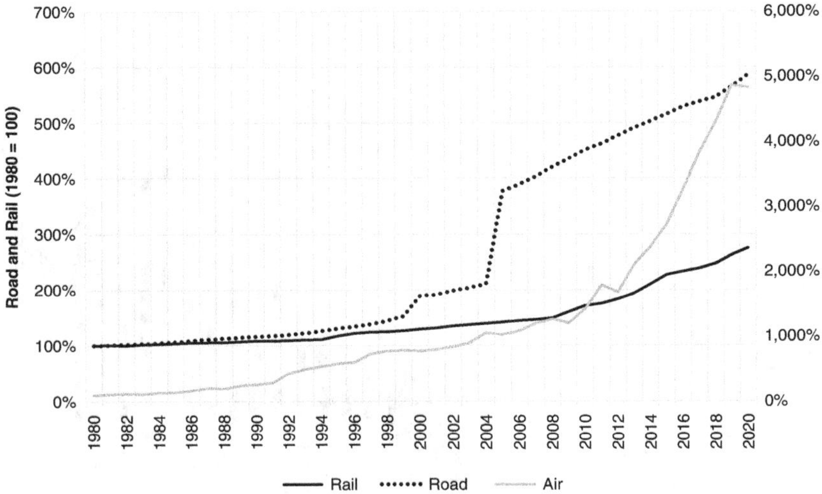

Figure 3.8 Improvements in transportation infrastructure, China, 1980–2020
Source: SYB, various years. Author's calculations.

3.66 billion, more than two-and-a-half trips per person per year for the entire country.

Unlike the railway network, which was built on a foundation laid prior to China's age of abundance, the country's highway construction is entirely new. At the end of the 1980s, China had about 1 million km of roads, with hardly any highways. Road construction took off in the 1990s, extending the total length by nearly 70 percent in one decade. By the year 2000, China had built up to 16,300 km of highways nationwide. The first decade of the twenty-first century saw the fastest pace in highway construction, when the total length increased by over 4.5 times to 74,100 km. In terms of the total length built, the next decade set the record. The 2010s saw more highways built in a single decade than the total at the start of the decade with 86,900 km constructed. By 2020, 161,000 km of highways connected all of China. This construction boom, as shown in Figure 3.8, as with increased air travel, came largely after 2010.

Cars came along with roads. Under socialism, private property ownership was virtually eliminated and privately owned vehicles were not heard of. That changed with the reemergence of the private economy. By the mid-1980s, privately owned vehicles began to appear on Chinese roads. For the whole country, in 1985 there were 284,000 cars registered as privately owned. A decade later, that number increased to only 2.5 million, still a rarity. At the turn of the century, privately owned cars rose to

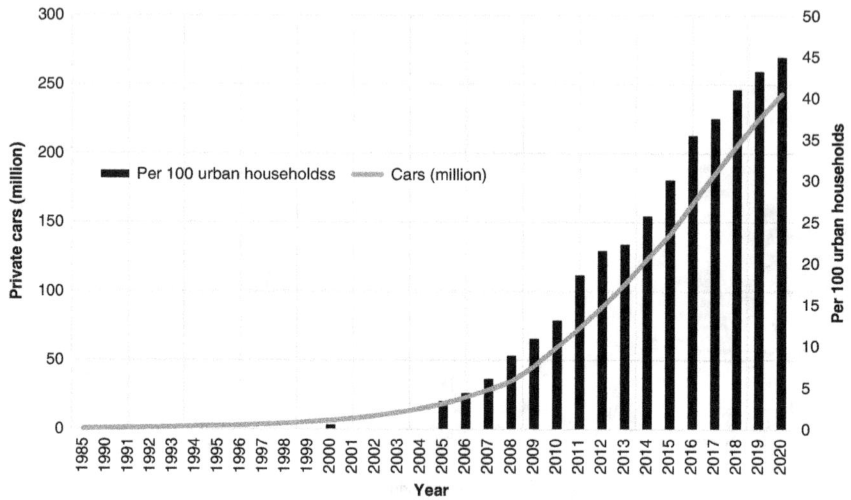

Figure 3.9 Rise of private vehicle ownership (per 100 households), China, 1985–2020
Sources: SYB 2018, tables 16–21; SYB 2021, tables 16–21; SYB, various years

6.25 million. Surveys of urban households reported still only 0.5 cars per 100 households. In less than 20 years after 2000, China witnessed an automobile revolution. By 2010, private vehicle ownership rose to close to 60 million. In the decade after 2010, the number of privately owned vehicles, over 90 percent of them being personal passenger cars, quadruped to 243 million in 2020, with 45 percent of urban households reporting having a car, up from 13 percent in 2010 (Figure 3.9).

Comparable to the vastly developed highway network that has connected all of China is air travel. In the early 1980s, few Chinese had ever seen an airplane with their own eyes let alone boarded one. Out of a population of nearly 1 billion Chinese, about 3 million flight trips were made in 1980, averaging 3.5 trips per 1,000 people. By 1990, the number of total trips increased fivefold to 16.6 million. That number was dwarfed by 2000, when the trips taken by airplane increased another fourfold, to 67.22 million a year. Still, such a number counted for only about 5 percent of the total Chinese population. In the next decade, air travel quadrupled again to an annual number of 268 million. By 2017, annual air travel person-trips reached 552 million, equivalent to 40 percent of the total population size of China.[84] This is still a small number, if

[84] SYB 2018, table 16–6. These are trips taken, not the number of persons taking trips.

compared with the United States, which – with a population less than one-quarter that of China – logged 965.4 million person-trips.[85]

Once the Chinese population started to travel, they also started to go far. Having experienced a rise in income and more comfortable homes, a large number of Chinese began traveling for pleasure, sightseeing, and shopping. Although gauging reasons for domestic travel is an inexact science, domestic tourism trips numbered 629 million in 1995 or about half of the total population size. The number nearly doubled to 1.21 billion in 2005. By 2015, the number increased to 4 billion, and only two years later, in 2017, to 5 billion.[86]

Overseas travel presents an entirely different experience from domestic trips, as it opens a traveler up to foreign landscapes, people, history, and culture. These trips are also much more clearly documented compared to other travels, as all citizens must pass border control and have their passports checked and stamped. Even in the late 1990s, overseas travel for personal rather than business or government reasons was extremely rare, with 3.19 million trips logged for the entire population of over a billion in the year 1998. Overseas tourism increased tenfold within the next ten years, rising to 34.92 million trips by 2008. That, however, was just the beginning. In the decade following, annual overseas tourism trips nearly quadrupled to 135.81 million, translating to one overseas tourist trip for every ten Chinese. In 2019, the year prior to the global COVID-19 pandemic, 162 million overseas trips for private reasons were recorded. With increased wealth, overseas travel for sightseeing was no longer the privilege of an exclusive few.

With international travel, the Chinese also started to spend and spread their recently amassed vast wealth to economies across the globe, creating economic opportunities beyond the Chinese borders. Chinese tourists are now ubiquitous worldwide from European historical centers to American national parks and from the North to the South Pole. By 2018, Chinese tourists became the largest group of visitors to Russia's Arctic region.[87] From 2008 and the 2017–2018 Antarctic tourist season, tourists number to the South Pole increased 100 times, with the number of Chinese rising from fewer than 100 to 8,273, up by 3,000 from just the previous year, accounting for 16 percent of visitors to the South Pole, second only to the United States by 2018.[88]

[85] Bureau of Transportation Statistics, "2018 traffic data for US airlines and foreign airlines US flights," www.bts.dot.gov/newsroom/2018-traffic-data-us-airlines-and-foreign-airlines-us-flights

[86] SYB 2018, table 17–10.

[87] "China's rich flock to poles for adventure travel," *Financial Times*, June 21, 2017, www.ft.com/content/ef791606-5262-11e7-bfb8-997009366969

[88] http://124.127.52.76/a/201901/12/WS5c395cb3a3106c65c34e4092.html

Connecting with the World

The new millennium also seemed to be a line of demarcation for the Chinese virtual world. More than traveling around the country via high-speed railways or taking airplanes to faraway destinations around the globe, in the first two decades of the twenty-first century the country expanded connections through invisible links such as phones and personal computers.

As with food, clothing, housing, and home appliances in the late 1970s, modes of communication among Chinese were scarce; connecting to people remotely was difficult, slow, and expensive. Long-distance communication was conducted via the country's postal system, which delivered letters and news materials to people's residences. Most often, mail was delivered to people's work organizations, such as production brigade headquarters in the countryside and mailrooms of work organizations in the cities. Nationwide there were only 1,863 telephone exchanges for long-distance call connections. In 1978, 300 people shared about one telephone. Operated by special staff, telephones were almost exclusively for institutional use. A one-minute long-distance phone call, if one had access, cost a fortune. Long-distance pricing was set up with a distance gradient. A one-minute call within 25 km cost 0.10 yuan, within 500–599 km cost 0.80 yuan per minute. With a monthly average per capita disposable income of less than 40 yuan in cities and less than 20 yuan in the countryside, a five-minute long-distance phone call could take away 10 percent of an urban resident's monthly living expenses. Even in 1990, there was barely 1 telephone per 100 persons. By 2000, the ratio had improved to 1 telephone for every 8 persons.[89]

Around the turn of the century, personal computers and mobile phones emerged on the Chinese social scene. By 1999, about 6 percent of urban households owned a personal computer and 7 percent had a mobile phone. In just five years, mobile phone ownership proliferated to near saturation in urban China, with 111 phones per 100 households in 2004. Personal computer ownership expanded to nearly one-third of all urban households (Figure 3.10). Among rural households, mobile phone ownership also rose quickly, from 4.31 per 100 households in 2000 to 34.7 percent by 2004, nearing a third of the urban prevalence. Rural households however rarely adopted personal computers; only less than 0.5 percent of all households in 2000 and 2.1 per 100 households in 2005.[90] By 2011, urban household personal computer prevalence reached 80 per 100 households, and mobile phone ownership exceeded

[89] Telephones per 100 persons was 0.38 in 1978, SYB 2018, tables 16–34 and 16–35.
[90] SYB 2006, tables 10–10 and 10–30.

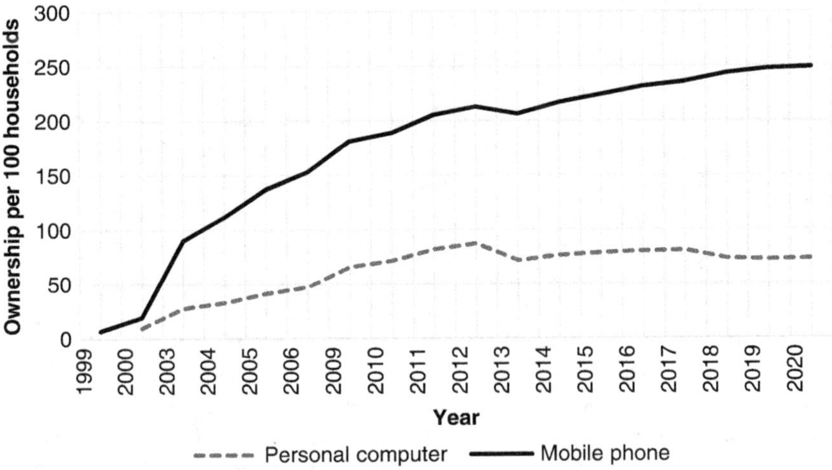

Figure 3.10 Arrival of new means of communication: personal computers and mobile phones (per 100 households), urban China, 1999–2020
Source: SYB, various years

2 per household. Mobile phone adoption in rural China quickly caught up with that in urban China, with about a five-year time lag. By 2005, nearly one-half of all households had a mobile phone; by 2011, prevalence reached 179.74 phones per 100 households, not far behind that for urban households. Personal computer ownership, however, always lagged in rural China, reaching only 17.96 percent by 2011.[91]

The combination of household expenditure going toward moving around and communication represents the most drastic change in Chinese consumption during China's ascendance to prosperity. Between 1990 and 2010, urban households' per capita spending on transportation and communication rose 53-fold from 40.5 to 2,149.69 yuan. Such an increase far outpaced income growth, which rose by 14.44 times for per capita disposable income, from 1510.16 yuan to 21,809.78 yuan, during the same period. The change in the share of urban household expenditure is also the most dramatic in this category, rising from merely 1.2 percent in 1990 to 14.18 percent in 2010.[92] The same shift in household expenditure took place among rural households, whose expenditure on transportation and communication rose from 1.44 percent of total per capita expenditure in 1990 to 10.50 percent in 2010.[93]

[91] SYB 2012, table 10–30. [92] SYB 2012, table 10–5. [93] Ibid., table 10–25.

Paths to Abundance

In less than half a century, over one-fifth of the world's inhabitants saw their lives transformed in a way that they, as well as the world, could hardly have imagined. Other countries and regions have realized rapid improvements in living standards before – Europe, North America, East Asia, and elsewhere – but not on this order of magnitude and rarely at this rapid pace.

The path to prosperity and abundance in China resembles largely what the world has seen elsewhere in its history. Figure 3.11 illustrates this process with a selection of living standards indicators chosen from the materials presented in this chapter. The process started with people eating better, first in quantity then in quality. This phase in China took only a decade, in the 1980s. By the late 1980s, consumption of vegetable oil, one measure of food intake, rose 400 percent from the late 1970 levels (right axis, Figure 3.11). Once well-nourished, the population became better and more stylishly clothed. The next phase, transforming the homes people live in, unfolded in the two decades of the 1990s and the 2000s. Modern household appliances from washing machines and color televisions to refrigerators and air conditioners began to outfit homes, first and in particular those in the cities (per 100 households, right axis, Figure 3.11). By 2010, nearly every household had a color television and most urban households had an air conditioner.

Once the Chinese people owned and outfitted their homes with comforts and conveniences, leisure became a part of life. They started to motor around in their own automobiles and travel beyond the Chinese

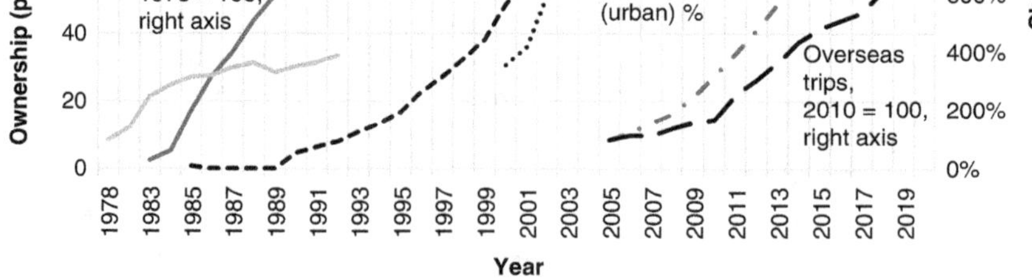

Figure 3.11 Paths to abundance, changes in selected indicators, China, 1978–2020
Source: SYB, various years

borders. The number of privately owned automobiles rose by over 13 times in the 15 years after 2005 (right axis, Figure 3.11). Similarly, the number of overseas trips by Chinese also increased by 6.5 times. Massive numbers of Chinese shoppers descended upon Rome, Milan, London, Paris, Tokyo, New York, and Los Angeles. Chinese tourists are now seen in almost every corner of the world, from the Serengeti to the North and South Poles. Instead of consuming goods bearing the three words "Made in China," the world began to feel the impact of the new Chinese affluence up close and in person.

There was, of course, no single path for every Chinese to march along the way to material abundance. Vast differences persisted, between rural and urban sectors, and across regions, provinces, cities, counties, work organizations, villages, and families. The largest divide, following the legacy of the socialist planned economy, was the two categories of citizens created within the same country, that between rural and urban residents.

Paradoxically, the vast and disadvantaged segment of the population, those in the Chinese countryside, not only led China's march to prosperity but were also its early beneficiaries. Living on a much more precarious margin of subsistence than their urban counterparts, as they were excluded from the government's guaranteed provision of food and other necessities for living under a rationing system, a large number of rural Chinese quickly turned around their lives as well as those throughout the entire country. Rural Chinese were the first to reap the fruits of their increased yields: from grains to vegetables to eggs and meats, and to new houses. While urban residents waited for their work organizations to build new housing, families in rural China built their homes, earlier and more expeditiously. In the 1980s and early 1990s, as urban households preferred washing machines, color televisions, and other household appliances to make their still crowded living spaces more livable, rural households with their increased income built more housing space than urban residents.

The march to abundance, however, will not and cannot be stopped outside the city walls. The next phase of the Chinese industrialization was about to begin. Rising productivity in the countryside motivated rural dwellers to look for new ways to realize their potential, to further improve their standard of living, and to create greater wealth and prosperity. This undertaking began with non-farming activities in the villages, in the form of village and township enterprises. Later, the pursuit of a better life propelled hundreds of millions of rural people into cities, as migrants without full citizenship in their own country. As a result, China's second industrialization at that moment became one of the largest migration and urbanization episodes in human history.

4 Ascendance

So, how did all of this happen?

The prevailing narrative of China's economic ascendance propagated by both the government and academics is its uniqueness. China was unique, as this narrative would proclaim, by virtue of its strong and efficient government: its ownership, control, regulation, and industrial policies.[1] Some attribute growth to two special characteristics of China's post-Mao political system: incentivizing local officials by economic performance under their jurisdiction and the tax-sharing arrangement between central and local governments.[2] These narratives ascribe the central role of the government in reorienting its overall objectives from revolution to economic growth, and they credit a wide range of institutional reforms for China's economic successes. Indeed, in the absence of this governmental reorientation and growth-facilitating policies, China's economic growth would not have happened.

Yet, while the China miracle was unexpected, the Chinese path to abundance was not that unique. The road to abundance in China was simply a process of (re)industrialization, an industrialization process from the bottom up. Its uniqueness can be characterized as a race-to-the-bottom competition.[3] Local governments relied on nontax measures, such as artificially suppressing land costs for industrial park use and loosening labor and environmental regulations to compete for economic opportunities. This growth came with the lion's share of costs paid by farmers who lost land, by rural migrant laborers whose labor was made

[1] As discussed in Chapter 1, Qian (2017) lists two schools of interpretation of China's success in reforming its economy – the School of Universal Principles and the School of Chinese Characteristics – and proposes a third perspective, focusing less on why but how the reforms worked. Qian takes the universal principles as the starting points. He also takes initial historical conditions for achieving "a constrained optimization" (7).

[2] Tao and Su 2021.

[3] Tao and Su (2021) question the evidence used to support these two arguments, and they offer a counterargument that it was the government-supported "double race-to-the-bottom competition" (13), both within China and globally, that best explains China's growth as well as its challenges.

cheap and whose rights were infringed upon, and by the population in general who bore the consequences of rampant environmental pollution.

From goods made to changes in work and in life, the Chinese process was not unlike other societies that had taken the road earlier. In Europe, North America, Japan, South Korea, and other industrialized economies, industrialization began with the production of textiles and then progressed to cement, steel, chemicals, and to machineries, automobiles, and electronics. In the process, the population moved away from farms to factories and from the countryside to cities.[4] The path was the same: it followed the process of industrialization and urbanization or of transforming from an agricultural to an industrial and post-industrial society.

A comparison with China's two East Asian neighboring countries, Japan and South Korea, makes this point abundantly clear. For both countries, as in China, the fastest economic growth occurred during a historical transformation of their economies, a transformation from farming to non-farming and to urbanization. For Japan, the pioneer among the three East Asian countries in this process, industrialization and urbanization unfolded in two phases, truncated in between by World War II. Between 1920 and 1940, the share of the Japanese population living in cities doubled from 18 percent to 37.7 percent. During those two decades, Japan registered its first phase of rapid income increase, with the size of the economy estimated to have expanded by 120 percent and its per capita GDP by 69 percent.[5] The war set back Japan's per capita income by 50 percent in 1945, compared to 1940, and the share of urban population also shrank, back to 27.8 percent.[6]

Japan resumed its transformation away from farming and to the cities after World War II. As shown in Figure 4.1, in the three-and-a-half decades of Japan's fastest economic growth period, between 1945 and 1980, per capita income increased nearly tenfold (by 9.98 times). During the same period, the share of urban population rose from 27.8 to 76.2 percent. In three-and-a-half decades, half of the nation went from farming to non-farming, from rural to urban living.

For South Korea, the transformation came later, if only at a faster pace. During its period of fastest economic growth, between 1965 and 2000, per capita income increased by 13 times, and the share of urban population rose from 32 percent to almost 80 percent. As in Japan, half of the nation moved out of farming within three-and-a-half decades.

4 Such shared experiences of the East Asian model of industrialization are well documented and analyzed in Vogel 1993; Overholt 1993; and Hung 2015, chap. 3.

5 From a per capita GDP of $1,696 in 1920 to 2,874 in 1940 (in 1990 international GK$). www.rug.nl/ggdc/historicaldevelopment/maddison/

6 Urban population numbers for Japan are based on Harris 1982.

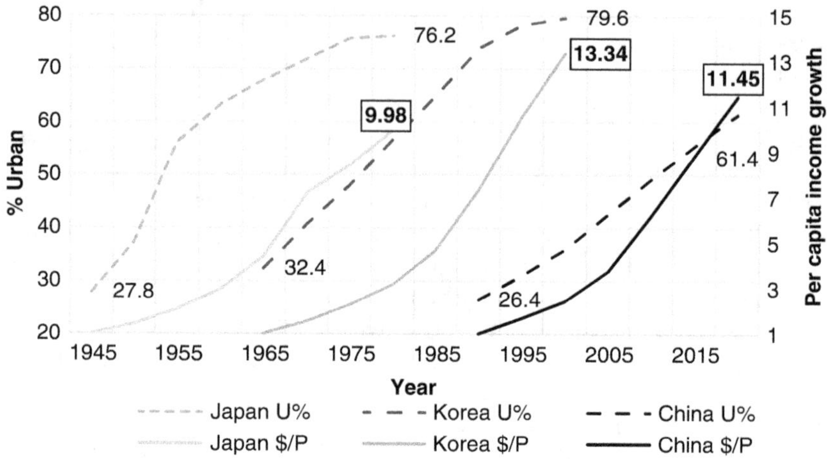

Figure 4.1 Industrialization with urbanization: Japan, South Korea, and China

Sources: Japan, urbanization numbers from Harris 1982, per capita income from Maddison (www.rug.nl/ggdc/historicaldevelopment/maddison/). South Korea and China, WDI. Per capita GDP increase is calculated with the initial year in the time period used set as 1.

China simply followed this path of industrialization with urbanization near the end of the twentieth century. In the three decades between 1990 and 2020, per capita income rose by 11.45 times and the share of urban population increased from 26 percent to 61 percent (Figure 4.1). Between 1980 and 2020, in just four decades, 45 percent of the entire population became urbanized, forming the largest migration and urbanization streams in human history.

For China, however, the industrialization that led to its abundance was its second drive since the middle of the twentieth century. As discussed in Chapter 2, China's first attempt at industrialization during its socialist planned economy years was a unique and deeply distorted one; it was an industrialization minus labor force transformation and an industrialization without urbanization. China manufactured goods in an industrial economy but not an industrialized society. An industrialized society is one where at least half of its labor force works in nonagricultural sectors and more than half of the population lives in cities.

China's success in leaving its short-lived socialist planned economy was aptly characterized as a process of "growing out of the plan."[7] Unlike the

[7] Naughton 1996.

former Soviet Union and most Eastern European socialist countries, China did not suffer a drastic downturn in economic output or a severe deterioration in the population's standard of living. The Chinese public endured and supported reforms because people's living standards were improving.

Ascendance to prosperity began in China's vast countryside. Growth initially came largely and disproportionately from China's countryside. The rapid increase in agricultural productivity and the profoundly swift transformation of the labor force away from agriculture into industrial production led China's growth and industrialization. Growth in rural China not only improved the lives of those in the countryside but more importantly lifted the whole nation by supplying urban residents with most of their essential daily needs: food, clothing, furniture, and construction materials.

China's second industrialization after 1980 unfolded on the foundation of the two legacies from its first industrialization under socialist rule. As discussed in Chapter 2, the first legacy was a vast reservoir of human energy in the Chinese countryside. Between 1950 and 1980, China's rural population expanded by about 300 million, yet arable land acreage remained essentially the same.[8] While overall agricultural output increased under the planned economy, productivity actually decreased; more and more rural residents lived on the margins of hunger and poverty. At the same time, as documented in Chapter 2, under socialism both the health and literacy levels of China's population, including the rural population, improved vastly. The energy of the rural population, which numbered nearly 800 million by the late 1970s, was thus suppressed during China's planned economy era. An able and hungry labor force was ready to work and ready to transform their lives. This collective energy was enormous, and it was ready to burst when opportunities emerged. China's second industrialization also took place with a second legacy of the socialist era; an industrialization that divided the society into two types of citizens, condemning the vast rural population as secondary citizens and confining them to the countryside. This segregation led a second industrialization process that originated in the rural areas.

China's rural population drove economic growth in two successive, sometimes overlapping, phases. First, industrialization took off in situ; farmers liberated from collective farming transformed into an industrial labor force. Instead of going to the cities, they engaged in manufacturing

[8] Total arable land used for agricultural production was reported to have only grown by less than 4 percent between 1952 and 1980 from 21.19 billion *mu* to 21.96 billion *mu* (SYB 1983, 154).

in their villages. By the mid-1990s, 40 percent of China's rural labor force was producing industrial goods in the Chinese countryside. Numbered at 182.6 million strong, this industrial labor force in China's countryside was nearly as large as China's total urban labor force at the time, which was 190.4 million. In 1995, China's rural laborers generated *more than half of all China's industrial output.*[9]

Then, in the second wave, a massive number of laborers moved into the cities. By the turn of the twenty-first century, the number of rural migrant laborers in Chinese cities reached over 100 million, *surpassing the combined number* of employees in state and collectively owned enterprises in the cities at that time.[10] These two phases – rural industrialization and then rural-to-urban migration – are often treated separately, as if they were just two phenomena for the same "surplus labor" looking for employment opportunities. Rather, these two phases were the continuation of the same process, with the same population, and driven by the same political-economy logics. In two phases – first working in the Chinese countryside at TVEs, then moving to cities as migrants – this massive number of rural Chinese launched China's prosperity.

Governments at all levels in China definitely played crucial and indispensable roles, creating essential institutional frameworks meeting the needs of a new economic regime. China's reforms relied on systematic changes throughout its whole economic system. These changes included acknowledging private property rights that allowed non-state ownership, a move decidedly away from the exclusive socialist-style public ownership. Another reform was a price mechanism driven by supply and demand in a so-called market, not predetermined preferences decided in the offices of government bureaucrats.[11] The government created the special economic zones to attract foreign direct capital investment, encourage exports, and allow private businesses in cities. Operating a functional, new market economy also required corresponding legal, banking, and other financial institutions.[12]

[9] The total number of people in the rural labor force in 1995 was reported to be 450.42 million, and the number working in TVEs was 182.62 million (SYB 2003, tables 12–4 and 12–30). The total number of urban employed was 190.4 million (SYB 2003, table 5–4). The total value added generated by rural industries was 1459.5 billion yuan in 1995 (SYB 2003, table 12–31), the total output from industry and construction was 2,853.8 billion yuan, and GDP for the same year was 5847.8 billion yuan (SYB 2003, table 3–1).

[10] The number of rural migrants in cities reached 152.8 million and migrant rural laborers were reported to be at 104.7 million in 2002 (Chan 2012). The total number of urban employees in state- and collectively owned enterprises was 82.85 million (SYB 2003, table 5–4).

[11] Weber 2021 chronicles debates and decisions during China's price reforms in the 1980s.

[12] On property right reforms, see Walder and Oi 1999; on foreign direct investment, see Y. Huang 2002. A broad collection on Chinese reforms is Brandt and Rawski 2008. A chronicle of major government decisions and policies is in Peng and Chen 2008.

Governments, however, do not create economic miracles. People do. As with breaking away from collective farming in the late 1970s, the two phases of industrialization and urbanization in the ensuing decades that propelled China to prosperity were *not* initiated or led by the government. To the contrary, an urban-based government more than often catered to the interests of the urban population and suppressed or restricted economic initiatives of the rural population. Hundreds of millions of poor Chinese farmers were not lifted out of poverty, they broke out of poverty and elevated their own standard of living with their own minds and hands, often at great sacrifice. While the Chinese ascendance would seem to be set in the glittering lights of the skyscrapers in the cities, the process started elsewhere: in the Chinese countryside.

Too often, the lens on China's age of abundance is trained on its cities, where the ever-rising skyscrapers, new airports, railway stations, and fancy boutique stores have sprung up. Cities are also the dwelling places of the bureaucrats who claimed to have designed the reform blueprints and the academics who wrote about them. The lens focusing on China's reforms is often trained on urban China also because the urban sector, from production to daily living, was where the socialist system was fully implemented. Although growth sprouted elsewhere, reforms had to be implemented in the cities.

To focus on the cities and the state-owned sector misses not just how China's march toward material prosperity began but also its foundation and the source of its energy. What drove China's second industrialization and its prosperity came from the bottom, not the top, of society. Modifications to the economic system are certainly necessary, but they are far from sufficient. Ronald Coase and Ning Wang emphasize two paths in their insightful analysis of the Chinese reform process: one state-led and one grassroots. As they observe:

> The presence of two reforms – one state-led, one grassroots – in China's economic transformation is beyond any doubt. The failure to recognize the dual-track structure of reform has become a source of confusion in understanding the "great story of our time." As the grassroots reform was often overshadowed by, and not explicitly distinguished from, the first, the Chinese government, which clearly orchestrated the first, was also credited as the planner and instigator of the second. This misattributes a grassroots movement to the state and gives rise to a state-centered misinterpretation of Chinese market transformation.[13]

[13] Coase and Wang 2012, 160.

Two paths led to China's ascendance to material prosperity. One path was followed by those who began the Chinese economic transformation in its vast rural areas. The path taken by the city dwellers was quite different. Urban employees and their families mostly struggled throughout the 1990s to adapt to risky, turbulent, and deeply painful reforms. To understand how the age of abundance began, one needs to begin in the Chinese countryside, to appreciate "capitalism with Chinese characteristics."[14]

Industrialization In Situ

For the families in Xiaogang village taking the risk to abandon collective farming out of despair in the late fall of 1978, the payoff was instant and handsome. The year after they converted to household-based farming, the farmers' yields were unprecedentedly rewarding. For thirteen consecutive years prior to household farming began, nearly 80 percent of the villagers' grain consumption relied on state subsidies. That changed in 1979, when the farmers had a bumper harvest equivalent to a total output of the five years between 1966 and 1970 combined; a harvest that allowed the villagers to sell their surplus grain output to the state after meeting their own needs.[15] The same change in agricultural output was soon realized throughout the country as families started to depart from collective farming. Just three years after Xiaogang village saw its first harvest in 1979, national grain output in 1982 rose to a level 16 percent higher than that in 1978.[16]

With instantly increased productivity and grain output, the farmers in Xiaogang village began to shift their energy elsewhere to make use of their additional labor and newly increased income. In 1983, the village head who led the families to venture into household farming began to plan for a factory, with initial plans for a brick kiln. When the plan became entangled in local politics, he pursued a different initiative, raised capital, and hired technical personnel from elsewhere for a plastics recycling factory. That factory was ordered to close as it threatened the village's reputation as a "model village" for household farming. Though unsuccessful, this shift from farming to village-based industrial production was but a microcosm of what was soon to engulf the vast Chinese countryside, especially in China's coastal areas. China's second industrialization, in the Chinese countryside, was launched. Liberated from farming, the rural labor force shifted to work in township and village enterprises (TVEs).

[14] Y. Huang 2008; 2012. [15] Chen and Wu 2009, 74.
[16] Calculated from SYB 1983, 158.

TVEs had their earlier roots in the people's commune years. Owned and operated by collectives, the limited number of small-scale shops were intended to serve agriculture production and the countryside, not to industrialize the economy or to compete with state-owned industrial firms in the cities. As miniature replicas of urban, state-owned enterprises, they were clustered into five small industries, producing iron and steel, cement, chemical fertilizer, hydroelectric power, and small farming equipment. Prior to rural reforms in the late 1970s, "the macroeconomic significance of rural industry remained small."[17] The two exceptions were in cement and chemical fertilizer production, for which rural factories produced up to half of the national output, and up to 60 percent by the early 1970s. Lacking capital, technology, and skilled labor, the small number of factories scattered across the Chinese countryside were inefficient and played a "surprisingly unimportant" role in the Chinese economy during the planned economy era. They employed a miniscule share of the Chinese labor force: in 1975 approximately 5 percent of the rural labor force was employed in these industries.[18] In 1978, less than 10 percent of China's total industrial output was produced in rural China. Moreover, 13.5 percent of the commune-level enterprises were operating at a loss.[19]

Leaving Farming

The swift shift from farming to manufacturing in the Chinese countryside was nothing short of striking. Only 1.52 million nationwide in 1978, the number of TVEs shot up eightfold in seven years, to 12.22 million by 1985, and further doubled in the next decade to nearly 25 million by 1994.[20] Between 1978 and 1989, the share of value added generated by rural enterprises as China's GDP more than doubled from 5.7 percent to 12.4 percent. A decade later, it reached 30 percent. As early as 1987, less than a decade after returning to private farming, rural households began to draw the majority of their income from non-farming activities. For the first time, the combined values of industrial production and services surpassed those of agricultural products in China's countryside. In 1995, value added from rural enterprises accounted for a quarter of the country's total economic output, up from less than 6 percent in 1978 and less than 9 percent in 1985. By the year 2000, rural enterprises contributed to 30 percent of the country's GDP. Measured as the share of output from the nation's non-farming sectors (secondary and tertiary sectors combined), the contribution

[17] Riskin 1987, 214. [18] Ibid. [19] Naughton 1996, 144–46.
[20] SYB 2003, table 12–29.

from rural enterprises rose from 8 percent in 1978 to 12 percent in 1985, 31 percent in 1995, and 36 percent by 2000.[21] By the early 1990s, the output from TVEs already accounted for 40 percent of China's total industrial growth, reaching 59 percent in 1995.[22] The 1980s were decidedly China's "entrepreneurial decade."[23]

A historical transformation of China's rural labor force had begun. In 1978, on the eve of rural reforms, of the roughly 280 million rural laborers, only 28.27 million were recorded as working in enterprises run by rural collectives.[24] Slightly more than a decade later, by 1990, more than one-fifth of the total labor force had switched to working in rural non-farming firms (Table 4.1). By the late 1990s, over 150 million, or over

Table 4.1 *Industrialization of rural employment, China, 1978–2002*

Year	Rural labor (million) (1)	Rural industry (million) (1)	% Rural industry (1)	Rural labor (million) (2)	Rural industry (million) (2)	% Rural industry (2)
1978	306.38			284.56	28.27	9.93%
1980	318.36			298.08	30.00	10.06%
1985	370.65			390.00	69.79	17.89%
1989	409.39			409.39	95.45	23.32%
1990	477.08	108.69	22.78%	420.10	93.67	22.30%
1991	480.26	113.41	23.61%	430.93	92.65	21.50%
1992	482.91	124.87	25.86%	438.02	96.09	21.94%
1993	485.46	145.42	29.96%	442.56	105.81	23.91%
1994	488.02	148.84	30.50%	446.54	123.45	27.65%
1995	490.25	163.87	33.43%	450.42	120.18	26.68%
1996	490.28	173.67	35.42%	452.88	128.62	28.40%
1997	490.39	171.72	35.02%	459.62	135.08	29.39%
1998	490.21	171.29	34.94%	464.32	130.50	28.11%
1999	489.82	175.00	35.73%			
2000	489.34	168.92	34.52%			
2001	490.85	169.02	34.43%			
2002	489.6	171.72	35.07%			

Sources: Rural labor and employed in non-farming firms and self-employed (1) from SYB 2003, table 12–30; rural labor and employed in industry (2) from SYB 1999, table 12–4, based on statistics from the Ministry of Agriculture.

[21] Calculated from numbers in SYB 2003, tables 12–31 and 3–1.
[22] J. Y. Lin and Yao 2001, calculated from numbers in SYB 2003, tables 12–31 and 3–1.
[23] Y. Huang 2008, 150.
[24] For years, the SYB published the number of TVEs and the number of people employed. The practice stopped in 2000. Then in 2003, the SYB published historical data from 1978 to 2002, thus offering a source to follow the changes, however imperfect the statistics might be.

30 percent of the entire rural labor force, were reported to be working in these rural industrial firms.[25]

The silent rise of the new nonagricultural labor force *in rural China* soon overtook the old industrial labor force in urban China, which was still under the state's dwindling protection and struggling for retransformation. By 1995, at 163.87 million strong, the number of people employed in rural enterprises was about to overtake the total number of employed individuals in urban China, who numbered 190 million. Rural enterprises by then employed *more workers* than the total number of employees in the state and collectively owned enterprises, which was 144.08 million. In the next five years, with the restructuring of the state-owned enterprises and layoffs, the difference became even larger. By 2000, the 128.2 million Chinese working in TVEs outnumbered the 96.01 million in state- and collectively owned enterprises in urban China by a margin of 33.53 percent.[26]

The vastly increased number of rural non-farm workers, nevertheless, does not capture the full extent of rural employment transformation. The non-farming individuals, whose number was estimated based on surveys, included only those counted as in full-time non-farming employment. The number does not include many others whose economic activities straddled farming and non-farming sectors. And these aggregate numbers do not differentiate employment by the age or gender of the rural laborers. Age and gender characteristics of non-farming employment offer additional insights that reveal the process of rural economic transformation.

A more detailed snapshot, from census tabulations not surveys, further informs the process of rural labor force transformation. This is the share of labor force registered in the countryside and whose primary employment was reported in non-farming sectors. The Chinese censuses classified employment by three residential types: in cities, towns, and the countryside. In the year 2015, for instance, out of the 11 million individuals employed nationwide (based on a 1/100 sample population mini census), 31 percent were registered in cities, 23 percent in towns, and the remaining 46 percent in the countryside. Out of those registered in the countryside, in 1990, China's population census reported 11 percent aged 15 and over

25 For 1990, the two different sources – statistics from the Ministry of Agriculture and from China's National Bureau of Statistics – both showed 22 percent of the rural labor force employed in rural industrial firms. While the number from the National Bureau of Statistics for the late 1990s shows over a third of all rural employment was in rural enterprises, the number from the Ministry of Agriculture was lower but still close to 30 percent (Table 4.1).

26 SYB 2003, table 5–4. The total number of non-farming workers in rural China, if including those listed as so-called private businesses and self-employed, was 168.92 million in the year 2000. The total size of the labor force in all urban China was reported to be at 231.51 million.

working in non-farming jobs, with the share at nearly 15 percent among those aged in their late 20s and early 30s (Figure 4.2).[27] By 2005, the shares rose to 17 percent for all employed. Among those aged 20 to 24, the share in non-farming employment rose to nearly 30 percent.

The decade after 2005 saw a sharp increase in non-farm work among the population registered in rural China. By 2015, with only less than half of all employed persons in China still registered in the countryside, 36 percent were no longer working in the farming sector, a share that had more than doubled from the decade prior. Among those under 30, over half reported working in non-farm sectors; for those older than their late 30s, the share was more than 40 percent (Figure 4.2). For the country as a whole (urban and rural populations combined), the share of labor force working in nonagricultural sectors reached 63 percent by 2015. Among young people who had left farming, the share reached 76.4 percent of 20–24 year olds, 79 percent for 25–29 year olds, and 76.3 percent for 30–34 year olds.[28]

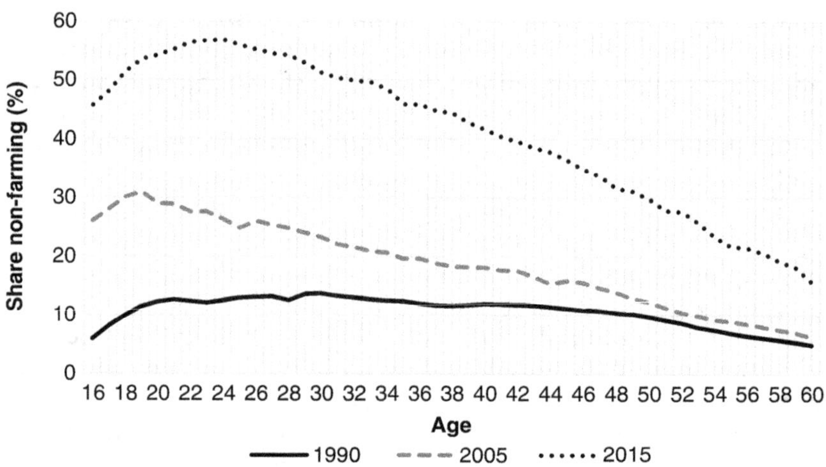

Figure 4.2 Labor transformation to non-farming, rural China, 1990, 2005, and 2015 (share of rural population working in non-farming jobs)
Sources: China Population Census 1990; 2005 and 2015 1/100 mini-censuses

[27] Calculated from China Population Census 1990. These numbers are substantially lower than those reported in the SYB, where the numbers are from surveys and may better capture types of employment. It is more likely that in a census a rural resident will simply resort to choosing "farming" as their employment.

[28] China 2015 1/100 Population Survey, table 5–2.

Another important feature of China's rural employment transformation was the gender gap in non-farming employment. This change was one of the most transformative social changes in post-Mao China. Over the two-and-a-half decades after 1990, female non-farm employment caught up quickly with that of males. Prior to large-scale out-migration in the mid-1990s, the share of females reporting to be engaged in off-farm work was sharply lower than that of males. In both 1990 and 2005, the share of females in rural China reporting in off-farm work was less than 50 percent of that for males at ages above 30 (Figure 4.3). In 2005, as compared with 1990, the gender gap actually increased, with the share of females in off-farm jobs at only 40 percent, a lower level than men (Figure 4.3). That change was likely due to the gendered pattern of out-migration from the 1990s to the early 2000s, as more young men than young women moved to the cities, leaving a disproportionately larger share of women in the countryside for farming and taking care of children. By 2015, however, the pattern reversed. The gender gap markedly narrowed in non-farming sectors among the rural-registered population. Among those aged 30 and below, the ratio between females and males rose to 0.8, nearly doubling from the level a decade before. Though not at parity, a very high share of both men and women were in non-farm jobs.

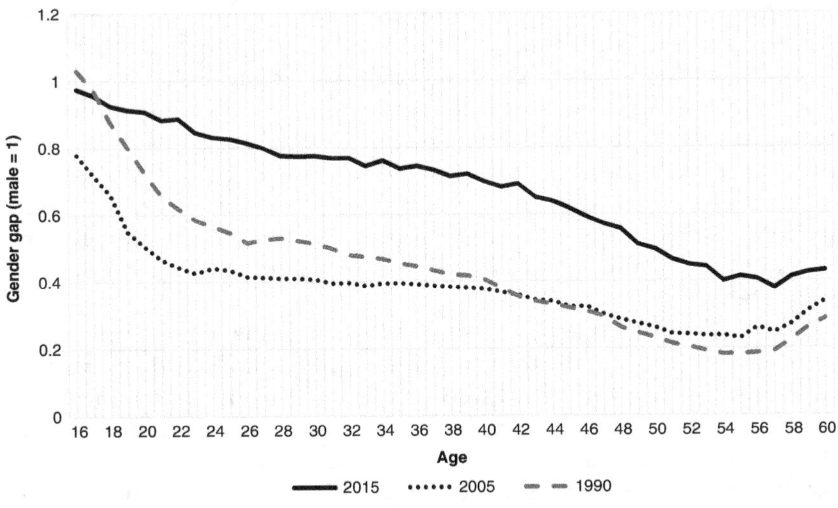

Figure 4.3 Gender gap (proportion of females vs males) in non-farming employment, rural China, 1990, 2005, and 2015
Sources: Author's calculation based on China Population Census 1990, 2005, 2015

The decade after 2005 saw both a trend in the rural population leaving farming and a closing of the gender gap in non-farm employment in the Chinese countryside.

China's in situ industrialization led to rapid increases in the rural population's income. With increased income, their living standards improved to unprecedented levels. As noted by Jean Oi in her book on China's rural transformation, it was "the sector of the rural economy that has been at the core of China's economic success" in the twenty years after the late 1970s.[29] Rural enterprises produced everything: from building materials, machineries, textiles, household goods, to coal and other mineral resources. As rural industrial firms flourished, rural industrial outputs provided a larger share of the rural population's income than did farming. By 1992, the industrial output value from non-state sources throughout China, largely from rural industries, outperformed the state sector for the first time.[30] During the 1980s and the early 1990s, as profiled in the previous chapter, rural living standards improved the fastest, as measured by rural residents' consumption of food and other products. Increased income, largely from non-farming activities, also allowed rural Chinese to invest in building new homes, improving their living quality further.

Making and Exporting

At first glance, China's rural industrialization bears some resemblance to Europe's proto-industrialization predating its industrial revolution. In different societies that later industrialized, peasants supplemented their income from farming by engaging in the cottage industry of manufacturing textile products, spinning and weaving in their homes and in the intervals when they were freed from farming. European and Japanese cottage industries served important functions in the development of capitalism in those settings from marketing networks to capital accumulation.[31]

Yet this is where the similarities end between China's in situ industrialization and the proto-industrialization elsewhere in the world. Workers in the Chinese countryside produced not only for themselves – they produced for all of China and for the entire world. Moreover, while China followed other East Asian economies in their early stages of economic takeoff with an export-oriented, manufacturing economy, much of that export – especially export growth – took place in China's vast rural areas. In 1978, exports accounted for less than 5 percent of China's GDP. The

[29] Oi 1999, 624. [30] Naughton 1996, 164. [31] Mendels 1972; Howell 1995.

share of exports in China's economy quickly gained importance, rising to 9 percent of GDP in 1985, 16 percent in 1990, and 25.72 percent by 2002, the year after China joined the WTO.[32] At its peak, Chinese exports to the world accounted for 30 percent of the country's entire GDP, with $143.70 billion worth of goods. While the volume of exports continued to rise to more than $220 billion by the late 2010s, exporting's share of GDP declined to less than 20 percent (Figure 4.4). Manufacturing for export, as in China's neighboring economies, proved to be a successful recipe for China's economic growth.

Rural industries drove and led China's export-oriented economy. The share of exports attributed to rural industries, as shown in Table 4.2, already accounted for nearly 20 percent by the end of the 1980s. During the years when rural industries grew the fastest, when exports as a share of China's GDP doubled from about 10 to 22 percent, the exported value from rural industries rose to more than 40 percent of China's exports to nearly half of all exports in 1996 (Figure 4.4).

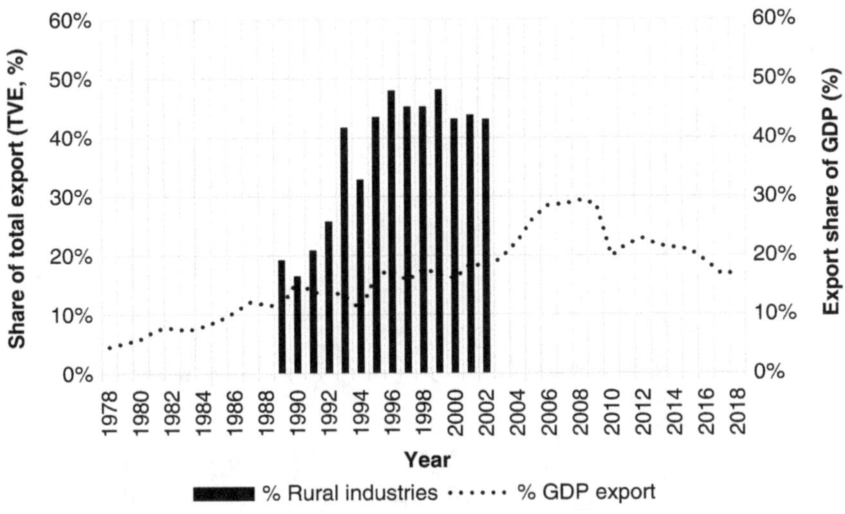

Figure 4.4 China's export economy and the role of rural industries
Source: Exports as GDP share, calculated from SYB 2019, tables 3–1 and 11–2; share of rural industry exports calculated from SYB 2003 (also see Table 4.2 in this book) and SYB 2019, table 11–2

[32] Calculated from SYB 2003, tables 3–1 and 17–3.

Table 4.2 *Export by township and village enterprises, China, 1989–2002*

Year	Value added as share of GDP	TVE share of exports	Combined value of exports (100 million yuan)	Composition of export					
				Chemical products	Machineries	Light industrial products	Food	Textiles and cloth	Crafts
1989	12.32%	18.99%	289.8	7.16%	6.15%	13.27%	12.05%	44.72%	16.65%
1990	13.50%	16.26%	391.7	6.31%	6.74%	16.22%	10.69%	44.38%	15.67%
1991	13.75%	20.62%	646.8	5.29%	6.27%	22.07%	8.34%	43.72%	14.32%
1992	16.84%	25.51%	968.6	6.91%	7.52%	19.20%	8.20%	44.51%	13.66%
1993	23.12%	41.50%	1780.4	6.16%	8.18%	25.06%	7.23%	41.28%	12.09%
1994	23.37%	32.61%	2659.8	7.01%	9.10%	25.65%	8.72%	37.81%	11.70%
1995	24.96%	43.32%	4222.3	7.02%	9.10%	25.65%	8.72%	37.81%	11.70%
1996	26.01%	47.77%	4702.4	7.02%	9.10%	25.65%	8.72%	37.81%	11.70%
1997	27.85%	45.03%	5378.4	6.81%	9.42%	27.19%	8.18%	37.22%	11.19%
1998	28.32%	45.02%	5325.6	6.50%	9.73%	27.73%	7.99%	35.50%	12.55%
1999	30.32%	47.92%	5995.3	6.43%	10.60%	31.34%	7.83%	32.60%	11.20%
2000	30.35%	42.98%	6665.2	6.61%	11.16%	30.66%	7.93%	32.66%	10.99%
2001	30.17%	43.58%	7341.2	6.46%	10.76%	32.90%	7.43%	32.53%	9.92%
2002	30.91%	42.91%	8909.2	6.26%	13.72%	30.16%	7.33%	32.41%	10.11%

Sources: Calculated from SYB 2003, tables 3–1, 12–34

The content of exports from rural industries also demonstrates a production upgrade from foods, textile products, and handcrafts to light industrial goods and machinery. In 1989, foods, textiles, and handcrafts accounted, respectively, for 12, 45, and 17 percent of all export value; a combined share of nearly three quarters of all exports (73.42 percent). By comparison, machinery combined with light industrial products accounted for only about 20 percent. By 1998, the share of the former dropped to 56 percent; the latter two categories rose to 37.46 percent. Then by 2002, the former further dropped to slightly less than half of exports, while the latter two accounted for 43.88 percent. At that point, rural industries were no longer mostly processing consumer goods – foods, textile products, and handcraft goods – for export. Many of these firms upgraded to manufacturing machines, tools, and other parts used for industrial production. These factories had a much higher level of capital, better technology than they had had a decade earlier, and a larger number of employees.

Just as the China economic miracle itself could not have been fully anticipated, the rise and eventual boom of rural enterprises was an utter surprise. It was never in any blueprint of the post-Mao Chinese leaders who oversaw the economic transformation.[33] Deng Xiaoping, who steered China's prosperity, said this much himself in 1987. By then, ten years after the start of China's economic reforms, the number of rural enterprises shot up by 10-fold from 1.5 to 15 million, when 20 percent of the rural labor force had already changed their employment to non-farming. In a meeting with a Yugoslav visitor in June 1987, Deng explained, "In the rural reforms our greatest success – and it is one we had by no means anticipated – has been the emergence of a large number of enterprises run by villages and townships. They were like a new force that just came into being spontaneously."[34] Deng was pleased to see that these rural industries helped solve the problem of surplus labor, employing 50 percent of the rural labor and keeping them from relocating to the cities.[35]

[33] Naughton 1996, 144: "as in the case of household farming, the shift in development strategy led to unanticipated institutional changes with profound consequences."

[34] Quoted in Vogel 2011. Vogel also notes in his biography of Deng (445): "Deng did not launch the TVEs experiment, but it fit his philosophy: when something works, support it."

[35] Zhonggong zhongyang wenxian yanjiushi 2004, 565. This conversation is also recorded in Coase and Wang 2012, 53: "Their annual output value has been increasing by more than 20 percent a year for the last several years. The increase in TVEs, particularly industrial enterprises, has provided jobs for 50 percent of the surplus labor in the countryside ... This result was not anything that I or any of the other comrades had foreseen; it just came out of the blue."

This rise of rural industries was made possible by a number of legacies from China's socialism. In rural China, an abundant pool of young, healthy, and literate laborers was more than eager to work toward improving their lives. And that pool expanded in leaps and bounds. The rapid increase in agricultural productivity raised the living standards of the rural population and increased the vast labor pool. Increased productivity led to both improved diet as well as increased investment in non-farming ventures. Once the collective farming system became history, the traditional Chinese family reemerged as the engine of economic growth.[36]

China's dual social system and the parallel reforms in rural and urban sectors also created tremendous opportunities for rural industries. Price reforms from government-set to market-driven prices adopted a dual-track approach; state and collectively owned factories in urban China were allowed to sell their products after meeting the planning quota at market prices and to retain profits. This dual-track reform not only enabled rural enterprises to produce much needed consumer goods at market prices, but it also created opportunities for rural enterprises to forge opportunities with urban firms and to benefit from urban firms' technology, personnel, and even capital.

In addition to their ready access to abundant labor and the market, rural industries also benefited from a number of other factors in the early years of their rise. Rural enterprises enjoyed a low tax rate and benefited both from their proximity to urban areas and from the struggling state-owned firms that were unable to meet the rising demands of consumers as well as producers. Importantly, in their early years of growth, rural firms had easy access to capital, which in part was made possible by the skyrocketing rise in rural household savings. Rural firms could rely on the rural financial institution of Rural Credit Collectives, who supplied up to two-thirds of total bank funding in the late 1980s, often under the active promotion and sponsorship of local governments.[37] For example, bank loans to TVEs rose from 2.88 billion yuan in 1985 to 11.28 billion in 1990 and to 44.41 billion by 1995 – a 15-fold increase within about a decade.[38] As new entrants to the market filling niches and operating under market conditions, rural industrial firms enjoyed a very high profit margin in the early years, further fueling growth in this sector. Return on capital was over 30 percent in the earliest years, in 1978, and was reported to still be as high as 15 percent in the mid-1980s, before dipping to only around 5 percent by the early 1990s.[39]

[36] Whyte 1995. [37] Naughton 1996; Oi 1999.
[38] Loan at the end of the year. SYB 2003, table 12–32. [39] Naughton 1996, 150.

Breeding Capitalists

China's rural industries produced not just goods but also people.[40] More specifically, they trained China's first post-socialist generation of capitalist entrepreneurs. The booming rural industrial firms spawned China's first and largest army of capitalists, who started in the countryside and expanded to every corner in China. Many of these first-generation capitalists were the most capable communists in Chinese villages, as former production team leaders and Communist Party secretaries. Local governments were crucial in facilitating, leading, and often taking rural enterprises to success, as investigated and summarized by Jean Oi, back in the 1990s:

> China's economic reforms took off in many parts of the countryside precisely because the key entrepreneurs leading the charge were those who had the economic and political resources – the cadres themselves. Rooted in the prior existence of collective and central planning, local state corporatism is the path of least resistance in the transition from a Leninist system.[41]

The capitalistic nature of these rural industries was evident in every aspect. Privately owned and individually operated businesses far outpaced those under the umbrella of "collectively owned" ones. While collectively owned firms were larger in scale and produced more value added in the early years of rural industrialization, the share of businesses explicitly classified as non-collective stood at 90 percent after the mid-1980s (Table 4.3). By the turn of the twenty-first century, barely two decades into the rural economic transformation, virtually all rural industrial businesses became privately owned.

Privately owned and capitalistic, rural industrial firms quickly surpassed those under the "collectively owned" businesses in employment and then in economic output. By 1990, they employed more than half of all individuals working in TVEs. In the same year, already a third of all value added by rural enterprises were produced by these private firms. By the late 1990s, these private firms, employing over 60 percent of the labor, began to deliver more than half of all value added from rural industries (Table 4.3). Even many of those TVEs under the collectively owned category were in fact privately owned. They operated under the "red-hat," as collectively owned, for purely political reasons.[42] Numbering more than 20 million, most of these rural-based firms continued their operations in the villages and townships in the Chinese countryside. Others expanded and transformed into new and larger businesses elsewhere. Many rural entrepreneurs later turned into business tycoons.

[40] Y. Huang 2008; 2012. [41] Oi 1999, 192. [42] As in Oi 1999; Y. Huang 2008; 2012.

Table 4.3 *Ownership type of township and village enterprises*

Year	Number of firms (million)	Firms private	Employed private	Value-added private
1978	1.5			
1980	1.4			
1985	12.2	87.2%	40.5%	27.1%
1989	18.7	91.8%	49.6%	33.6%
1990	18.7	92.2%	50.4%	33.2%
1991	19.1	92.4%	50.4%	32.1%
1992	20.9	92.7%	51.3%	32.9%
1993	24.5	93.1%	53.3%	35.8%
1994	24.9	93.4%	50.9%	35.8%
1995	22.0	92.6%	52.9%	35.9%
1996	23.4	93.4%	55.9%	41.9%
1997	20.1	93.6%	59.2%	51.5%
1998	20.0	94.7%	61.5%	55.1%
1999	20.7	95.5%	65.6%	60.2%
2000	20.8	96.2%	70.1%	65.3%
2001	21.2	96.8%	74.2%	68.9%
2002	21.3	96.6%	71.4%	62.7%

Source: Calculated from SYB 2003, tables 12–29 and 12–31

As non-farming employment and economic output increased at an unexpectedly rapid pace in rural China throughout the 1980s and into the early 1990s, this industrialization remained in the countryside. The socialist legacy of one-country, two-systems was still in full force, and city gates were closed to those without an urban household registration. Jobs at state-owned firms and government organizations were still kept off-limits to persons without a city household registration. Even those who studied and were enthralled by rural industrialization advocated in situ industrialization. This was the disposition of China's best known sociologist Fei Xiaotong at that time. Returning to his native Jiangsu province in the early 1980s, where he investigated rural economy and social relations back in the 1930s, Fei documented the fast improvement in villagers' lives along with different types of rural industries under rapid development. He identified small towns as a social entity "located in between the rural communities and the urban centers, and an entity both different and inseparable from the countryside,"[43] and endorsed "vigorously developing small towns."[44] The preference of in situ industrialization lasted well

[43] Fei 1986, 18. [44] Ibid., 14.

into the early 1990s, with government policies of keeping farmers at their natal soil, in the villages or in nearby small towns. This slogan best summarizes the government's preference at the time for in situ industrialization: "leaving farming land but not the village, entering factories but not cities."

Into Cities

Just as the rise of rural industrialization was revolutionary in the 1980s, the rise of China's megacities, rather than small towns, also exceeded expectations. Instead of remaining in their native villages and forming small towns, rural Chinese pressed into cities, especially large cities. By 2001, over twenty years after they signed that desperate piece of paper to begin household farming, the households in Xiaogang village were transformed. Only twelve of the original eighteen households still maintained roots in the village. And, out of the remaining twelve households, only three had adult children who had stayed with farming. Young people in the other households almost all abandoned village life, not as panhandlers but as migrant laborers working in cities and towns elsewhere. In one household, three out of four sons and their wives set up life in nearby Jiangsu province. In another, all three children made a life in Zhejiang province. In the most mobile household, six adult children spread out all over China, five outside of their home province: with the eldest in Nanjing, Jiangsu province; the second son in Beijing; the third in Tianjin; the fourth in nearby Fengyang, in the same province; the fifth in Shanghai; and the sixth in the city of Zhangjiagang, Jiangsu province. The village that made its name as the pioneer in household farming had few people left on its farms.[45]

As rural industrialization grew rapidly in the 1980s and 1990s, two forces were forging to set the stage for the second phase of China's post-socialist industrialization. In contrast to the first phase where industrialization mushroomed in the countryside, this second phase extended to cities. It converted China not only into an industrialized *economy* but also – for the first time in its history – into an industrialized and urbanized *society*. As with the first phase of China's post-Mao industrialization, the second phase also unfolded with its enduring legacy created under socialism. While the vast population from rural China continued to play a dominant role in building China into prosperity, they did so while being treated as secondary citizens in their own country.

[45] Chen and Wu 2009, 294.

The two forces that set the stage of this second phase of industrialization were both a push and a pull. Rural industries flourished in the 1980s, unexpectedly, under relatively favorable institutional conditions. This outcome was attributable to a rising demand from consumers both from the countryside as well as in the cities. As incomes increased, so did the vacuum resulting from the dearth of consumer goods produced in the rigid planned economy system. From nails to knitwear, shoes to shirts, briefcases to bedding, sunflower seeds to hard liquor, everything was in short supply. State-owned enterprises were not equipped or were too inefficient to meet the rising demand. Born into a new era, these rural industrial firms were producing goods in response to consumer demand and were doing so under market conditions.

A force began to push rural laborers out of the countryside. Besides the abundant labor pool, other institutional factors favorable to rural industrialization were changing in the late 1980s. As economic reforms in urban China ran into more turbulence, rural industrial firms were singled out as targets of economic rectification, to cool off an overheated economy, and to protect enterprises in the cities. The Chinese government once again focused their resources on supporting employees and their families in the cities. A report, carried in the influential internal circular by Xinhua News Agency in July 1989, advocated "cooling off the temperature of setting up rural industrial firms." The report claimed that rural industrial firms harmed agricultural growth by competing for labor, resources, and investment. It further blamed rural industrial firms for the problems experienced by state-owned firms in cities.[46] Even Deng Xiaoping, who had marveled at the miracle of TVEs just two years earlier, vowed "to shut down absolutely those rural industrial firms that were wasting electricity and raw materials."[47]

Hostile policies toward rural industries were openly and resolutely meted out. An explicit government order capped growth rates at 15 percent annually. Tax relief favoring light industrial goods produced by rural firms was phased out.[48] To protect state-owned enterprises, banks were ordered at the start of 1989 to implement a policy of "zero lending" to rural firms, causing significant problems for some firms.[49] By the early 1990s, collectively owned enterprises became liabilities to themselves.

[46] Peng and Chen 2008 (645): "TVEs took away supplies of coal, electricity, transportation means, and raw materials from large- and medium-sized enterprises. As a result, in 1988, roughly 40 percent of these large- and medium-sized enterprises could not fully utilize their production capacities, reducing their output by more than 400 billion yuan, roughly the same as the output from TVEs, and reduced profit and tax contribution to the state by over 50 billion yuan."

[47] Translation based on Peng and Chen 2008, 645.

[48] Cai Fang, Wang, and Du 2008, 91. [49] Peng and Chen 2008.

Some were privatized, others were transformed into "shareholding cooperatives." Rural informal financing, which had become an increasingly important funding source for local governments, was under scrutiny and subject to frequent crackdowns. Government-controlled bank loans to rural enterprises were more difficult to acquire. Rural industrial firms' capital investment started to decline. Rural income growth, faster than that in urban China in the 1980s and largely driven by non-farming income, began to lag that of urban residents.[50] Between 1989 and 1991, rural income increased at an anemic annual rate of 0.7 percent. In some locales, income growth turned negative.[51]

At the same time as their income growth slowed, rural residents continued to shoulder a heavy burden from the government. Despite price increases for agricultural products, farming remained the disadvantaged sector of the economy, as was the case during the earlier planned economy years. In the 1980s, the price scissors continued and got wider. One estimate put the gap in pricing to have increased by more than 10 percent in the decade, estimated to be 102 billion yuan in the year 1989, 2.1 and 1.1 times of that in 1978 and 1985, respectively. Per capita taxation burden in 1990 reached 10.9 percent of net income.[52] These institutional biases incentivized abandoning the farm and country life altogether.

Enter a pull force at the very same time. A decade earlier, in the early 1980s, city doors had cracked if not swung open for rural Chinese. Farmers started to sell their surplus agricultural goods, meeting urban residents' rising demands. Urban employment, however, was still off-limits to them; as was housing, education, health care, and other social services. With the rise of China's special economic zones after the early 1980s, and as reforms of state-owned enterprises unfolded, demand for labor also rose over the decade. Entering the 1990s, from manufacturing and construction to retails and services, opportunities further emerged in cities. With the notable exception of the construction industry, however, state and collectively owned work organizations were still off-limits to rural migrants.

By the early 1990s, the removal of food rationing, a practical and crucial barrier of rural-to-urban migration, facilitated the pull of the rural labor force to cities. Prior to their exit, food rationing coupons, issued only to urban residents, prevented rural Chinese from purchasing food in cities, even if they had cash on hand. People from the countryside needed to bring their own food when traveling to cities to sell their products or to find work. With the increasingly abundant supply of food

[50] Y. Huang 2008, chap. 3, documents these reversals in detail.
[51] Peng and Chen 2008. [52] Niu 1992.

items following successive growth in agricultural output in the 1980s, food rationing was phased out. By 1993, food rationing was fully eliminated, closing a chapter of the socialist planned economy that was characterized by the chronic shortage of food and other consumer goods.

With both push and pull forces, China's rural population flocked to the cities en masse. Beginning in the late 1980s, and accelerating in the 1990s, rural Chinese out-migrants formed the largest ever human migratory stream in world history. The rise started slowly, then surged nearly exponentially. In 1982, the number of migrants within China was estimated to be only 46.5 million, comprising less than 0.5 percent of China's total population at the time. The number of migrants rose slowly in the 1980s, reaching only 66.3 million by 1990, before further rising to just 69.5 million in 1995, still far less than 1 percent of the population.

The first sharp rise in rural migrants came in the second half of the 1990s, during which the number of rural migrants to cities nearly doubled, to 136.6 million (Figure 4.5). The number rose gradually again in the early 2000s, then a second sharp rise came, toward the end of the decade, jumping to 221 million by 2010. With the number of migrants reaching 241 million in 2018, nearly one out of every five Chinese was then a migrant.[53] Among rural residents, the share who migrated out was certainly more than one in five, as the overwhelming majority of Chinese migrants were from the countryside.

Combined, these push and pull forces generated the steep increases in the number of rural migrants in Chinese cities in both periods. The first spike in the second half of the 1990s, when the number exceeded 100 million, coincided with the rural industrial slowdown. Urban reforms in the late 1990s also opened more opportunities for rural labor, when the need for construction shot up, tacking with the urban residential commercial market and the start of China's construction boom in general.

The second sharp rise in the number of migrants, in the late 2000s, followed the boom of Chinese manufacturing for international markets, after the global financial crisis in 2008. It was during this second spike of migration that the number of migrants in Chinese cities first surpassed 200 million. Massive government funding for investment in infrastructure building created more opportunities for construction, stimulated domestic consumption, and accelerated exportation. It was at this time

[53] Chan 2012; Liang 2016; SYB 2019. Migrants are generally defined as those who have been away from their place of household registration for six months or longer. Statistics based on migrant labor surveys, which began in 2008 and were carried out by China's National Bureau of Statistics, gave higher numbers of migrant laborers. See, for instance, www.stats.gov.cn/tjsj/zxfb/202004/t20200430_1742724.html

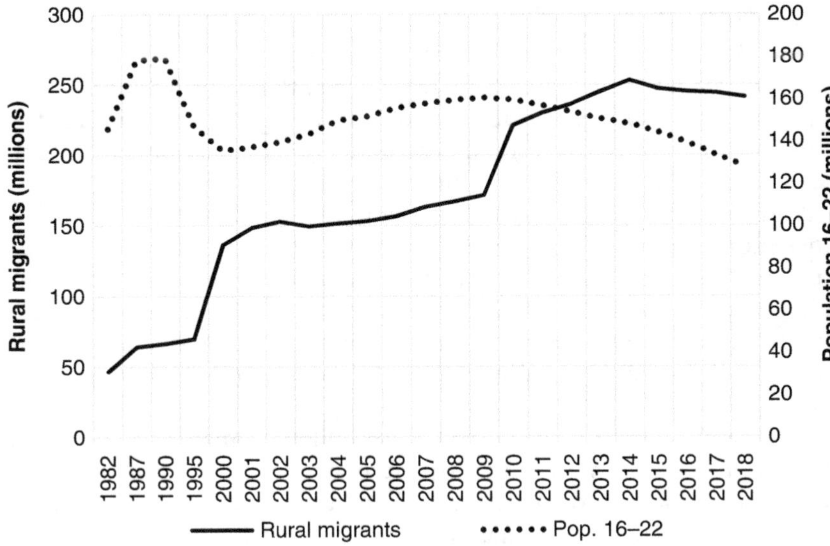

Figure 4.5 Rise of rural migrants in urban China
Note and sources: Migrants are defined as those with a rural household registration living in cities and away from their original residence for six months or more. The numbers for 1982–2009 are estimated by Chan (2012); 2010 and later are from SYB 2019, table 2–3. The National Statistics Bureau only provides data for 2010 and later. The number published by the National Statistics Bureau for 2010, 221 million, is close to Chan's estimate, 205.6 million. Population numbers aged 16–22 in this figure are projected by Cai Yong.

when manufacturing products such as the iPhone for the global market began to take place in the industrial parks across China.

Changes in population age structure also played a role in the rise and fall in the number of rural migrants. Figure 4.5 also plots the number of people aged 16–22 over a period of more than three decades, at an age when young people begin to enter the labor force. The number of people in this age group sharply increased, from 145 million in 1982 to 179 million in 1990, due to the post-famine baby boom and high fertility in the 1960s. The number in this age group then dropped after the peak. It expanded again, gradually, from 135 million in 2000 to a peak of 160 million in 2009. The two periods of rapid increase in migrants both followed the increase in the number of young adults entering the labor force. The total number of rural migrants stabilized and started to drop after the mid-2010s, in part driven by this downward demographic trend.

Building Up China

Migrant laborers from rural China built a new China. From roads, railways, bridges, and skyscrapers to airports, the entire Chinese landscape was thoroughly redrawn. It is not just the length or the number of roads and airports that was significant. Railways, roads, railway stations and airports all got bigger and a lot better. In the 2010s alone, 220,200 road bridges were built, including the world's longest, at 164 km, as well as five more of the world's ten longest.[54] By 2020, five of the world's top ten cities with the largest number of skyscrapers were in mainland China. Out of the 2,026 buildings taller than 150 m in the ten cities, 796 are in China. Of the ten tallest buildings on earth, five are also in mainland China, all exceeding 500 m in height and completed after 2015.[55]

Residential housing development was similarly remarkable. Between 2005 and 2017, nearly 14 billion square meters of commercial building space were sold, including nearly 300 million square meters of office space.[56] That was over 10 square meters for each person in the country, or more than 20 square meters for each person residing in urban China. By the early 2010s, China's steel output was approaching roughly half of the world's total.[57] In just three years between 2011 and 2013, China used more cement than the United States had in the entire twentieth century.[58]

Over time, construction became an increasingly important sector of the Chinese economy. One measure to appreciate the importance of the construction sector is to compare its output value to that of industrial production, which rose sharply by 3.24, 5.22, and 3.43 times in the three decades of the 1980s, 1990s, and 2000s, respectively.[59] At the start of the 1980s, the ratio of output between the construction and industrial manufacturing sectors was about 1:9, or construction was just 10 percent of

[54] www.statista.com/statistics/258358/number-of-road-bridges-in-china/; https://seasia.co/2020/08/26/top-10-world-s-longest-bridge-2020

[55] Together with buildings in Hong Kong, China's special administrative region, which has the highest number at 480, the total number would be 1,276, 63 percent of all the tallest buildings in the ten cities. Shenzhen has the second most, 292, surpassing New York's 287. Wuhan, tenth on the list, has 96. https://en.wikipedia.org/wiki/List_of_cities_with_the_most_skyscrapers; https://en.wikipedia.org/wiki/List_of_tallest_buildings#Tallest_buildings_in_the_world

[56] Calculated from SYB 2018, table 9-8.

[57] World Steel Association, "Global crude steel output increases by 3.4% in 2019," Jan. 27, 2020, https://bit.ly/45L2BTr

[58] Ana Swanson, "How China used more cement in 3 years than the US did in the entire 20th century," *Washington Post*, Mar. 24, 2015, www.washingtonpost.com/news/wonk/wp/2015/03/24/how-china-used-more-cement-in-3-years-than-the-u-s-did-in-the-entire-20th-century/

[59] Calculated from SYB 2019, table 3-1.

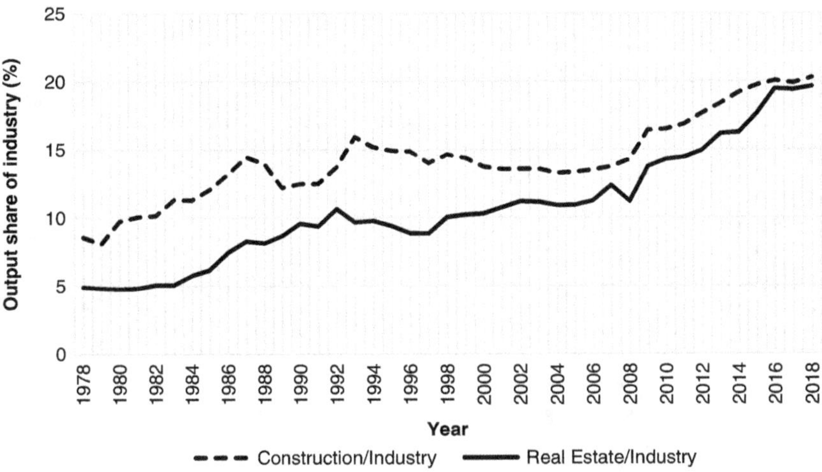

Figure 4.6 Expansion of construction and real estate (output share compared with industry)
Source: Author's calculations based on SYB 2019, table 3–1

industrial production (Figure 4.6). An initial boost came in the 1980s, during which the share increased to 15 percent. After 2008, a second major boost took place, during which construction output was equal to 20 percent of the value generated by industrial production. The real estate sector grew even faster, increasing from a ratio to industrial production of 5 percent in the early 1980s, to 10 percent in the early 1990s, and then rising sharply to 20 percent by the late 2010s. Combined, the total output of these two construction-related sectors reached 40 percent of that generated by all industrial production.

China's abundant migrant labor pool formed the mighty army for this building boom. The mammoth building boom relied on a huge number of workers, from producing construction materials to actually completing construction-related projects. The first major influx of rural migrants coincided with the beginning of China's construction boom in the cities. In the mid-1990s, when urban construction took off with 25,000 registered construction firms nationwide, these firms employed about 15 million people. Virtually all construction companies then were state or collectively owned; many of them had already started using migrant labor as employees. By the early 2000s, the number of construction companies nearly doubled; the number of people employed in the construction business increased to nearly 20 million (Table 4.4).

Table 4.4 *Domestic private companies in construction industry*

	Number of firms	Share "other"	Employees (million)	Share "other"	Value generated (100 million yuan)	Share "other"
1980	6604		6.48		287	
1985	11150		9.12		675	
1990	13327		10.11		1345	
1995	24133	2.5%	14.98	2.1%	5794	2.7%
2000	47518	26.9%	19.94	23.0%	12498	25.9%
2001	45893	38.4%	21.11	36.4%	15362	39.4%
2002	47820	54.8%	22.45	49.5%	18527	50.7%
2003	48688	63.3%	24.14	56.8%	23084	58.5%
2004	59018	72.3%	25.00	65.3%	29021	64.1%
2005	58750	74.5%	27.00	68.1%	34552	66.2%
2006	60166	77.6%	28.78	71.6%	41557	69.6%
2007	62074	79.4%	31.34	74.2%	51044	71.7%
2008	71095	83.1%	33.15	77.1%	62037	74.0%
2009	70817	84.2%	36.73	78.6%	76808	75.0%
2010	71863	85.3%	41.60	79.7%	96031	76.4%
2011	72280	85.9%	38.52	82.2%	116463	77.7%
2012	75280	86.8%	42.67	83.7%	137218	78.9%
2013	78919	89.6%	45.28	86.7%	160366	83.5%
2014	81141	90.2%	45.37	87.4%	176713	84.1%
2015	80911	90.7%	50.94	88.0%	180757	84.8%
2016	83017	91.2%	51.85	87.8%	193567	84.8%
2017	88074	92.2%	55.30	88.9%	213944	85.0%

Source: SYB, various years

Government statistics suggest that most of these new construction workers were migrants. In 1995, at the start of the urban construction boom, almost all construction companies were registered under state or collective ownership; only 2.5 percent were listed as "other," namely not under state or collectively owned (Table 4.4).[60] By 2002, the total number of registered companies nearly doubled, and the share of companies registered as "other" exceeded 50 percent. So did the share of total value generated by the construction sector. By the late 2000s, over 90 percent of the over 80,000 registered companies, with nearly 90 percent of the 50 million employees, were domestic privately owned companies. They generated 85 percent of all value from the construction sector (Table 4.4).

[60] Official Chinese statistics classify ownership type of construction companies into five categories: state, collective, overseas Chinese, foreign, and other. Here by exclusion, I treat those in the "other" category as domestic and privately owned companies.

Real estate development is listed in official Chinese statistics under a separate category from construction, as the sector also involves those working in design and management as well as in sales. In 1998, the year China implemented urban housing reforms, government statistics reported about 25,000 real estate companies in existence, employing roughly 820,000 individuals. Over half of all employees that year were reported to be in state- or collectively owned companies. By 2005, the number of companies more than doubled to 56,290; the workforce rose to more than 1.5 million, 80 percent of which were employed by domestic private firms. In 2015, the number of real estate development firms increased to more than 90,000, employing over 2.7 million, 90 percent in privately owned domestic companies.[61] Many if not most of these real estate sector employees were migrants, especially migrants from rural China.

The true share of rural migrants working in the construction sector was likely much higher, as many migrants worked as temporary hires not employees. Surveys of migrants offered some hints. For instance, up until the late 1990s the main source of employment for migrants was in the construction sector. The earliest government policy permitting migrant laborers to be hired in cities, issued in the mid-1980s, was to allow state-owned construction companies to hire migrant workers.[62] Though the work had been termed "the most bitter and tiring of the jobs, … it was surely the most popular," as it "was probably the one demanding the least investment and the lowest risk, and promising quick returns."[63] By the early 1990s, one-third to two-fifths of all migrant laborers worked at construction sites.[64] A survey in Shanghai in 1995 estimated over a quarter of male migrant workers were employed in the construction sector, a sector that also paid the highest wages compared to other jobs at the time.[65]

Manufacturing for the World

Silicon Gold

During the world's first industrialization two-and-a-half centuries ago, one product stood out. That item was textiles, for clothing. As the world could feed a growing population with an increased food supply, attributable to the addition of crops from the "New World," the population then looked for better clothing for themselves, another essential human need.

[61] Calculated from SYB 2018, tables 19–2 and 19–3. [62] www.asianlii.org
[63] Solinger 1999, 207. [64] Ibid. [65] F. Wang, Zuo, and Ruan 2002.

That need was met by a revolution beginning in England, with the invention and application of new power sources and new textile weaving machineries. That industrial revolution elevated the world to a different era, transforming what once was a craft cottage industry. It vastly increased the productivity of textile making and spread capitalism and colonialism throughout the world.

What served as the basis of that revolution and the rise of global capitalism was one product – cotton – also known as "white gold." In the United States, which became a major source of cotton, production grew explosively, from merely 1.5 million pounds (680,389 kg) in 1790 to 36.5 million pounds (16.57 million kg) in 1800 and to 7 times more a decade later. Forty years later, total cotton production in the United States reached 3 billion pounds (1.36 billion kg), making cotton the top export commodity (up to 75 percent) and the country a top global cotton trade origin (up to 80 percent).[66] Cotton exports from the United States were said to supply materials to clothe "half of the civilized world."[67] The United States reached global dominance in cotton production in such a short time because of "planters' command of nearly unlimited supplies of land, labor, capital, and their unparalleled political power."[68] Capital was foreign, from England, and slaves were the forced labor.

The United States' ascendance to dominance in global cotton production was built on the backs of slave labor. The needs of cotton plantations accelerated the slave trade in the United States. Prior to the arrival of mechanized harvesting in the 1840s, cotton production was labor intensive. During the early phase of the United States' explosive cotton production, between 1790 and 1820, a quarter million slaves were forcefully relocated to grow cotton. Moreover, prior to the British abolition of the slave trade in 1807, an estimated additional 170,000 slaves were brought to the United States, accounting for a third of all slaves brought in since the slave trade began in 1619. Altogether, up to 1 million slaves were sold and forcefully relocated to the Deep South, primarily to grow cotton.[69] Of the 3.2 million slaves in the United States' fifteen states in 1850, 1.8 million were producing cotton.[70] Slavery and cotton production became two inseparable constructs in US history. "It was on the backs of cotton, and thus on the backs of slaves, that the US economy ascended in the world."[71]

66 Beckert 2014, 104, 106. https://courses.lumenlearning.com/suny-ushistory1os2xmaster/chapter/the-economics-of-cotton/
67 Beckert 2014, 119. 68 Ibid., 105. 69 Ibid., 109.
70 https://courses.lumenlearning.com/suny-ushistory1os2xmaster/chapter/the-economics-of-cotton/
71 Beckert 2014, 119.

The "white gold" worldwide in the first decade of the twenty-first century was a handheld device made for the Internet age. It was the smartphone, a device that can make phone calls, send emails, take photos, play games, watch movies, and view videos. It was a device that relied on the silicon chip. Manufacturing this device was the modern-day equivalent of gold mining. No other smartphone succeeded like the iPhone, manufactured by Apple Inc. The product's market expansion was massive, reminiscent of cotton production two centuries earlier. Between 2007 – the year Apple launched the iPhone – and 2018, Apple sold 2.2 billion units worldwide. China was not only a supplier but also a huge market for the iPhone. It was reported in 2017 that China had 228 million iPhone users, nearly double that of the United States' 120 million.[72] The iPhone was hugely profitable as well. In the year 2020, nearly 200 million iPhone units were sold, and iPhone sales accounted for over half of Apple's annual revenue of $365 billion.[73]

As the cotton economy had been at the root of industrialization and global capitalism two centuries ago, this time around, land, labor, and political power also converged to make the iPhone. This time, they converged in China. Whereas labor came from overseas in the cotton economy era, land and labor were abundant in China, guaranteed by Chinese political power. The modern Chinese government did not need to acquire foreign land or exact concessions from Native Americans, as was the case during cotton production in the United States. The government owned land and had the power to convert farmland into industrial parks by relocating the farmers.

As for labor, China had an abundant and capable pool; migrants hailing from the countryside to cities and industrial parks. It was reported that more than 3 million Chinese worked at Apple in the late 2010s.[74] Apple's main supplier in China and for years China's leading exporter, Foxconn, alone employed up to 1.3 million people in its twelve factories across China. Foxconn's first large-walled campus, established in 1988 at the Longhua Technology Park in the Shenzhen Special Economic Zone, employed anywhere from a quarter to close to a half million workers.[75]

[72] Damjan, "How many iPhones have been sold worldwide? – iPhone sales analyzed," May 17, 2022, https://kommandotech.com/statistics/how-many-iphones-have-been-sold-worldwide/

[73] www.businessofapps.com/data/apple-statistics/

[74] "Half of iPhones manufactured in central China's Zhengzhou city," *China Daily*, Sept. 19, 2017, www.chinadaily.com.cn/business/tech/2017-09/19/content_32191283.htm

[75] https://en.wikipedia.org/wiki/Longhua_Science_and_Technology_Park Charles Duhigg and Keith Bradsher, "How the US lost out on iPhone work," *New York Times*, Jan. 21, 2012, www.nytimes.com/2012/01/22/business/apple-america-and-a-squeezed-middle-class.html

Its mammoth-sized second one, located in Zhengzhou city, Henan province, in central China, was known as "the iPhone City." Foxconn began production there in 2010, with an eye on the labor pool, less expensive than in the Pearl Delta region where labor and land costs had already risen. To attract "the iPhone City" built in Zhengzhou, the local government offered huge incentives, including: a $250 million loan; a $10 billion pledge to expand a nearby airport; and a reduction of the company's payment for social insurance and other payments for workers, as much as $100 million a year.[76]

Assembling these highly profitable iPhones relied on millions of Chinese laborers, mainly migrant laborers from rural China. Of Apple's 766 global suppliers in 2016, 346, nearly half, were from the Chinese mainland.[77] The iPhone city in Zhengzhou alone employed up to 350,000 migrant workers, who reportedly cranked out as many as 350 iPhones a minute, and a half million iPhones per day on 94 production lines.[78] In 2021, this factory alone produced 166 million iPhones, accounting for 70 percent of all Apple's latest model of iPhones worldwide.[79] After making shoes and clothing in their private businesses in rural China, young rural Chinese relocated to cities to make high-tech products for the world marketplace. Into the twenty-first century, China not only became the world factory but also became enmeshed in trade wars. In 2017, when the US government launched a trade war against China, China's top yielding exports to the United States were cellphones and other household goods, totaling $70.36 billion, 14 percent of China's exports to the United States in the previous year.[80]

The Apple iPhone's enviable profitability was partially attributable to cheap Chinese labor. In 2016, for instance, an iPhone (Model 7) was sold for $649. The factory cost was $237.45, yielding a gross profit of $283 per phone from the retail price. From the factory cost of making an iPhone,

[76] David Barbosa, "How China built 'iPhone City' with billions in perks for Apple's partner," *New York Times*, Dec. 29, 2016, www.nytimes.com/2016/12/29/technology/apple-iphone-china-foxconn.html

[77] "Half of iPhones manufactured in central China's Zhengzhou city."

[78] Ibid.; Harrison Jacobs, "Inside 'iPhone City,' the massive Chinese factory town where half of the world's iPhones are produced," *Business Insider*, May 8, 2018, www.businessinsider.com/apple-iphone-factory-foxconn-china-photos-tour-2018-5

[79] Yimou Lee and Brenda Goh, "Foxconn apologises for pay-related error at China iPhone plant after worker unrest," *Reuters*, Nov. 25, 2022, www.reuters.com/technology/apple-supplier-foxconn-apologises-hiring-blunder-covid-hit-china-plant-2022-11-24/

[80] "We estimate China only makes $8.46 from an iPhone – and that's why Trump's trade war is futile," *The Conversation*, July 7, 2018, https://theconversation.com/we-estimate-china-only-makes-8-46-from-an-iphone-and-thats-why-trumps-trade-war-is-futile-99258; Fred P. Hochberg, "The iPhone isn't made in China – it's made everywhere," *Wall Street Journal*, Jan. 31, 2020, www.wsj.com/articles/the-iphone-isnt-made-in-chinaits-made-everywhere-11580485139

only a tiny portion went to China: $8.46 per phone, or about 3.5 percent. This compares with $68.69 per phone, nearly 30 percent of the total cost, that went to the United States. The share of production costs that went to China was only about one-eighth of what went to Japan, about half of what went to South Korea, and one-sixth of what went to Taiwan.[81] China contributed its inexpensive labor.

Not So Free Labor

Unlike the cotton farming slaves of the Deep South who propelled the economic ascendance of the United States during the Industrial Revolution of the West two centuries ago, rural Chinese labor had their personal freedoms. The latter could not be traded or mortgaged. Yet, their labor was made cheap, and their freedoms were limited. As with slaves imported from Africa centuries ago, better paying jobs were simply off-limits to Chinese rural migrant labor. In place of cotton plantation owners who ruled the unfree labor, governments in China openly and blatantly enforced labor market discrimination to exclude migrants.

One particularly glaring example of exclusion was a government edict issued in the capital city of Beijing in the late 1990s. On January 12, 1998, Beijing's municipal Labor Bureau announced a comprehensive list, 198 specific jobs in twelve sectors, for which a migrant was not eligible to work in the city.[82] The list included all jobs in the public sector, including those in finance, insurance, the postal service, and government offices. Other excluded positions were: accountants, tellers, salespersons, data entry workers, and those considered posing a risk to city residents, such as driving a bus, guarding a warehouse, cleaning rooms in a star-rated hotel, even operating an elevator. Rural migrants could be hired for some construction work, mining, or loading and unloading in the transportation sector. Migrants could wash corpses in city morgues but not clean fancy hotel rooms; they could guard city cemeteries but not warehouses.

These discriminatory policies were formulated to protect urban employees, many of whom in the late 1990s were under threat of being laid off amidst urban enterprises reforms. During this time in Shanghai, China's largest city, an employer was required to pay a 50 yuan fee for each migrant worker hired. This amount was roughly one-tenth of a migrant laborer's average monthly wage at the time. The charge was framed as a contribution to help employment of urban workers. City

[81] "We estimate China only makes $8.46 from an iPhone."
[82] http://law.51labour.com/lawshow-24390-4.html

governments also stipulated that wages paid to laid-off urban workers could not be lower than wages paid to hire migrant workers.[83]

The jobs filled by migrant workers often required long hours with low wages and no benefits. Those hired in factories that manufactured exports were packed into factory dorms. China's first post-Mao era labor law, passed in 1994, nominally covered all workers, regardless of their residential status. Coverage and protection, however, differed vastly in practice depending upon residential status. In 2005, while an estimated 15 percent of urban workers were in the informal sector, without a labor contract, the share for migrants without a labor contract was reported to be 90 percent.[84] Near the end of the 2000s, the majority of migrant workers were still denied labor contracts by their employers and hence could not expect any contractually enforceable terms. According to the first government survey of migrants, conducted in 2009, 57.2 percent of all migrant laborers had no labor contract with their employers. Those employed in the manufacturing sector had the largest share of contracts at 51.7 percent; the service sector was at less than 35 percent, and the construction sector at only 26 percent . At this time, nearly 90 percent of surveyed migrants were working long hours, ironically in violation of the Labor Law, which stipulated no more than 44 working hours per week. Migrant laborers' average hours worked per week were 58.4.[85] These ubiquitous and forced violations continued, even after new labor laws, the Labor Contract Law, were revised and adopted in 2008 and 2013. By 2015, 60 percent of the migrants working away from their home townships still reported not having a labor contract.[86]

Migrant workers were made cheap because they were dispensable and lacked recourse. In the wake of the 2008 global financial crisis, as Chinese exports declined, nearly 30 million migrant workers were laid off.[87] With no insurance or a foothold in cities, migrants not only needed to earn money but were also under threat of losing their jobs. A pervasive slogan hanging over workers said so much: "If you do not work hard at your job today, you will be looking hard for a job tomorrow." In the Foxconn factory assembling iPhones for Apple, most migrants were in their late teens and early twenties, with a starting salary of 1,999 yuan (or about $300) per month. After a forty-five-day probation period, the monthly salary increased to between $390 and $500. Such a wage level was 50 percent lower than for the average urban employee in 2015. Workers

[83] F. Wang, Zuo, and Ruan 2002. [84] Gallagher 2014.
[85] www.stats.gov.cn/ztjc/ztfx/fxbg/201003/t20100319_16135.html
[86] 2016 National Migrant Survey, China National Bureau of Statistics, www.stats.gov.cn/tjsj/zxfb/201704/t20170428_1489334.html
[87] Gallagher 2014.

could increase their pay to $676 a month if they worked as many as 20 hours overtime per week. Eight workers would share four bunk beds in one dorm room. On the assembly line, the same task would be repeated over an eight-, ten-, or even a twelve-hour shift. Stress resulting from long working hours and "prison like" living conditions in this company led to a wave of suicides by young workers in early 2010.[88] Migrant laborers also staged strikes as well as other forms of protests.[89] In the midst of the COVID-19 pandemic, in October 2022 riots broke out. Workers in the Zhengzhou Foxconn factory were seen fighting back security guards, abandoning their jobs and belongings, forming lines of exodus along highways and farm fields to flee the city.[90] These workers simply walked out because they were squeezed in a tiny space between a strict state Zero-COVID policy that required them to be quarantined when infection cases were reported and an employer that was simply unprepared to provide the space and food supplies for the workers.

With an abundant pool of young labor, despite an annual turnover rate of 30 to 40 percent, new replacements could be quickly found.[91] Migrant workers were dispensable because for the most part they did not have the same protections as their urban counterparts. Studies of labor disputes reported that migrants often received worse settlements compared with workers with urban residential status. From their experiences migrants were made fully aware of their vulnerable lot in the cities.[92]

It is clear who the producers and builders of China's age of abundance were. China's vast rural population produced and built: from food, clothing, and housing to skyscrapers, roads, bridges, airports, and iPhones. Migrant workers, hundreds of millions of them originating from the Chinese countryside, transformed China into a land of abundance. What has not been told enough is how they were taken advantage of in the process, the fact that they were paid less, exploited, and not protected because of their social status.

Rural Chinese served as the backbones of China's ascendance, and they did so in two phases, first switching from farming to manufacturing

[88] David Sarno, "Firm shaken by suicides," *Los Angeles Times*, May 26, 2010, www.latimes.com/archives/la-xpm-2010-may-26-la-fg-china-suicides-20100526-story.html; Sun Yu, "Chinese migrant workers face crackdown for 'malicious' protests over unpaid wages," *Financial Times*, Jan. 24, 2023, www.ft.com/content/779512aa-6a73-47ce-b924-471fa63dc5a1

[89] Feng 2017.

[90] Wenxin Fan and Selina Cheng, "Inside a Chinese iPhone plant, Foxconn grapples with Covid chaos," *Wall Street Journal*, Oct. 30, 2022, www.wsj.com/articles/inside-a-chinese-iphone-plant-foxconn-grapples-with-covid-chaos-11667097816

[91] "Light and death," *The Economist*, May 27, 2010, www.economist.com/business/2010/05/27/light-and-death

[92] Feng 2017; P. Xie, Wang, and Cheng 2017.

in the Chinese countryside when the invisible walls of Chinese cities kept them out. Once they were needed and allowed into cities, rural migrant laborers came in large numbers. However, they worked and lived as a distinct social group – outsiders in their own country. Numerically in the majority, these rural migrants were by no means allowed to share any power. While they were not the only ones who made Chinese material prosperity possible, they were the members of society at the margin, and their contributions were not confined to their hard labor.

In contrast to these migrant laborers from the countryside, China's urban population experienced China's ascendance in a rather different way. The two categories, or two classes, of people in China marched on two different paths to prosperity.

5 Two Paths

The vast number of rural migrants to cities was not the only propelling force of China's economic ascendance and abundance. These migrants certainly were not the only ones who saw their living standards improved. While comprising an increasingly larger share of residents in Chinese cities, migrants from rural China were just one component of the urban population.[1] As outsiders in Chinese cities, rural migrants relied mainly on their labor for income and wealth accumulation. For most urban Chinese, however, while income from work constituted a major source of income and wealth, it was far from the only source. Ascendance to abundance for the Chinese population differed for these two segments of society.

The rural origin of China's economic ascendance was well noted. So were the two paths taken during China's economic transformations. As summarized by Yasheng Huang, the author of successive groundbreaking studies of China's economic transformations, "In its very essence, the story of economic transition is one of two Chinas – the rural and more market-driven China versus the urban and more state-controlled China."[2] The same observation was made succinctly by two other scholars:

> Chinese capitalism is rural in origin. The expense of a more arm's-length, entrepreneurial type of private sector, and rural capitalism is highly entrepreneurial in a Schumpeterian sense. Urban China, by contrast, is far more state-controlled. The urban reforms since the early 1990s have led to a politically-connected, rent-seeking private sector (the most prominent example of which is the real estate private firms), whereas the reversals of rural reforms have been at the expense of a more arm's-length, entrepreneurial type of private sector.[3]

[1] In 2018, the total number of employees in urban areas as reported by the government was 434.19 million (SYB 2019, table 4–1), and the number of migrant laborers of rural origin was reported to be at 290.77 million, with 174.25 million counted as working away from one's township of household registration and 135 million living in urban areas. www.stats.gov.cn/tjsj/zxfb/202004/t20200430_1742724.html

[2] Y. Huang 2008, 105. [3] Coase and Wang 2012, 166.

The path taken by urban Chinese was at times treacherous, such as when their iron rice bowl was under threat during reforms in the 1980s and 1990s, but eventually they returned as the true winners. Deeply trapped in a planned economy system that dominated every aspect of their lives, urban residents needed to break free from the shackles of the old system and face an entirely new economic environment. Unlike their rural counterparts, who had practically next to nothing to lose, urban residents lived a much more protected and privileged life under socialism and had to adapt. As documented in Chapter 3, while lagging in measured income growth compared with urban residents, rural residents experienced more notable improvements in their living standards once the Chinese reforms began, both in what they ate and how they were housed. They also saw and seized more opportunities, first in the countryside and then through moving into the cities, as outlined in the Chapter 4.

Pain before Gain

As discussed in the previous chapter, by the early 1990s more people in the Chinese countryside were engaging in off-farm economic activities than working in state- and collectively owned firms in the cities. Enterprises in rural China were producing more industrial output than state-owned firms in cities. In contrast to the rapid industrial transformation in rural China, however, urban China continued struggling with the onerous planned economy system. A market economy was nevertheless emerging, following both price reforms in the late 1980s and early 1990s and nascent foreign and private entrepreneurship.

The hardest-fought and the most painful reform was perhaps the price reform, which restored or created prices for products in line with production costs and demand, not by government planning. Administratively set prices not only arbitrarily favored certain economic sectors, over time the yawning gap between cost and pricing created economic distortions and inefficiencies. As with other reforming socialist planned economies, transitioning to a market economy brought on rampant inflation and corruption, culminating in widespread social dissatisfaction and protests. Urban retail prices, for instance, rose by 12.5 percent in 1985, 21.3 percent in 1988, and 16 percent in 1989. Food prices increased even faster: 16.5 percent in 1985, 12 percent in 1987, 25.2 percent in 1988, and 14.4 percent in 1989.[4] Hyperinflation and the associated corruption contributed to the massive 1989 demonstrations and the bloody crackdown. Aside from the political factors that drove the demonstrations,[5] double-digit hyperinflation

[4] SYB 1993, table 7–5. [5] Su 2023.

likely created a pervasive sense of uncertainty fueling the massive turnout of urban residents. Hyperinflation returned, for the last time, in the early 1990s, with urban consumer prices rising by 16, 25, and 16.8 percent in 1993, 1994, and 1995, respectively.[6] Those were unsettling times.

Even more unsettling was the crumbling of the employment security known to urban residents during the socialist years. Employment in a state- or collectively owned organization was equivalent to holding an iron rice bowl; a rice bowl that guaranteed a constant food supply and could never be broken. Along with lifelong employment security was guaranteed income. Work organizations also provided welfare benefits such as housing, education, health care, and pensions. This was the case for urban residents up until the early 1990s. In 1990, virtually all the urban workforce was still employed by state- and collectively owned organizations (nearly 95 percent, Table 5.1), not much different from 1978. In 1995, the share was still over 80 percent. As of that point, "many workers and their families were still being served by their old work units."[7] The cracks, however, were beginning to open. Also in 1995, nearly 3 percent of the total urban labor force was already employed by foreign or overseas Chinese invested companies; one in ten reported as self-employed.

Large-scale transformation in urban employment did not begin until the 1990s. Enterprise reforms, to transform work organizations into firms that could survive and prosper in a newly emerged market environment, came with a high cost. Unprofitable firms, which were numerous, were to be shut down or reorganized. Insolvency of state-owned enterprises stood at about 10.9 percent in 1988, increasing to 16 percent in 1989, 27.6 percent in 1990, over 30 percent in 1993, and 40 percent by 1995.[8] By 1996, 45 percent of state-owned firms were operating at a loss, and collectively, state-owned firms were losing more money than they took in.[9]

Drastic and often painful reforms proceeded in the 1990s, especially in the late 1990s, resulting in large-scale unemployment and underemployment. In the five years between 1995 and 2000, 48 million employees were removed from state- and collectively owned doles, amounting to nearly one in four of all state employees in 1995. By the turn of the century, the share of employment in state- and collectively owned organizations had been reduced by a third, to 64 percent. The share of the urban labor force in the private business and self-employment sectors rose sharply to more than one in four, over 40 million (Table 5.1).[10] Some

[6] SYB 2006, table 9–1. [7] Solinger 2022, 11. [8] Peng and Chen 2008.
[9] Solinger 2022, 12. [10] Calculated from SYB 2017, table 4–2.

Table 5.1 *Transformation of urban employment by ownership type (%), 1978–2018*

	State/Collective	Joint	Private	Foreign	Self
1978	99.8				0.2
1980	99.2				0.8
1985	96.1				3.5
1990	94.3		0.4	0.4	4.2
1995	83.1		2.8	3.0	9.0
2000	64.1	9.0	8.5	4.3	14.3
2001	60.4	10.3	10.3	4.5	14.4
2002	54.7	12.1	13.2	5.0	15.0
2003	50.1	13.2	16.2	5.5	15.1
2004	46.2	14.0	18.2	6.3	15.3
2005	41.8	15.4	19.8	7.1	15.9
2006	39.0	15.6	21.4	7.6	16.3
2007	36.3	15.6	23.3	8.0	16.8
2008	34.3	15.7	24.7	7.8	17.4
2009	31.8	16.2	25.1	7.7	19.2
2010	30.5	16.4	26.0	7.8	19.2
2011	27.9	17.7	26.3	8.2	19.9
2012	26.5	18.6	26.9	7.9	20.1
2013	21.5	24.6	25.6	9.2	19.1
2014	19.6	23.5	28.3	8.5	20.1
2015	18.2	22.6	30.4	7.6	21.2
2016	17.3	21.7	31.5	7.0	22.5
2017	16.2	20.7	33.3	6.4	23.4
2018	14.7	20.6	33.7	5.7	25.2

Sources and notes: Calculated from SYB 2017 for 1978 to 2016, and SYB 2019 for 2017 and 2018. Shares were calculated based on the sums of these categories. Sums for urban employment published in SYB starting in 1990 differ from the sums here.

employees of state-owned firms shifted to work in the newly created category of joint-stock or limited liability firms, while tens of millions were laid off. In 2002, an estimated 20 million urban residents were relying on government minimum-livelihood guarantee subsidies at an amount that was less than 30 percent of the average disposable income for urban employees. An overwhelming majority, 70 percent, of these new urban poor were laid-off workers and other unemployed.[11]

By the late 2000s, the urban employment transformation was largely complete, with only less than a third of the urban labor force remaining in state-owned organizations. While many of the remaining state-owned

[11] Solinger 2022, 35–36.

firms were later organized into state monopolies, which were more profitable and better compensated, the rise of private businesses and self-employment also brought about unprecedented opportunities for others, who accounted for more than half of all urban employment after the mid-2010s (Table 5.1).

Power and Property

At the same time as enterprise reforms inflicted pains on urban residents, new opportunities for moneymaking also emerged. Profits from private businesses and self-employment became important sources of new wealth, as were rent-seeking opportunities and corruption by government officials. In 2015, a study of wealthy individuals reported that "55 percent of Chinese millionaires derived their wealth from private businesses, and 20 percent are property speculators who have jumped on the crest of the rapid hike in home prices. About 15 percent are stock gurus, while the remaining 10 percent are high-earning salaried executives."[12] The majority of ordinary urban residents, however, derived their wealth mainly from a new source unavailable under socialism: private ownership of housing.

The privatization of urban housing turned out to be the most consequential wealth creation and redistribution in modern Chinese history. With the iron rice bowls smashed, all the benefits associated with them were also going to be phased out. Chief among the benefits was the virtually free housing provided by work organizations during the planned economy era. Analogous to the land reforms that redistributed farming land from landlords to landless peasants back in the late 1940s and early 1950s, the privatization of urban housing transformed urban residents from a property-less to propertied population. As late as 1980, nearly all urban residents lived in government-controlled housing; private ownership was virtually nonexistent under socialism. Starting in the late 1980s and accelerating by the end of the 1990s, in slightly over a decade the urban Chinese housing market was practically all privatized. The privatization process first allowed urban work organizations to use their own funds toward housing construction, instead of waiting for government allocation. Later, still lacking funds from the government for new construction, individual employees were allowed or encouraged to contribute their own funds and improve their housing conditions. Finally, in the late 1990s, the last phase of urban housing reforms converted almost all

[12] F. Wang 2019; Bain & Company, "China's population of high net worth individuals swelled to more than one million in 2014, doubling from just four years ago," May 26, 2015, https://bit.ly/3MaIWp6

government-owned housing to private property, selling them at very low prices to the current occupants.

Concurrent with urban housing reforms, the government permitted commercial housing construction and sales, hence allowing apartments and houses built for sale at market prices. China's 2000 census, only two years after the end of government-provided housing and the first to include questions on housing, reported that nearly three-quarters of all urban households had already managed to take possession of the housing units they were residing in.[13] Surveys confirm this shift in private housing ownership among urban households. China's Household Income Project (CHIP) surveys reported in 1995 that 57 percent of surveyed urban households lived in houses rented from the state. By 2002, the share dropped to 18 percent.[14] By 2018, at 89.68 percent, China was ranked eighth in the world in housing ownership, higher than neighboring Japan (80.5) and South Korea (56.8), and also much higher than in the United States at the time (65.3).[15] In 2017, according to China's Household Finance Survey, housing ownership in urban China reached 92 percent, with 22 percent of households owning more than one unit.[16] Into the twenty-first century, both wealth and wealth inequality increased at a rate much faster than income and income inequality.[17]

Unlike land distribution in rural China decades earlier, urban housing privatization was not a process of equalization but of stratification. The initial wealth bestowed in the form of housing varied enormously, by location (where a family lived – city and district) and by size (how much space they occupied). The size of the occupied housing unit was generally a function of their position in the society (work organization and rank) at the time of the conversion. Households headed by government officials acquired larger apartments, at costs well below the market price. By 2000, urban households with close associations to the government had the highest housing ownership: 82 percent among households headed by government officials, 77 percent for those headed by professionals, and 73 percent for staff members. These households accounted for nearly 40 percent of all urban households. For the remaining urban households, the ownership share was only about 40 percent or less.

Housing ownership also varied by education and occupation. As also reported by the 2000 census, over 50 percent of urban households headed by a person with a college education purchased their apartments from their work organization, compared with one in four among those with

[13] F. Wang 2003. [14] Xia, Li, and Song 2020, 271.
[15] https://en.wikipedia.org/wiki/List_of_countries_by_home_ownership_rate
[16] https://chfs.swufe.edu.cn
[17] Meng 2007; Y. Xie and Jin 2015; F. Wang 2019; Knight, Li, and Wan 2020.

a junior high school education, and one in five for those with a primary education. The share of households that purchased apartments from their work organizations was twice as much or higher among those headed by a government official, a professional, or a staff member in a government organization than those headed, for example, by an ordinary service or production worker.[18] The windfall was enormous as the price paid for purchasing government-owned housing was well below market price. One study put the ratio of market price to official selling price at an average of 7:1.[19] Households headed by government officials and those with a college degree were also much more likely to have purchased and to reside in newly built apartments. Over half of government officials and staff members in cities reported living in newly built apartments they purchased in 2020, compared with only about 25 percent among households headed by a person working in the manufacturing sector.[20]

Excluded from this wealth creation and distribution was China's rural population, including the large number of those residing and working in Chinese cities as migrants. They were not only outside of the initial distribution but remained so during the massive wealth creation in the following decades. They were not part of the initial redistribution when the government sold their housing stock to urban households at very low prices. The rural population's outsider status rendered most of them ineligible to purchase real estate property. At the early stage of urban private real estate development in the late 1990s, individuals who purchased a high-end apartment in cities were given local household registration as an incentive for investment. The prices for these units were high; hence very few rural migrants received urban household registration status.[21] Over time, however, purchasing an apartment in many Chinese cities required local resident status in that city. The restrictions were especially strict in the largest cities where prices went up the most.

Increases in real property values were estimated to have accounted for 40 to 50 percent of the rising wealth-to-income ratio between 1978 and 2015.[22] A minority of rural residents, mostly in the suburbs, benefited from the wealth boom when their land was acquired for urban construction and they were compensated. The vast majority of the rural population, however, did not have the right to join this massive wealth creation and redistribution. Rural migrants in cities were also mostly denied the

[18] F. Wang 2003. [19] Knight, Li, and Wan 2020, 111.

[20] Calculated from China Population Census 2020, table 9-9a.

[21] F.-L. Wang 2004. The average purchasing price for a unit was 30 times the average annual wage in Beijing. In 1999, compared with 2.37 million temporary *hukou* holders, only 715 households obtained a local *hukou* via purchasing a housing unit (120).

[22] Piketty, Yang, and Zucman 2019.

wealth benefits during the urban housing boom due to their household registration status, when urban real estate prices skyrocketed after the year 2000.

Housing was by far the most important and fastest source of new wealth. Not only does housing ownership remain high in China, but its importance in overall household wealth is entirely new. It emerged only after socialism. Using the standard of net housing wealth as a share of total housing wealth, China measures at about 80 percent compared to the average in OECD countries of less than 50 percent.[23] As private housing ownership emerged, housing wealth started to accumulate and quickly became the dominant source of household wealth. In just one decade, between 2002 and 2012, housing wealth as a share of total household wealth rose from 53 to 73 percent.[24]

Housing wealth grew at a staggering rate of 20.1 percent annually, outpacing overall net per capita wealth, which was 16.7 percent in the decade after 2002. The share of net housing wealth for urban households was even higher: 62 percent in 2002 and 78 percent in 2013. By comparison, the share of household financial assets was much smaller; and it became smaller still in the 2000s, falling from 27 percent in 2002 to only 12 percent in 2013. Urban net housing wealth, expanding at a rate of 19.4 percent annually between 2002 and 2013, also increased much faster than the overall wealth per capita growth rate of 16.8 percent, which itself was already remarkable.[25]

Personal effort made little difference in the newly grown urban housing wealth. Most benefited by virtue of pure luck, the location of their household, or their position in the social hierarchy. The luck fell mostly on those living in cities, especially in the most desirable cities where economic opportunities were abundant and real estate price rose mostly rapidly. Such opportunities were themselves in part created by specific government policies and resource allocations, such as in the capital city of Beijing and in Shanghai, Shenzhen, and Guangzhou, which were named as special economic zones. By 2020, these four cities were among the most expensive cities in the world in terms of housing. The ratio of property price to household income was 33 for the city of Guangzhou, 41 for Shanghai, 44 for Beijing, and 45 for Shenzhen. In comparison, the ratio was only 21 for London, 14 for Tokyo, 11 for New York, and 8 for San Francisco.[26]

[23] "Housing, wealth accumulation and wealth distribution: Evidence and stylized facts," OECD Economic Department Working Papers, No. 1588, 2019, fig. 8.

[24] Knight, Li, and Wan 2020. [25] Ibid., 118.

[26] www.numbeo.com/property-investment/rankings.jsp?title=2020

In the first decade of the private urban housing expansion in China, real estate prices skyrocketed. Price increases were fastest in its top-tiered cities. In much of the country, in cities that were designated as "tier 2" or "tier 3," the average housing price increased at an annual rate of 8 to 10 percent, following increased purchasing power (per capita income growth).[27] In the four "tier 1" cities – Beijing, Shanghai, Guangzhou, and Shenzhen – the annual housing price increase was much faster at 13.1 percent between 2003 and 2013. Housing prices increased at twice the rate of per capita disposable income growth, which averaged 6.6 percent annually. Such a rapid increase in real estate prices was only comparable to the other well-known historical boom in the world – in neighboring Japan during its boom between 1955 and 1990. Even China's tier 3 cities posted impressive price increases at an annual rate of 7.9 percent; surpassing even the tier 1 cities in the United States during the same period.[28] Annual return rates were even higher: ranging from 11 percent for tier 3 and 13.5 percent for tier 2 to 15.7 percent for tier 1 cities during the 2003–2013 decade.[29]

How sizable was this once-in-a-lifetime windfall for China's urban residents? While it is hard to assign an exact monetary value on this massive wealth explosion, one can attempt a rough approximation to appreciate the magnitude of this wealth creation and redistribution. The exercise in Table 5.2 offers such an example based on the two most exclusive and privileged Chinese cities – Beijing and Shanghai – between 2003 and 2013. This decade began five years after the 1998 whole-scale urban housing reforms. The initial housing stock in 2003 is used to calculate the rising wealth due to price increases in the decade following.

Housing wealth estimated in 2003 in these two most expensive cities in China was equivalent to about 24 percent of China's GDP in that same year. Housing asset values are estimated by using the reported per capita housing space (measured by construction space), which was reported at 24.77 m^2 in Beijing, behind Shanghai at 29.25.[30] One can generate an estimate of total residential housing space by multiplying population size and per capita housing space. Beijing reported a total urban population of 11.51 million, out of 14.56 million total long-term residents; Shanghai had 10.41 million out of 13.42 million. Multiplying

[27] Fang et al. 2015. Based on 31 out of the 35 tier 2 cities and 85 tier 3 cities, encompassing a population of 220 million and 370 million, respectively, in 2004.

[28] Glaeser et al. 2017. [29] Fang et al. 2015. Real growth rate.

[30] "Beijing renjun zhufang mianji 24.77 pingfangmi zai neidi ju di san" 北京人均住房面积24.77平方米在内地居第 (Beijing's per capita housing space reaches 24.77 m^2, ranked no. 3 in the country), *Xinjing bao* 新京报, June 26, 2004, http://news.sina.com.cn/c/2004-06-26/01433524107.shtml

Table 5.2 *Calculation of housing wealth growth due to price increases*

	Beijing	Shanghai
Urban population (million) 2003 [(a)]	11.51	10.41
Per capita housing space (m^2) 2003 [(b)]	24.77	29.25
Estimated total housing space (million m^2) 2003 [(c = a*b)]	285.10	304.49
Price per m^2 (yuan) 2003 [(d)]	4,456	4,987
Estimated value (million yuan) 2003 [(e = c*d))]	1,270,418	1,518,504
Price increase index (2003–2013) [(f)]	7.6	4.43
Estimated value (million yuan) 2013 [(g=e*f))]	9,655,174	6,726,973
"Housing wealth" created (million yuan) [(h = g – e)]	8,384,756	5,208,469
US$ million (6.7 yuan = US$1)	1,251,456	777,383
"Housing wealth" gained per capita (US$)	108,728	74,677

Sources: (a) (b): Statistical Yearbooks for Beijing and Shanghai (New China 60th Year); (d): SYB 2004, table 6–50; (f): Fang et al. 2015

the total residential housing space by price per square meter, based on numbers published by government report, gives an estimated total worth of housing wealth. In 2003, at the start of the decade for this exercise, Beijing's housing stock totaled an estimated value of 1.27 trillion yuan; Shanghai's was 1.52 trillion (see Table 5.2). China's GDP in that year was reported to be 11.66 trillion yuan.

By 2013, a decade later, the estimated market value of *the same housing stock* in these two cities rose to 13.6 trillion yuan, staying at an equivalence of 24 percent of China's GDP in 2013, which rose to 56.88 trillion following a decade of hypergrowth. It is important to note that in this calculation, price changes are based on housing stock in the same residential areas and exclude new construction, which tends to be higher quality and more expensive.[31]

Rapid real estate price increases in these two cities created immense wealth on paper. With staggering price increases, by 7.6 times in Beijing and 4.43 times in Shanghai within a decade, the same housing stock in 2003 (not the total market as it had expanded over the decade) rose to an estimated value of 8.4 trillion yuan for Beijing and 5.2 trillion for

[31] Unit selling price increases for new construction could reflect increases in building quality. This is not the case for the price increase index reported in Fang et al. 2015, which followed price changes in the same residential areas in each city. In addition, average selling price per square meter (construction space) used here is for ordinary (excluding luxury) residential units (SYB 2014, table 15–11; SYB 2019, table 19–12). In 2003, the selling price of luxury units was much higher, about 85 percent and 80 percent higher than common or ordinary residential units in Beijing and Shanghai. The price difference narrowed to only 30 percent in Beijing, while it increased to 2.26 times in Shanghai in 2018.

Shanghai, or $1.25 trillion and $0.77 trillion, respectively.[32] Combined, at $2.02 trillion, in one decade the "housing wealth" generated in the top two Chinese cities alone was larger than the entire size of China's GDP back in 2003.

City residential status, especially in Beijing or Shanghai, was extremely valuable, particularly when compared with a hard-working migrant laborer from the countryside. On a per capita basis, in US dollar terms, the windfall from property price increases was approximately $110,000 per resident in Beijing, whether the person was an adult or a child. In Shanghai, the windfall was roughly $75,000 per person. These are just the averages based on the initial existing housing stock at the start of a decade, in 2003. Acquiring newly constructed apartments, an opportunity reserved for those with more resources and with local residential status, created more wealth during the real estate price boom and further contributed to an even more unequal wealth distribution.

A migrant worker, by comparison, would have to labor for three decades in order to acquire the same wealth gained by Beijing or Shanghai urban residents from the housing windfall in one decade. The wealth gain from property price increases was exclusive to residents in Beijing and Shanghai. Migrants were mostly excluded from the housing market in these top-tier Chinese cities, where purchasing an apartment required local residential status. The average annual wage for a migrant laborer in 2003 was 10,000 yuan ($1,400) and 31,000 yuan ($4,600) in 2013. Adding up the annual income of a migrant worker for the entire decade, the sum would be 240,000 yuan (about $36,000). This amount is only around one-third of the average wealth windfall due to real estate price increases for the average resident in Beijing and one half of that in Shanghai. Even this comparison remains vastly conservative as many urban dwellers initially acquired their government-owned apartments at prices substantially below the market.

Sharp increases in real estate prices continued beyond 2013. In the six years following, between 2013 and 2019, average selling prices in Beijing more than doubled again, and they rose by nearly 80 percent in Shanghai. Between 2000 and 2018, the average selling price for new residential housing units rose by 8.2 times in Beijing and by 8.7 times in Shanghai, substantially surpassing the increase in per capita income, measured by PPP, which rose by 6.27 times.[33] Beijing and Shanghai

[32] Based on the price increase index reported in Fang et al. 2015. China's SYB, which reports average selling prices for newly constructed units, shows a slower but also fast rise in prices, 3.89 times in Beijing and 3.25 times in Shanghai between 2003 and 2013.

[33] Chinese housing price data from SYB 2001 and SYB 2019; China per capita data from WDI.

residents amassed considerable wealth simply by virtue of their residential or citizenship status.

Costs and Profits

"Cheap Labor"

In contrast to China's urban residents, who gained a windfall of wealth simply by living in the apartment they were allocated or bought, the path to prosperity for most rural migrants was one of hard labor. A sizable number of rural migrants did become successful private business owners in Chinese cities, riding the chariot of China's economic boom. The vast majority of rural migrants, however, were hired laborers. In 2009, the first survey of migrant labor by China's National Bureau of Statistics reported that self-employed migrants in Chinese cities accounted for only 6.4 percent of all migrant laborers surveyed, whereas 93.6 percent worked as employees.[34] Even as their income and living standards improved considerably compared with their farming counterparts, migrant workers never received a fair share of the benefits their hard labor created for urban residents and capital owners in and outside of China. Their labor, as was widely known, was cheap.

Just how cheap was their cheap labor, and how did such cheap labor help to fuel the Chinese economic boom? This approximation can be derived by aggregating the labor cost savings from migrant laborers' undercompensated wages and benefits, compared with those of workers with an urban household registration status. This comparison is again only an approximation as it cannot fully account for the differences in personal backgrounds between migrant workers and urban workers, differences that affect earnings.

Working and living side by side in the same locales, Chinese employees with an urban household registration status enjoyed a consistently higher level of compensation and social benefits than migrant workers. One meticulous study traced wage disparities between migrant labor and urban employees over China's migration history from 1985 to 2010.[35] In Figure 5.1, the comparison is extended to 2018, with newly available data for both migrant laborers' average income and wages for urban employees in the non-private sector.

Prior to the mid-1990s, when the number of migrants rose sharply (Figure 4.5), the wage ratio between urban employees and migrant workers, excluding benefits received by urban employees, was roughly around

[34] www.stats.gov.cn/ztjc/ztfx/fxbg/201003/t20100319_16135.html [35] F. Lu 2012.

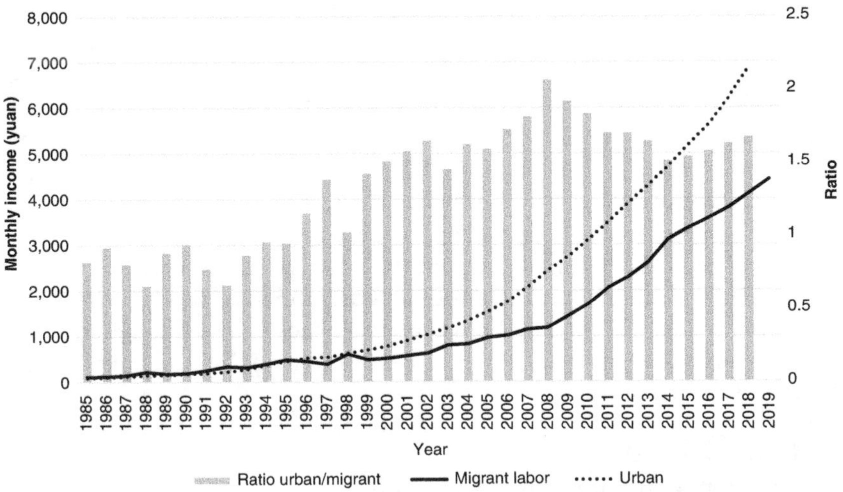

Figure 5.1 Migrant worker monthly wage, comparison with urban workers
Sources: 1985–2010: F. Lu 2012; after 2011, migrant labor: see various years of National Statistics Bureau Migrant Labor Survey, www.stats.gov.cn/tjsj/zxfb/202004/t20200430_1742724.html; urban (non-private sector) employees: calculated from SYB 2019, table 4–12

1:1. Such a ratio was possibly due to the selectivity of migrant laborers, who were relatively few in number then.[36] As rural migrants began to pour into cities, the wage gap soon expanded, with urban employees making about 50 percent more than migrant laborers by the end of the 1990s. Wage levels for both migrant laborers and urban employees rose sharply starting in the early 2000s, an increase that was driven by increased demand from domestic construction and global manufacturing for exports, and by the tightened supply of young labor. Average monthly income tripled for migrant laborers between 2000 and 2010; earnings for urban employees increased even faster, nearly quadrupling. The wage gap between urban employees and migrant workers continued to rise, reaching a peak of 2:1 in 2008, the year of the global financial crisis (Figure 5.1). The ratio dropped afterward, back to a level of around 1.6:1, a reversed trend coinciding with the reduction of young migrant labor (Figure 4.5).

Migrant laborers and urban employees understandably are not exactly comparable. They have different educational and skills backgrounds;

[36] An explanation is given in F. Lu 2012.

they work in different industries and occupations. At the same time, however, migrant workers are also known to work longer days and more days per week, and most of them receive little or no benefits. Comparisons between urban resident labor and migrant labor in the city of Shanghai in the mid-1990s, for instance, report a monthly income difference of nearly 1.4:1 in favor of urban employees, and an hourly income difference of 1.8:1.[37] For pension and health insurance coverage, it was 91 percent and 79 percent, respectively, for urban employees, versus 10 and 14 percent for migrant workers.[38] In 2005, aside from differences in benefits, of which migrants continued to receive very little, the hourly income difference between employees with a Shanghai *hukou* and those without was still 1.7:1. Considering the differences in personal characteristics, migrant workers in Shanghai still suffered a net "migrant penalty" of 25 percent in hourly wages, a finding similar to an analysis for 1995.[39]

In contrast to the early days of migration, when migrants were discriminated against blatantly with lower pay and no benefits, migrant laborers were channeled over time into specific industries and occupations with suppressed pay and benefits. The wage penalty continued into the late 2010s. A study analyzing data from China's 2015 employer–employee survey in two provinces reported that migrant workers earned 22.3 percent less monthly and 32.2 percent less per hour than nonmigrant workers. Taking into account individual characteristics, including educational levels, migrants were still paid 24 percent less in hourly income. The wage gap was especially large for workers in state-owned enterprises and among college-educated workers.[40]

The "savings" in the cost for labor, a product purely due to the residential-citizenship bias against Chinese rural migrant labor, amounts to an enormous sum. This low cost fueled China's economic boom, benefiting not only the migrant laborers and their families but also all Chinese and foreign businesses in China. Suppressed labor costs enabled China's urban residents to avail themselves of cheap goods and services. Cheap Chinese goods fueled worldwide consumption. Most notably, capitalists in and outside of China benefited handsomely from huge capital returns. The iPhone story was but one example among numerous other products and stories.

It is a complicated task to account fully for the savings reaped from the suppressed wages of migrant workers. The magnitude of these "savings"

[37] Y. Lu and Wang 2013, table 1. [38] F. Wang, Zuo, and Ruan 2002.
[39] Y. Lu and Wang 2013; also see Liang 2016.
[40] H. Cheng, Hu, and Li 2020. Based on 2015–2016 Employer-Employee Surveys in two provinces (Hubei and Guangdong), about 1,700 firms and nearly 8,000 migrant workers.

can however be illustrated with the following approximation. The calculation starts with the wage differences reported in Figure 5.1. By applying a very conservative and generous assumption, this calculation assumes that only 25 percent of the observed mean monthly wage differences between migrant workers and their urban counterparts was due to identity-discrimination, attributable to migrants' outsider status (column C, Table 5.3), an assumption that can be considered rather conservative. Of the total number of migrant laborers (column D), only a portion were working away (column F). Multiplying this share with the average monthly wage of a migrant laborer, and then with the number of migrant laborers working away from their own townships, the estimation approximates the annual labor cost savings (columns G and H).

Over the period of China's second industrialization, the labor cost savings due to migrant laborers' "outsider" status aggregates to a staggering amount. The numbers under column G in Table 5.3 are the direct calculations based on reported annual wages. In Column H, the numbers are adjusted for migrant workers' extra hours spent at work to earn the annual income compared to urban workers. Even with these conservative assumptions, the estimated total labor cost

Table 5.3 *Estimating migrant labor's cost savings*

Year	Migrant labor (A)	Ratio urban/ migrant (B)	Adjusted difference (C)	Migrant labor total (D)	Migrant labor away (E)	% Away (F)	Estimate 1 (billion yuan) (G)	Estimate 2 (billion yuan) (H)
2008	1180.5	2.1	0.27	225.4	140.4	0.6	528.7	727.0
2009	1421.7	1.9	0.23	229.8	145.3	0.6	569.5	783.1
2010	1690.0	1.8	0.21	242.2	153.4	0.6	646.6	889.1
2011	2049.0	1.7	0.17	252.8	158.6	0.6	682.5	938.5
2012	2290.0	1.7	0.18	262.6	163.4	0.6	787.8	1083.2
2013	2609.0	1.6	0.16	268.9	166.1	0.6	837.8	1151.9
2014	3108.0	1.5	0.13	274.0	168.2	0.6	801.7	1102.3
2015	3359.0	1.5	0.13	277.5	168.7	0.6	916.1	1259.6
2016	3572.0	1.6	0.14	281.7	169.3	0.6	1045.7	1437.8
2017	3805.0	1.6	0.16	286.5	171.9	0.6	1231.2	1692.9
2018	4107.0	1.7	0.17	288.4	172.7	0.6	1430.0	1966.3

Sources and notes: (A) and (B), see Figure 5.1; column C: percent of monthly wages penalty due to migrant status, 25% of the observed difference (B–1)*.25; (D), (E), and (F): National Bureau of Statistics, China: (G): (A)*C*(E)*12, for annual number; (H): (G) *1.375, assuming migrant laborers work 55 hours per week, compared to a 40-hour work week. www.stats.gov.cn/tjsj/zxfb/202004/t20200430_1742724.html

"savings" ranges from over 700 billion yuan ($72 billion) in 2008 to nearly 2 trillion yuan ($290 billion) in 2018. What does this number compare to? The cost savings alone amounted to 15 to 20 percent of the total wage bill of China's other urban employees.[41]

As with approximating the wealth windfall enjoyed by urban residents, calculating the cost paid by rural migrants is likely vastly underestimated. These comparisons do not consider migrant workers' long work schedules. In 2009, the average number of days worked by migrant employees was 26 per month, with one day off per week versus two days off per week for urban employees; migrant workers on average worked 58.4 hours per week versus 40 hours for urban employees. In 2009, for instance, a migrant worker in a manufacturing job averaged 58.2 hours' work per week, in construction 59.4 hours, and in food and hotel services 61.3 hours. These comparisons, moreover, do not include employment-related benefits. Nationwide, in 2009 only 7.6 percent of migrant laborers had pension insurance coverage, 12.2 percent had medical insurance, and 3.9 percent had unemployment insurance.[42] These insurance costs could add up to 40 percent of the wages.[43] The "identity-discrimination" assumption, a 25 percent penalty for migrants compared with their urban counterparts, can hence be a vastly conservative one.

Without these huge savings from the suppressed wages of hundreds of millions of Chinese rural migrant labors, the Chinese economic ascendance would not have been possible, certainly not at this vigorous pace. By the turn of the twenty-first century, the global economy propelled by the massive Chinese exports would have been entirely different. By leaving farming and land, rural migrants increased their incomes drastically and improved their own living standards and that of their families. Yet, were it not for the status-based discrimination that lowered their wages and allowed little or no benefits, the alternative labor cost would have been much higher. China's economic ascendance likely could not have been so rapid; the profits enjoyed by capital owners would certainly not have been as handsome. China's good labor was further *made* cheap by its peculiar social institutions.

[41] The total wage bill for China's urban employees in 2008 was 3,371 billion yuan for its 115 million employees; SYB 2009, tables 4–1 and 4–21. In 2018, the total wage bill for non-private-sector employees with an urban resident status was 14.1 trillion yuan; SYB 2019, table 4-10.

[42] www.stats.gov.cn/ztjc/ztfx/fxbg/201003/t20100319_16135.html

[43] "Best guide to China's social security system in 2023," www.hrone.com/guide-chinas-social-security-system-pays/

Contributions Social

Around the year 2010, Shanghai – China's fastest growing and richest city – was feeling a fiscal pinch. In that year, the city's government allocated 10.74 billion yuan from its annual budget to make up for the deficit in the city's pension program, as payout (81.15 billion yuan) exceeded collection (70.79 billion yuan).[44] The amount was not that large, only about 3 percent of the total government spending that year, which stood at 330.29 billion yuan.[45] Yet, the government knew well that it was only an early sign of a troubling trend that had been gathering momentum. The total payout for pensions in 2009 grew by 15.5 percent from 2008 and increased again by 14.2 percent in 2010. The payout for health care expenses was accelerating even faster, from an annual increase rate of 9 percent between 2008 and 2009 to 23.3 percent between 2009 and 2010. With a total payout of 111.16 billion yuan, Shanghai's retirees' pension and health care expenses were already equivalent to a third of the city's total government spending, and the reserves were drying up quickly.

The root problem, a problem that was expected to worsen over time, was the aging of its local residents, those with a local *hukou* and entitled to the benefits. Shanghai's demographic profile was not in the government's favor. The fertility level of the city's residents had been below the level of replacement of 2.1 children per couple for nearly four decades since 1971. The population census in 2010 reported a fertility level of 0.7 births per couple, about a third of the level required to maintain a stable population size in the long run. For nearly two decades, deaths exceeded births among the population with a local household registration status. Had there not been the continued influx of migrants, Shanghai's population size would have shrunk. By the late 2000s, the number of retirees accounted for almost one in four of the city's population with a local household registration. In contrast to the overall negative growth rate of the population with a local *hukou*, the elderly population was growing at about 4 percent a year. The population aged 65 and over, at 15.86 percent in 2010, was projected to increase to 25.97 percent by 2020 and 36.37 percent by 2030.[46]

Not to let this runaway aging population absorb more government expenditure, Shanghai's government directed its attention to others living in the city: migrants. Shanghai's reemergence as China's most dynamic

[44] Pension reserves stood at only 15.63 billion yuan in 2010, compared with a payout of 81.15 billion yuan, and had grown by only 2.6 percent from the year before, compared with a payout growth rate of 14.2 percent; http://rsj.sh.gov.cn/tqtwj_17340/20200617/t0035_1389008.html

[45] www.czj.sh.gov.cn/zys_8908/czsj_9054/zfyjs/zxqk/201509/t20150910_151204.shtml

[46] F. Wang, Shen, and Cai 2019b.

and prominent global city was powered largely by a huge influx of migrants from all over China. In 2010, migrants accounted for 40 percent of all residents in the city, up from less than 5 percent in 1990 and less than 20 percent in 2000 (Figure 5.2). The influx of migrants was especially massive during the first decade of the twenty-first century; increasing from 2.87 million to 8.91 million. While China's population growth between 2000 and 2010 was less than 6 percent, in Shanghai it was more than 50 percent, attributable to migration. Only a small share of migrants to Shanghai were granted a local *hukou*. Shanghai's total resident population (including both those with and without local *hukou*) more than doubled between 1980 and 2017, from 11.52 to 24.18 million, while the segment of the *hukou* population rose by only 27 percent, from 11.47 to 14.55 million.

The two populations in Shanghai, both those with a local *hukou* and the migrants, had vastly different age profiles. In 2010, for instance, Shanghai's local residents (those with a Shanghai *hukou*) had a top-heavy age composition with large shares in the older age groups (see the shaded shape in the age pyramids, Figure 5.3). Migrants, by comparison, were heavily concentrated around the prime working ages between twenty and fifty. These same migrants, mostly laborers, were denied social benefits such as pensions and health care in the city in which they resided, as was also the case for migrants elsewhere in China.

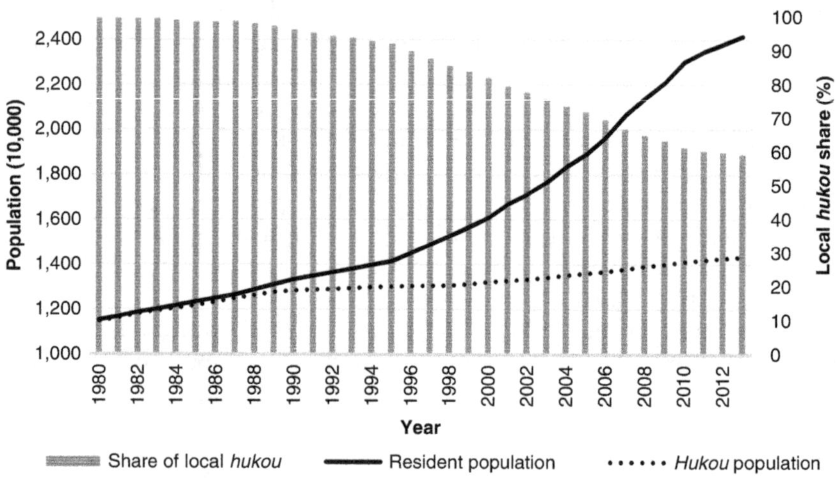

Figure 5.2 Migration and changing population composition, Shanghai, 1980–2013

Sources: F. Wang, Shen, and Cai 2019b. Population (left axis) and share of local *hukou* (right axis).

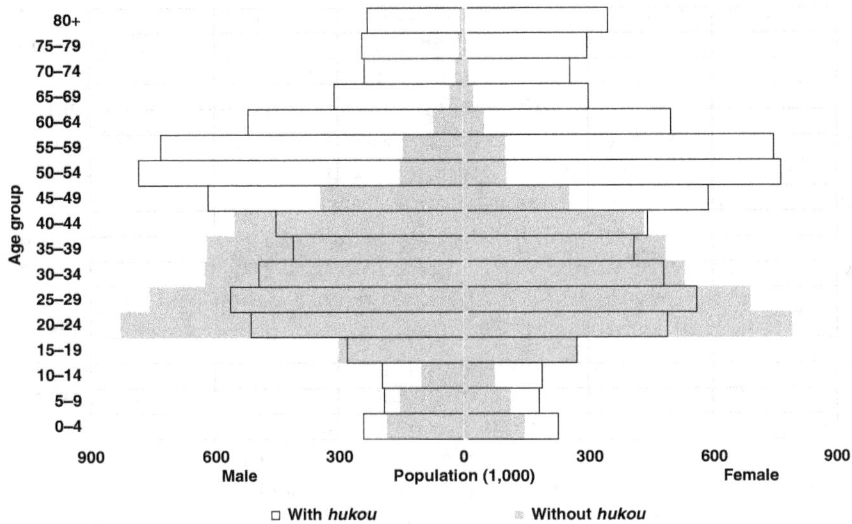

Figure 5.3 A city of two peoples: age and sex profiles of local residents and migrants, Shanghai, 2010
Sources: F. Wang, Shen and Cai 2019b.

These young and working migrants were a ready and ideal source to draw from to pay for the rising pension and health care costs of local residents. Government officials in Shanghai readily understood this math. The Shanghai city government enacted new rules, requiring from July 2011 that local employers pay social security and health care contributions for migrant laborers they employed, at a rate of 22 percent of wages. Prior to this new rule, employers had only had to pay social insurance contributions as such for local employees with a Shanghai household registration. Pension and health care contributions rose sharply as a result, up by 25.75 percent for pensions and 27.72 percent for health care in 2011 compared with the year before, and by 62.95 percent and 63.65 percent, respectively, in 2012 if compared with 2010, when enforcement gained more success. Payouts, however, were not increasing at the same pace, as one would expect, because migrant laborers were too young to receive pension benefits and most were not using local health care facilities. In contrast to this high increase in contributions, the payout rate stayed in the low 10 percent range.

A miracle emerged. Rather than being trapped in a deficit hole, pension reserve funds in Shanghai doubled in one year between 2011 and 2012, from 23.37 billion yuan to 50.09 billion yuan, and it doubled again in just three years to 110.39 billion yuan in 2015. Migrant laborers, in addition to powering Shanghai's booming economy, were made to shoulder the city's pension and health care burdens for those with a local *hukou*. By the end of the 2010s, Shanghai's pension fund was flush with 227.63 billion yuan in reserves. In contrast to being less than 20 percent of the payout amount in 2010, the reserve grew to reach 83 percent of the annual payout by 2019. Health care insurance reserve funds similarly rose tenfold between 2010 and 2018, from 20.34 billion yuan to 238.94 billion yuan. The reserve funds were large enough to pay for 2.89 years of benefits at the payout level of 2018, up from a deficit of 33 percent in 2010.[47] In contrast to the 10.74 billion yuan government subsidies back in 2010, while total government spending rose in 2019 by nearly 2.5 times that in 2010, to 817.9 billion yuan,[48] the city government only contributed 1.37 billion yuan into pension funds, about one-eighth of the amount a decade prior.[49] Shanghai's pension and health care systems, serving almost exclusively residents with a local *hukou*, were saved. Migrants not only supplied labor propelling Shanghai's booming economy but also shouldered social benefits for its local residents with their contributions to the pension and health care funds.

Shanghai's surplus in pension funds was so flush that it became one of the seven "net contributors" among the thirty-one mainland provinces in 2020 to help pay for pension deficits elsewhere in the country. Starting in 2018, faced with increasingly sharper regional disparities in pension reserves across provinces, attributable to different demographic profiles and pension revenues, the central government in Beijing implemented a system of centralized pension funds redistribution. In 2020, twenty-one of the thirty-one provinces ran a pension fund deficit. Northeast China, a region that has already descended to low fertility levels in the 1980s, racked up the worst deficit. For instance, in 2019 the share of population aged 65 and over was 16.23 percent in Liaoning province, compared with the national average of 12.6 percent and only 9 percent in Guangdong province, a province that attracted a large number of young migrants. Economic growth in Northeast China had been sluggish compared to other regions in China, in part being plagued by a high concentration of state-owned enterprises during the planned economy years. Its demographic profile was further confounded by young people leaving the region in droves in pursuit of better opportunities elsewhere. This top-heavy population age structure with a high share of elderly, combined

[47] Calculated from published city finance reports, e.g. www.czj.sh.gov.cn/zys_8908/czsj_9054/dfczsz/202001/t20200120_181886.shtml

[48] Ibid. [49] http://rsj.sh.gov.cn/tsbxxpl_17347/20200617/t0035_1377033.html

with a weak revenue base, bankrupted their pension reserve a long time ago. In 2020, Liaoning province ran a deficit of 55.56 billion yuan, accounting for three-quarters of its entire pension reserve.[50]

After having faced difficulties meeting pension payouts the previous decade, Shanghai emerged as the national leader in collecting pension contributions by the end of the 2010s. In contrast to provinces in Northeast China, provinces attracting migrants had a favorable pension revenue base and enjoyed pension fund surpluses. In 2020, Shanghai's pension revenue totaled over 200 billion yuan, ranking fourth in the nation after Guangdong, Jiangsu, and Zhejiang provinces, all of which are migrant inflow provinces. In that same year, Shanghai handed over 10 billion yuan in pension reserve surplus to the central government, which went toward subsidizing urban pensioners elsewhere.[51] In terms of total contribution, Shanghai ranked six in the country. On a per capita basis, Shanghai had the highest level of pension revenue; it was also among the highest per capita pension contributors to subsidize pension deficits elsewhere in the country.

Long-Awaited Convergence

Three Decades, Three Names

On March 25, 2005, the website of the Chinese Embassy to the United States posted an important news item. The news had nothing to do with Sino-US relations or any particular national news from China. It was rather a news announcement from the capital city of Beijing. The embassy in Washington DC deemed the content important enough to broadcast to the world.[52] Beijing's local legislative body, the Standing Committee of the People's Congress, announced an end to restrictive regulations against migrants, regulations that had been enacted in 1995.

The abolished regulations best exemplify how urban bureaucracies in China viewed and treated migrants from elsewhere. In addition to being excluded in the job market, migrants were put under "control and management" by urban bureaucracy. According to the 1995 regulations, migrants were to obtain upon arrival a "temporary resident permit" in the public security station at their destination. To obtain such a permit, the migrant needed to supply the required documents, in particular, proof

[50] "Yanglao jin zhongyang tiaoji, 7 shengshi jing gongxian, 22 ge diqu shoubudi zhi" 养老金中央调剂, 7省市净贡献, 22个地区收不抵支 (Pension redistribution by central government, with 7 provinces making net contributions and 22 in deficit), *BJ News*, June 30, 2020, www.bjnews.com.cn/graphic/2020/06/30/743595.html

[51] Ibid. [52] www.china-embassy.org/chn/xw/t188969.htm

that they were obeying birth control regulations. Neither an urban firm nor an individual was allowed to rent living or business space to migrants who did not have a temporary resident permit. To be eligible for work, a migrant worker was also required to apply for a "work permit" from the local labor bureau. Employers and individuals in the city were forbidden to hire workers without such a work permit. Moreover, migrants were responsible for paying "management" fees to local city offices.[53] Altogether, for a migrant to reside and to work legally, the person needed to obtain six to seven permits to cover "management fees" every year, costing up to 400 yuan. Other large Chinese cities followed suit, introducing similar regulations.[54]

Rural migrants were distinguished from city dwellers with an invisible mark: their household registration (*hukou*) status was "agricultural." During the socialist planned economy era this designation had barred them from access to food, employment, and housing in cities – such items were rationed and provided only to those with a "non-agricultural" status – but this time it was different. Thanks to increased food output produced by the rural population, food rationing was abolished by the early 1990s, and rural migrants could purchase their food and other daily necessities without restrictions. But housing allocation in cities remained off-limits to rural migrants. For decades, migrants and their family members were not eligible for social services such as education and health care in cities. They were segregated residentially, living in rented basements, construction sites, dorms, or urban villages that were constructed explicitly for them. In most cities, especially the largest ones, purchasing an apartment required a local household registration, regardless of the migrants' ability to pay. Not being able to enter the urban housing market, many migrants were deprived of the most prevalent and the easiest path to wealth creation and accumulation, as illustrated earlier in this chapter.

Over three decades, rural migrants to cities in China were designated three names. First, in the 1980s and early 1990s, came the label *mangliu* (blind wanderers). Official media portrayed them as aimless wanderers flooding into the cities, fanning fears that these countrymen were not just poor, dirty, and illiterate but also sources of urban crime. In addition, migrants served as the laughing stock for urban folk's entertainment broadcast on television. Although views varied among the leadership, the recurrent message was to return these wanderers back to the

53 http://law.51labour.com/lawshow-23188-1.html

54 Such fees were also reported to become a source of graft in the cities. Solinger 1999, 86–89.

countryside.[55] In March 1989, a State Council document – "Emergent Order on Strictly Controlling the Outflow of Migrant Labor from the Countryside" – was published on the front page of *The People's Daily*. The document required local officials to turn migrants back from train and bus stations to their villages and even suggested reducing the number of trains in operation to prevent the outflow of rural migrants.[56] A month later, the Ministry of Public Security and the Ministry of Civil Affairs jointly issued an "Order on Further Improving the Work of Controlling Blind Outflow of Rural Migrant Labor." To curb migration to Guangdong province in the Pearl Delta, which encompassed the special economic zone of Shenzhen, in February 1991 the State Council issued a special order entitled "On Persuading Migrant Labor Blindly Flowing into Guangdong."[57]

Out-migration from the vast rural hinterlands started to accelerate as efforts to curb the so-called blind wanderers proved futile and as China entered a new phase of reforms following the 1992 tour of Deng Xiaoping to Shenzhen to reenergize the reforms (see Figure 4.5). By then, the pejorative label "blind wanderers" was replaced by a more neutral, and factual, expression. Rural migrants began to be classified as *liudong renkou* (the floating population), a label they carried well into the twenty-first century. The term was factual because the tens of millions of rural migrants were not real migrants who could change their residence in a more permanent fashion. They were simply "floating" amidst China's urban society, lacking the capacity to settle. Migrants from rural China, mostly young and increasingly women as well as men, moved to cities for work. They left behind their families, including many young children, back in their home villages. In the cities, rural migrants worked long hours with low pay and little benefits, in jobs that urban youths did not want. They lived in rented basements, sometimes provided by their employers; others lived in "urban villages," low-quality housing built by urban residents to collect rents from migrants. Even for those who had adequate savings, they were not qualified to buy an apartment without the local household registration. This was particularly the case in large cities such as Beijing, Shanghai, Guangzhou, and Shenzhen; cities posting the most rapid real estate price increases.

[55] Such was the call from China's premier Li Peng in March 1989, in a report read to the Standing Committee of the National People's Congress: "Peasants entering the cities in large numbers isn't a way out; for the past few years we have specified a policy of 'leaving the land but not the countryside'; I think this policy is still very feasible. In the rural areas, continue to develop agricultural production, engage in the tertiary industries and town and village enterprises, absorb this labor power, create wealth, improve livelihood." Cited in Solinger 1999, 52.

[56] https://cn.govopendata.com/renminribao/1989/3/6/1/#823471

[57] Huang 2017, 109.

By the start of the twenty-first century, when the number of migrant laborers exceeded half of all non-farming employees in the country and made up to 80 percent in construction, urban policies toward rural migrants began to be more accommodating and welcoming. Hence, a third name for rural migrants emerged – *nongmin gong* (workers of rural origin). In 2003, the State Council issued documents requiring children of migrant families to be admitted to public elementary and middle schools in cities; though they were still required to take college entrance exams back in their hometowns in the countryside. The 2003 document and subsequent documents removed restrictions on hiring rural migrants and discontinued various charges imposed upon migrant workers and their family members. Migrants were allowed and even encouraged to purchase housing in small cities, in part to help absorb the surplus housing supply due to overbuilding. It was not until 2010 that the term *xinyidai nongmingong* (new generation of migrant labor), referring to those born after the mid-1980s, was first used in an official document.[58] This new generation of migrant laborers had been born after the revival of rural out-migration; many of their parents were among the first generation of rural migrants.

Within roughly three decades, from the early 1980s to the early 2010s, China finally succeeded in completing its industrialization and urbanization transformation.[59] Unlike attempts made earlier in the twentieth century, prior to and during the socialist planned economy system, the hallmarks of this transformation were that for the first time in Chinese history the majority of its population no longer relied on farming as their main source of livelihood; a larger share of the population lived in areas classified as urban rather than in the countryside. And unlike the industrialization under socialism, in this historical transformation incomes and the standard of living improved for the majority, not only the minority of the population. Chinese industrialization and urbanization was also particular to Chinese historical legacies and characteristics. In other words, as discussed previously, it developed in two phases: first in the countryside and then in the cities as well.

Yet, throughout this transformation, China's rural population continued to work and live as secondary citizens in their own country. This is the human or the social face of China's historical industrialization and urbanization. Chinese rural migrants' treatment invited comparisons with undocumented immigrants in other countries, including the

[58] Ibid.

[59] In 2011, for the first time in Chinese history, more than 50 percent of China's population was classified as living in urban areas, according to official Chinese statistics.

United States. Rural Chinese migrants shared several salient features with undocumented Mexican immigrants in the United States.[60] There was the proximity between sending and receiving areas and a very large gap in wages and in standards of living between the two. Migration in both cases was predominantly a circular, not permanent, process. At their destinations, migrants faced a complex system of work and residence restrictions, ranging from discrimination to outright illegality, preventing their settlement. And finally, there was similarity in the conditions that created surplus labor in agriculture while maintaining migrants' link to the land. Once arriving in the cities, migrants were segregated into separate jobs, with long work hours and lower pay. They were denied basic social benefits such as health care, pensions, and education for their children.[61]

Gendered Paths

Migration out of villages was not gender blind. Rather, it was a highly gendered process for female migrants themselves, their families, and for society. Migration opened up unforeseen, life-changing opportunities for women, especially young women. In the 1980s and early 1990s, male migrants disproportionately outnumbered female migrants at a ratio of 2:1 or even higher. Men left villages to work as construction workers; women stayed behind to farm or, for married women, to raise children.

This gender asymmetry soon changed. Manufacturing lines, such as those making iPhones in the Foxconn factories, employed a disproportionately high share of young, single females. Known as "maiden workers" (*dagongmei*), these young, single female factory workers were preferred by capitalists over men; they were perceived to be "more docile, more dexterous, and cheaper laborers for labor-intensive work than men."[62] In comparison to female workers outside mainland China, these female migrant laborers' toiled in a regime that was characterized as localistic despotic control.[63] Into the twenty-first century, food and household services further increased the demand for female migrants. By the mid-1990s, with the large influx of rural migrants into the cities, the share of female migrants rose to 40 percent.[64] Surveys of migrants conducted by the National Bureau of Statistics confirm that after 2010 over 40 percent of all migrants were female. The example of migrants in Shanghai in Figure 5.3 shows that this was the case for Shanghai in 2010; female and male migrants were almost equally represented in every age group.

[60] Roberts 1997.
[61] Solinger 1999; F. Wang, Zuo, and Ruan 2002; Lu and Wang 2013; Murphy 2020.
[62] C. K. Lee 1998, 161. [63] C. K. Lee 1998. [64] Solinger 1999, 243.

The occupational breakdown among migrant workers, drawn from the national surveys of migrants, highlights these differences into the 2010s. Female migrant laborers' occupations were distinctively different from their male counterparts. Males dominated jobs in transportation, construction, and as security guards. Females were concentrated in manufacturing and domestic services. As shown in Table 5.4, at the start of the 2010s, manufacturing and commerce were the two top occupations among all migrants; at 18.5 and 15.8 percent, respectively, among all migrant laborers. In both occupations, females were overrepresented, with their shares as total workers in those categories (61.68 and 47.29 percent) higher than their overall share (40.91 percent). In contrast, female migrants' shares in leadership and professional positions were below their overall share among migrants, a pattern that continued across much of the decade, as reported in the four surveys. Women were overrepresented in jobs such as food services and clerical jobs and in cleaning and housekeeping.

For many young women in the countryside, leaving their villages and families provided an opportunity to flee their patriarchal homes. Migration to the cities gave young women an opportunity to seek economic independence and social freedom, away from parental control, especially with respect to dating and marriage. Migration also afforded these young women an opportunity to be exposed to city life. In most rural areas, girls were forced to end their schooling earlier than boys as parents saw little value for girls to have more education in a society where males were preferred over females in both the labor market and the political arena. By leaving the countryside, young women could also save their parents the trouble of arranging marriages. Working in cities allowed young female migrants a "relatively independent, modern, and romantic lifestyle in anticipation of marriage and adulthood."[65] Many rural parents were also happy to see their daughters leave as they could not only support themselves but also send remittances back to subsidize the education of or building new houses for their brothers, a practice also found in other East Asian societies, such as in Taiwan and South Korea during their processes of industrialization.

Down the Paths

Two decades after the city government in Beijing issued its edict making nearly 200 types of jobs unavailable to migrant workers, and over a decade after the city's legislature removed many of the restrictions, migrants and their urban counterparts continued their lives on two different paths.

[65] C. K. Lee 1998, 136.

Table 5.4 *Occupational composition of migrant workers and gender composition, China, 2011–17*

	2011		2013		2015		2017	
Occupation	Total	Female	Total	Female	Total	Female	Total	Female
Government/ company officials	0.67%	33.84%	0.52%	33.94%	0.40%	29.24%	0.63%	41.25%
Professionals	12.59%	27.48%	6.05%	29.24%	7.15%	32.78%	9.26%	38.25%
Staff and clerical	5.35%	**52.98%**	1.15%	**56.04%**	1.93%	**53.61%**	1.75%	**58.54%**
Business	1.35%	**49.94%**	19.11%	**42.12%**	18.09%	**44.24%**	23.93%	**43.94%**
Small vendors	0.53%	**46.47%**	5.02%	**42.47%**	5.85%	**43.65%**	2.70%	**43.89%**
Food services	8.85%	**52.96%**	11.04%	**49.98%**	10.52%	**48.27%**	9.79%	**51.12%**
Housekeeping	0.46%	**89.55%**	0.50%	**84.62%**	0.42%	**83.04%**	0.53%	**86.43%**
Cleaning	2.00%	**76.94%**	1.35%	**76.82%**	1.53%	**73.98%**	1.78%	**74.59%**
Security	1.56%	4.15%	1.14%	5.68%	1.23%	7.55%	1.35%	6.87%
Repairs	2.45%	9.51%	3.95%	14.35%	3.39%	15.97%	3.57%	13.12%
Deliveries							0.85%	16.51%
Other commerce	15.80%	**61.68%**	16.93%	**53.91%**	18.97%	**53.38%**	15.33%	**58.05%**
Agrobusiness	1.67%	39.92%	2.44%	40.02%	2.14%	**42.07%**	1.64%	39.03%
Manufacturing	18.50%	**47.29%**	14.51%	**43.57%**	13.06%	**44.53%**	10.54%	**44.92%**
Transportation	3.13%	5.93%	2.83%	8.77%	2.55%	7.07%	2.47%	7.95%
Construction	8.70%	10.85%	5.26%	13.29%	4.56%	14.00%	4.39%	13.87%
Other production/ transportation	10.28%	37.17%	4.39%	32.56%	5.00%	30.99%	4.32%	33.18%
No stable occupation	2.54%	32.46%	2.87%	36.38%	1.53%	30.82%	2.39%	38.51%
Others	3.56%	**45.00%**	0.94%	**45.00%**	1.66%	**45.65%**	2.77%	**51.71%**
Total	99.99%	40.91%	100.00%	40.64%	100.00%	41.70%	100.00%	42.89%
Sample size	58,675	24,006	167,916	68,247	158,768	66,201	138,044	59,211

Sources and notes: National Surveys of Migrants; migrants are defined as those with rural origin and with no local non-agricultural household registration status at their place of residence.

Table 5.5 *Occupational distribution: urban residents vs. migrant workers, China, 2011–17*

	Urban resident		Migrant labor	
	2000	2015	2011	2017
Party/government/company heads	4.43%	3.44%	0.67%	0.63%
Professional/technical personnel	14.17%	16.14%	12.59%	9.26%
Staff/clerks	9.69%	9.49%	5.35%	1.75%
Commerce/service workers	23.32%	42.00%	33.00%	59.84%
Workers in agrobusiness	14.44%	4.07%	1.67%	1.64%
Production/transportation	33.84%	24.63%	40.62%	21.72%
Others	0.11%	0.22%	6.10%	5.16%
Sample size	Census	1/100 survey	58,675	138,044

Sources and notes: For urban residents: from published census and 1/100 survey tabulations; urban residents are defined as having a local non-agricultural household registration status. For migrants: from National Surveys of Migrants; migrants are defined as those with rural origin and no local non-agricultural household registration status.

Migrant workers and their urban-household-registered counterparts continued to have two distinctively different occupational profiles.

Comparisons of occupational distribution among urban employees between the year 2000 and 2015 show a shift from the manufacturing sector to the service sector while the shares in government and professional sectors remained largely the same (Table 5.5). Among migrants, for whom systematic data became available with national surveys of migrants in 2011, a similar shift from manufacturing to services occurred, over a shorter period between 2011 and 2017. By 2017, the share of migrants working in production and transportation dropped to the same share as urban residents, about 20 percent. The share of migrants working in the commercial and service sectors rose much faster, however, accounting for six out of every ten migrant workers. As in 2011, when survey data first became available, the share of migrants employed in leadership positions remained minuscule (less than 1 percent).

Two decades after being barred from guarding city warehouses, security guards became one of the more common and the fastest growing occupations for migrants. Estimated to be close to 2 million nationwide, these security guards were ubiquitous, guarding entrances to office buildings, construction sites, kindergartens, university campuses, and gated urban residential communities, large or small.[66] This profession was in demand: from 2012 to

[66] The 2017 national migrant survey reported an estimated number of 137.1 million migrant workers in cities, based on a sample survey with a sample size of 138,044

2017 the number of security guards increased by 40 percent, while the overall size of the migrant labor force rose just 4 percent. Another common profession for migrant workers was "sanitation and cleaning," with an estimated 2.5 million workers, increasing by 33 percent in the same five years. Jobs serving the needs of urban residents accounted for more than 1 in 10 of all working migrants. Having worked at construction sites to build Chinese cities, many migrant workers then shifted their employment to guarding and cleaning what they had built, still serving cities and their residents.

Entering the third decade of the twenty-first century, China positioned itself as the global leader in e-commerce. With a per capita income level of only 30 to 40 percent of that in the United States, South Korea, or Britain,[67] China surpassed them by a wide margin in e-commerce. In 2020, about 45 percent of all retail sales in China was from e-commerce, a share forecasted to surge to over half of all retail sales the following year. The expansion of e-commerce was swift, reminiscent of the speed at which roads and bridges had been built in the decades earlier. In 2010, only about 5 percent of China's retail sales had been through e-commerce, a share comparable to the United States at the time. In 2018, the share of e-commerce in retail sales in China was 29.2 percent, a level that South Korea and Britain were not projected to reach until 2021. The share in the United States that year was only 15 percent.[68] After 2018, within just three years, the share of e-commerce in retail sales in China rose from to over 50 percent. In 2018, a reported 50 billion packages were express-delivered in China, more than half of the world's total – close to 40 packages for every Chinese person. Between 2010 and 2018, express delivery grew at a staggering rate of 46.9 percent annually.[69] The same is the case with online food delivery; between 2015 and 2020 the number of online food delivery users increased from 113.6 million to 421.2 million.[70] At the top of this rapid growth and vast network were the privately owned e-commerce giants such as Alibaba, JD, and Pinduoduo, propelled by entrepreneurial and technical ingenuity. At the base to support this booming industry,

respondents, suggesting a sample ratio of 1/1,000. Among surveyed respondents, 1,862 reported a profession as security guards, translating to about 1.8 million nationwide. www.stats.gov.cn/tjsj/zxfb/201804/t20180427_1596389.html

[67] Adjusted for purchasing power parity. GDP per capita PPP (current international $) for 2020, China: $17,312; South Korea: $43,124; Britain: $44,916; United States: $63,544. https://data.worldbank.org/indicator/NY.GDP.PCAP.PP.CD

[68] Ethan Cramer-Flood, "In global historic first, ecommerce in China will account for more than 50% of retail sales," *Insider Intelligence*, Feb. 10, 2021, https://bit.ly/474yVBS

[69] "How can China deliver 50 billion packages every year?" *Xinhua net*, Sept. 9, 2019, www.xinhuanet.com/english/2019-09/17/c_138397454.htm

[70] www.statista.com/statistics/1117698/china-number-of-internet-food-delivery-service-users/

however, were the tens of millions of migrant laborers, working in the warehouses, delivering goods, and driving the taxis.

Delivery, along with taxi services, became the newest and the fastest-growing profession for migrant workers in cities. In 2017, over 1 million migrant workers became delivery drivers, based on estimates from a national survey. Another report put the number at 3 million for 2018, with a fast growth of 50 percent in just two years between 2016 and 2018.[71] In addition to the millions of delivery drivers across cities in China, there were also tens of millions of ride-hailing drivers, a disproportionately large share of whom were migrants.[72] Delivery workers, often seen on their motorbikes, were ubiquitous around Chinese city streets and alleys, delivering packages, groceries, and restaurant foods. As in factories and at construction sites, an 8-hour working day was not on these workers' schedules. To meet delivery quotas, they delivered around the clock, working through searing heat as well as pouring rain. More than half of all delivery workers were reported to work on average for 10 hours a day or more, with 20 percent working 12 hours or more on an average day. They had little choice.

Workers in China's new informal sector were often more exploitable than those working on production lines. They were paid by the number of deliveries completed, not by standard, hourly wages; few had basic protections under labor law, nor did they receive overtime pay. To compete for orders and to earn a decent income, food delivery workers were reported to work up to 15 hours a day; rushing every minute in city traffic, and making as many as 50 deliveries a day or 1,500 deliveries a month.[73] China could realize such a rapid growth in express-delivery services, again because of the abundant supply of low-cost labor. It was estimated that in 2018, the Chinese courier averaged $880 per month in income, a third of a comparable worker's earnings in the United States.[74] Migrant delivery workers, many of whom are children of China's first-generation migrants, are the backbone of China's

[71] Emily Feng, "For China's overburdened delivery workers, the customer – and app – is always right," *NPR*, Dec. 1, 2020, www.npr.org/2020/12/01/938876826/for-chinas-overburdened-delivery-workers-the-customer-and-app-is-always-right; "2019 nian quanguo kuaidi congye renyuan zhiye diaocha baogao: 75.07% de kuaidi congye renyuan yue-shouru zai 5,000 yuan yixia" 2019年全国快递从业人员职业调查报告: 75.07%的快递从业人员月收入在5000元以下, *CNR*, Jan. 2, 2020, http://m.cnr.cn/news/20200102/t20200102_524923032.html

[72] The largest ride-hailing company, Didi chuxing, claims to have 13 million drivers using its platform, providing 25 million trips per day. https://finance.sina.cn/tech/csj/2021-06-12/detail-ikqciyzi9156145.d.html

[73] Zhang Jialin, "The fast and frustrating lives of China's food delivery drivers," *Sixth Tone*, July 26, 2019, www.sixthtone.com/news/1004343/the-fast-and-frustrating-lives-of-chinas-food-delivery-drivers

[74] "How can China deliver 50 billion packages every year?" Xinhuanet, Sept. 17, 2019, www.xinhuanet.com/english/2019-09/17/c_138397454.htm

new economy, just as their parents' generation, who manufactured for the world and built China into a new country. These new platform workers, from delivery drivers to ride-hailing drivers, are indispensable in creating and maintaining the lifestyle of China's new middle class, who have achieved a certain income threshold and are making use of the fast-expanding e-commerce sites and services for their own consumption.

By the early 2010s, a "global middle class" had formed in China. The term "middle class" is admittedly arbitrary and elusive. One classification relied on income brackets used in Western societies (in this case, countries in the European Union). Applying Western criteria, a person was considered "middle class" if they lived above the European (EU) cut-off level of being poor and below the upper-income designations. The income range was between $36 and $120 per person per day, in 2013 prices. By this definition, China's global middle class made up less than 1 percent of its total population in 2002. The share of China's population falling under global middle class increased to 7 percent in 2007, then 19 percent by 2013. In absolute numbers, the size of this global middle class rose from fewer than 12 million to 64 million then to more than 254 million, a size that was projected to expand to over 500 million by 2020.[75]

Most of China's new global middle class dwells in its cities. Urban Chinese accounted for 90 percent of all those classified as middle class in 2013, far exceeding their share of China's total population. The same applies to the upper-class category.[76] Property was an important marker of this global middle-class status as well. Those who achieved the status of China's "global middle class" not only earned middle incomes but also acquired more housing wealth. Individuals in this class lived in housing that averaged three times the value of the lower class and almost ten times the value of the poor category. The upper class, those with a per capita per day income above $120, lived in housing with an average rental value double that of the middle class.[77]

The path to material abundance and prosperity brought almost all Chinese people to a life that was simply unimaginable when the journey began, as well as along most steps thereafter. However, depending upon a person's social status, the path was by no means a singular one and the same. The two classes of citizens created under socialism followed two vastly different paths to material abundance, whether through labor or by luck. After four decades of ascendance, the two paths have yet to converge.

[75] Gustafsson, Sicular, and Yang 2020, 89, 94. The cut-off points are that this middle class would not be considered poor or upper class by European standards (between 60 percent and 200 percent of the per capita median income for fifteen European countries in 2013).

[76] Ibid., 98. [77] Ibid., 97.

6 Surplus

With more than a third of its population ascended to the global middle class, by the 2010s China became the third largest consumer market in the world, behind the United States and the European Union. In just three decades, China transformed from a land of scarcity to a reservoir of vast wealth. Faster growth in income and wealth than in consumption had given rise to a surplus for most Chinese families.

No longer pressured by daily concerns over living necessities, the majority of Chinese families and individuals could for the first time in centuries contemplate making long-term plans for their futures: accumulating wealth, investing in their children, and preparing for their own old age. Although a minority, the more fortunate in society had already started converting their surplus into even more wealth: investing in the real estate market, purchasing stocks, or experimenting with other financial means not known to them just recently. After decades of cutthroat economic growth at all costs, the public as well as the government started to shift their attention from creating physical infrastructure to creating a social living environment compatible with an upper-middle income society: cleaner air, water, and soil, and a publicly supported social benefits infrastructure, from education and health care to pensions.

The country also moved along with its demographic transformations. Wealth and surplus creation in China benefited from its demographic fortunes. At the start of its economic ascendance, China was blessed with a historic demographic window. Rapid improvement in population health and decline in fertility prior to 1980 prepared China with a population characterized by a large, young, and productive labor force, while the elderly and the very young cohorts were both quite small. A healthy and literate population, though deeply divided socially, formed the most critical foundation for China's economic ascendance.

That demographic fortune is no longer present. Just as China's economic ascendance relied on its historical demographic opportunities, the close of this demographic window now threatens to deplete the surplus created and accumulated. The vast number of young laborers who propelled China's economic boom are now entering their post-working-age life phase. As China's post-boom generations enter adulthood, the surplus (or deficit) they inherit depends not just on how they produce and consume but also on how their parents' generation will be supported. The social contract, an intergenerational one, is now being put to the test.

Honoring this intergenerational contract or sustaining the intergenerational bond is not just an individual obligation. It is not confined to each family or between each child and their parents. Rather, the test also falls on the state. Just as most educational costs up to high-school level are already afforded by the state, so is the lion's share of health care expenditure, as well as income during old age in the forms of pension and other assistance. As young people moved away from villages to become non-farm workers and city residents, the traditional arrangement of familial old-age support became obsolete and undependable. Will the Chinese state, which has resumed its role as a dominant force controlling key economic sectors and positioning itself as a new paternalistic protector, be able to play the roles of fair guardian and redistributor?

A Lifecycle Approach to Surplus Generation

Surplus creation, more than income increases, was far more than just an economic process. As illustrated in previous chapters, the process of income and wealth accumulation was both social and political. Different social groups followed separate paths in improving their living standards and in acquiring wealth. These paths were separated by barriers of political institutions. As a result, inequalities in surplus have been and continue to be more pronounced than those of income. Such inequalities also bear far more significant and long-term implications.

Surplus generation and depletion follow the individual life span. In all societies and for every person born, an individual's life begins as a dependent, whose survival and well-being relies on transfers from others, whether from family, kin, the community, or the state. Whereas an individual can draw on their savings for old-age support, such cannot be the case during infancy and childhood as a child comes into the world with no savings. To examine surplus generation and depletion in a society, one needs to adopt a lifecycle approach.

A lifecycle approach allows the incorporation of intergenerational transfers across an individual life, transfers that are essential for members of a society to be sustained and to thrive. As transfers depend on more than just the individual, and increasingly on the family and the state, this perspective also incorporates the roles of population age composition. The surplus, past as well as future, is not a simple equation of income minus consumption for each individual. It is an outcome of the aggregate accounts in a society, affected by the relative numbers of producers and consumers, or the population age structure.

Surplus generation comes from income growing faster than consumption. In the early years of China's economic ascendance, consumption growth among Chinese families lagged behind income growth, yielding a substantially increased surplus. At the society level, increase in surplus was possible by virtue of a favorable population age composition: when the population in the prime labor force age was abundant and the share of the elderly population was still small. As income continued to grow and the cohorts born after the ascendance began to reach adulthood, a new generation of consumers arrived. Consumption increase began to outpace income growth. As a result, the accumulation of surplus started to decline. Changes in population age structure, with more people entering old age, drew down the surplus at the societal level.

After investing heavily in building highways, bridges, and airports, the Chinese government shifted investments in the first decade of the twenty-first century to rebuild a social welfare system; a system expected to meet the demands of the upper-middle-income level of society. The close of the hyper-growth era, combined with the arrival of accelerated population aging, presents a true challenge to the state's ability to sustain and to improve this nascent social welfare system, a challenge that is not just fiscal but also political. Replacing economic growth, welfare provision and redistribution are now increasingly more important sources of the government's political legitimacy.

Assessing surplus generation during China's age of abundance hence begins with considering income and consumption of the individual, then changes in population age structure at the societal level. As wealth generation in China's age of abundance followed different paths, so did surplus redistribution. Riding the tide of wealth expansion and benefiting from an unexpected government revenue windfall, since the start of the twenty-first century the Chinese state resumed its role as a social benefit provider and income redistributor. As China leaves its age of fast growth and steps into a society that is rich and increasingly old, has the Chinese state stepped up to perform its role as a fair redistributor?

Labor, Income, and Consumption

Surplus exists when income exceeds consumption. At the start of China's age of abundance, with little private savings and wealth available, labor income was the most essential income source. China at that time also had one of the highest labor force participation rates in the world, with near-universal employment of both women and men (Figure 6.1, for 1982). This high-level participation did not translate into a correspondingly high standard of living. Employees of China's state and collectively owned companies in cities and members of the peoples' communes in the countryside worked long hours year-round. The fruits of their labor were barely adequate for food, clothing, and shelter, as illustrated in Chapter 3 of this book. The savings from suppressing consumption was used for state investment, mostly in the heavy industrial sector. A large share of the national income was used for capital accumulation, a share that made up a quarter of total national income in 1957 and rose to more than 30 percent in the 1970s and the 1980s.[1]

As productivity and income increased in the decades after 1980, labor force participation also changed. The share of the population in the labor force shrank. That reduction in the labor force participation rate, however, was more than compensated by the increase in labor productivity. The most noticeable change in labor force participation was the substantial drop among the population in the very young and older age groups

Figure 6.1 Changes in age and gender patterns of labor force participation, 1982 and 2010
Sources: China Population Census 1982; 2020

[1] It was as high as 43.8 percent in 1959, during the Great Leap Forward (SYB 1990, table 2–20). Also, between 50 and 60 percent of state expenditure was used for economic construction.

(Figure 6.1). In the early 1980s, more than two-thirds of 15–19 year olds had already left school and started working (Figure 6.1, 70.5 percent females and 77.8 percent males). About four decades later, these numbers had sharply reduced, with only around a tenth of those in this age group reported to be working, dropping to 8.6 and 12 percent, respectively. The same changes were seen among those aged 20–24, whose labor force participation rate nearly halved from 90.3 to 46.5 percent for females and 96.2 to 56 percent for males (Table 6.1).

These sharp drops in labor force participation among young people are largely an outcome of China's rapid expansion in education, a change attributable to China's prosperity. They reflect a fundamental transformation in the population's lifecycle income and consumption profiles. Back in the early 1980s, few if any rural youngsters in their late teens were not already working in the fields. The 30 percent or so of 15–19 year olds not

Table 6.1 *Labor force participation rate (%), China, 1982–2020*

			Female		
	1982	**1990**	**2000**	**2010**	**2020**
15–19	77.8	68.3	51.7	32.0	8.6
20–24	90.3	89.6	85.4	69.3	46.5
25–29	88.8	90.8	86.7	82.1	67.4
30–34	88.8	91.0	87.9	83.2	70.0
35–39	88.5	91.1	88.3	84.4	71.7
40–44	83.3	88.3	86.2	84.8	72.2
45–49	70.6	81.1	79.9	80.1	68.3
50–54	50.9	62.0	67.1	62.4	51.5
55–59	32.9	45.1	54.5	53.8	36.6
60–64	16.9	27.3	38.8	40.6	25.1
			Male		
	1982	**1990**	**2000**	**2010**	**2020**
15–19	70.5	61.6	49.1	34.8	12.3
20–24	96.2	92.6	90.2	76.2	56.0
25–29	98.6	97.9	97.9	95.8	83.8
30–34	98.8	98.6	98.1	97.0	90.6
35–39	98.9	98.8	97.9	97.0	91.3
40–44	98.6	98.7	97.4	96.5	90.2
45–49	97.5	97.7	96.4	95.1	87.9
50–54	91.4	93.3	90.9	89.8	82.5
55–59	83.0	83.6	80.3	80.4	71.7
60–64	63.7	63.2	60.3	58.3	42.5

Sources: China Population Census 1982; 1990; 2000; 2010; 2020

working were mostly urban youths privileged enough to stay in school at that age. As living standards improved, young children, rural as well as urban, no longer needed to contribute to the household income at an early age.

School enrollment at all levels above primary school grew exponentially. Annual enrollments of junior high school students nationwide rose more than 60 percent between 1990 and 2000, from 13.7 million to 22.6 million (Table 6.2). This increase in junior high school enrollment was followed by an expansion in senior high school enrollment soon after, with annual enrollments increasing more than 300 percent between 1995 and 2010, from 2.7 million to 8.4 million. Enrollment in vocational schools similarly experienced a rapid increase, with annual enrollments rising from 2.9 million in 1990 to 4 million by 2010 and to 6.5 million by 2020. The total number of high school and vocational school students was 14.8 million in 1990, 24.9 million in 2000, 46.7 million in 2010, and 41.6 million in 2020. As a share of the population aged 15–19 in those years, they correspond to 40.1 percent in 1990, rising to 79.4 percent in 2000, 76.4 percent in 2010, and 57.2 percent in 2020.[2]

Enrollments grew fastest in higher education. In just a decade, between 1995 and 2005, annual enrollment in colleges and universities shot up by five times, from merely less than 1 million to 5 million (Table 6.2). Annual enrollments in tertiary institutions reached 9.7 million by 2020,

Table 6.2 *Annual enrollment (millions) by school type, China, 1990–2020*

Year	College and university	Senior high school	Junior high school	Vocational school	Primary school
1980	0.28	3.83	15.58	0.58	29.42
1985	0.62	2.58	13.67	2.34	22.98
1990	0.61	2.50	13.70	2.86	20.64
1995	0.93	2.74	17.52	4.98	25.32
2000	2.21	4.73	22.63	4.08	19.47
2005	5.04	8.78	19.77	6.56	16.72
2010	6.62	8.36	17.15	8.70	16.92
2015	7.38	7.97	14.11	6.01	17.29
2020	9.68	8.76	16.32	6.45	18.08

Source: SYB 2021, table 21–7

[2] School population numbers are from SYB 2021, table 21–8; population numbers are from China Population Census. Calculated by author.

not far below the number of births in the same year, which was 12 million. The total number of students enrolled in higher educational institutions rose correspondingly from 2.1 million in 1990, to 5.6 million in 2000, 22.3 million in 2010, to 32.9 million in 2020. In the same year, there were also 25 million students enrolled in high schools and 16.6 million enrolled in vocational schools.[3] As a share of the college-age population, aged approximately 19–22, college students accounted for only 2 percent in 1990. That number increased moderately to 7.5 percent in 2000, then rose sharply to 24 percent in 2010, and more than doubled to 56 percent in 2020. By 2020, more than half of all young persons in this age group were in college, compared with 1 in 50 only two decades previously.[4]

At the other end of the age range, the over-50s, the change trended in the opposite direction with increased labor force participation until 2010. Such an increase was seen only for females, however. Labor force participation for women aged 45 and older increased consistently over the three decades between 1982 and 2010, and by a large margin (Table 6.1). For women in their late 40s and early 50s, the share rose by 10 percent; for those between 55 and 64, the increase was 20 percent or more. Whereas in the early 1980s only a third of women aged 55–59 were reported to be in the labor force, by 2000 over half were employed. Even at ages 60–64, 40 percent of all women were reported to be employed by 2010, substantially closing the gender gap. The low labor force participation rate for females back in 1982 could be attributed to a reporting issue, namely that women's work in the informal sector or family farming back at that time was not counted. The substantial increase in women counted in the labor force, however, is nevertheless real. Older women's labor force participation increased in part in response to a demand for them to handle farming, as many of their husbands had left the countryside for work in the cities. By 2010, the young women who left the countryside to work in cities in the 1980s and 1990s reached ages 40 or older. Many of these female migrants remained in the labor force, employed as factory workers and service providers. With the transformation of the economy, especially with rural-to-urban migration, women's work changed; their work was finally more recognized and better counted.

Changes in labor income reflect vividly the changes in the Chinese economy and society. Figure 6.2 illustrates this shift with age profiles for individual labor income between 2002 and 2014, a period of rapid income growth. These profiles use both the aggregate national statistics

[3] Total enrollment numbers from SYB 2021, table 21–8.

[4] College enrollment numbers are from Ministry of Education, *Educational Statistics Yearbook of China* (ESYB). Population numbers are based on China Population Census. Calculated by author.

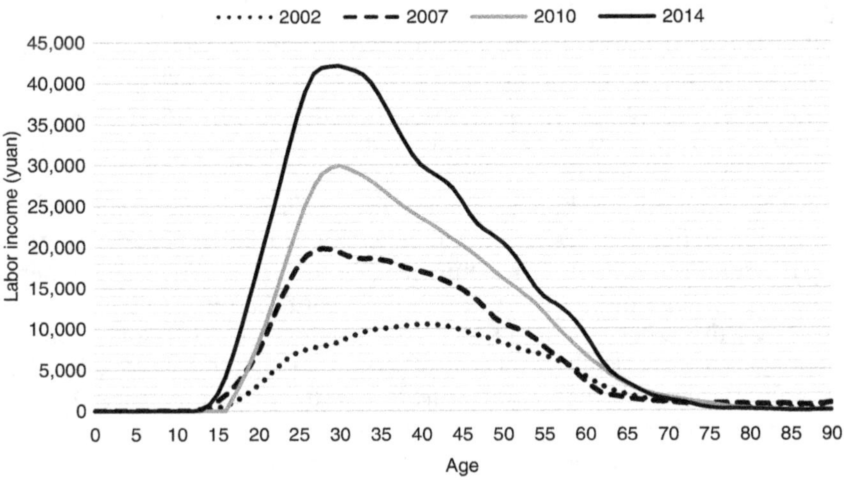

Figure 6.2 Per capita labor income change, China, 2002–14
Sources: Author's calculations based on official Chinese statistics and surveys (see Methodological Notes at the end of this chapter for technical explanations). In 2002 prices. See also Shen Ke 2019.

from the government and individual earning profiles from surveys (see Methodological Note for a brief description of the approach at the end of this chapter). Individual labor income levels rose sharply during this period, which was the fastest growing decade (Figure 6.2). Per capita labor income, adjusted for inflation, rose 35 percent between 2002 and 2007, followed by a more rapid increase of 53 percent between 2009 and 2014.[5]

Two features stand out in the age profiles of labor income: stagnant earnings in old age and an earlier arrival of the peak earning age. During the decade that saw the fastest labor income growth over a four-decade period, the increases in labor income concentrated in the young and middle-aged groups, while people aged above 60 years saw only moderate income increases. This pattern is partly due to older persons' low participation in the labor market, which is due to the early retirement regime in urban China and the depressing effect of improving social security benefits on labor incentives.[6]

China's young population were the true beneficiaries of the economic boom. The peak income earning age shifted to the younger population, and the shift was rapid. As shown in Figure 6.2, in 2002, the age profile of

[5] Income levels adjusted for inflation, set at 2002 price. [6] Gruber and Wise 2001.

labor income resembled a normal distribution, with the peak earning age at 41, an age that fell between South Korea (35 in 2000), and Japan, Germany, Sweden, and the United States (45–47).[7] By 2007, the peak earning age for Chinese laborers dropped swiftly to only 28. It moved up slightly, to 30, in 2009 and 2014, an age that was still extremely young by international comparison.

This downward shift in peak earning age was an outcome of labor force changes from two sources: one for rural labor and another for urban labor. For the rural population, it was further due to two factors: employment type and demographic shift. The first decade of the twenty-first century witnessed the fastest labor transfer and urbanization in recent Chinese history, with rural dwellers – especially rural young people – leaving the agriculture sector for the manufacturing and service sectors. By 2015, for instance, the share of 25-year-old males working in non-farming jobs in rural China reached 60 percent, more than triple the level of 1990 (16 percent; see Figure 4.2). This was by far the largest exodus from agriculture in Chinese history. A higher non-farming wage income among the younger rural laborers, compared to the older laborers' agricultural income, was one of the reasons for this shift. The income advantage of those young rural workers was further amplified by the shrinkage of labor supply. Between 2004 and 2006, for instance, unskilled labor wages increased in double digits, a much faster increase than in the preceding years.[8]

The shift in income age profile among the urban population, while possibly also being affected by the push-up effect of declining cohort size, was more likely due to another source: rapid expansion of higher education and increased human capital among the younger urban employees. In the two decades following 1990, China engineered the fastest expansion in higher education in its history. The share of the labor force population with a college education doubled from 2.6 percent to 5.3 percent between 1990 and 2000, and doubled again to 12.5 percent by 2010. This increase in higher educational attainment as documented in Table 6.2 was concentrated mostly among urban youth. China's 2010 census revealed that while only about 7 percent of the population aged 40–49 received a college or higher education, the share was three times as high among those aged 20–29, at over 20 percent. In urban China, nearly 40 percent of those aged 20–24 in 2010, and nearly one-third among those aged 25–29 were college educated. The corresponding numbers

7 R. Lee and Mason 2011a. The peak earning age in Indonesia was 37 in 1996, 46 in Nigeria in 2004 (Olaniyan, Soyibo, and Lawanson 2011).

8 Du and Pan 2009, from Shen Ke 2019.

back in 1990 were only 9.8 percent and 8.5 percent, respectively.[9] With an economy that was fast moving toward high-tech and services, these young people with fresh college educations were positioned to get into the higher paying jobs. In other words, there was a generational shift in earning capability as well as in outcomes.

As incomes rose at an unprecedented pace, consumption began to catch up. Chapter 3 of this book profiles the process of rising consumption during China's ascendance to material abundance. Yet, compared with income growth, consumption increase initially came with a time lag. Between 2002 and 2007, for instance, per capita consumption at all ages changed little, even though fast income growth was already under way (Figure 6.3).[10] Per capita consumption rose during this period by only 25 percent, compared with per capita labor income, which rose by 35 percent.[11] By the decade's end, however, changes in consumption accelerated, catching up and even outpacing labor income increases. Between 2010 and 2014, per capita consumption rose by 55 percent, compared with a 53-percent income increase.

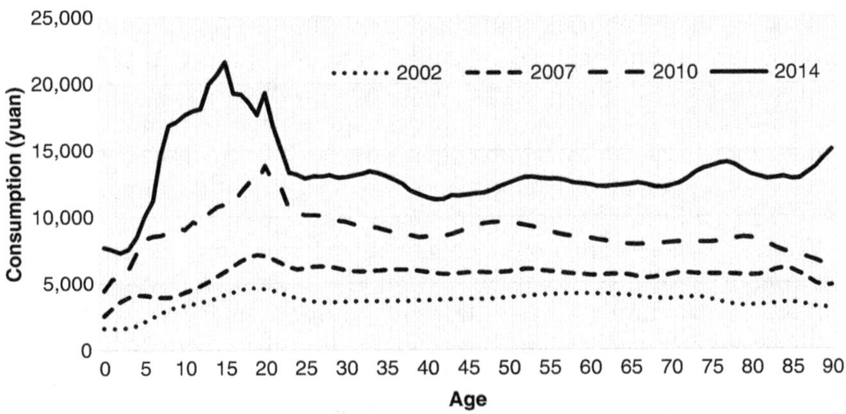

Figure 6.3 Per capita annual consumption by age, China, 2002–14
Sources: Author's calculations based on official Chinese statistics and surveys (see Methodological Notes at the end of this chapter for technical explanations). In 2002 prices. See also Shen Ke 2019.

9 These numbers are based on China Population Census 1990; 2000; and 2010.

10 Per capita consumption displayed in this figure differs from consumption data collected from household surveys directly. Rather, as with labor income presented in Figure 6.2, it was calculated by using the total consumption in society, based on national accounts, and distributed across ages utilizing data obtained from surveys. The per capita consumption level in other words included private as well as public spending.

11 National labor income levels and consumption levels increased in parallel by 82 percent and 79 percent, respectively, between 2002 and 2007.

Consumption increase was not evenly distributed across ages and population groups of different income levels. Rather, it varied by age and social group. As shown in Figure 6.3, the age gradient in consumption was flat in China for adult ages in most years, similar to cases seen elsewhere during income increase, such as in Taiwan.[12] After 2007 and as incomes reached a new high level, consumption rose most notably among those aged 10–20. This increase, including both expenditures by private families and by the government (public consumption), derives mostly from increased educational expenditure. The share of spending on education as total consumption over all ages rose from 15 percent to 16 percent between 2010 and 2014. Another notable change in the age pattern of consumption was in health care among the older age groups, where the share of spending rose from 10.9 percent to 11.9 percent.

Increased spending in education was made possible by income growth, and it was also made imperative by changes in the economy. Chinese parents were no doubt clear-eyed about the changes in the labor market, as shown in Figure 6.2. Education replaced seniority as the most important factor for high income in a fast-changing economy that was moving away from manufacturing. Jobs in the new economic sectors, such as information technology and finance, required proper training and became increasingly competitive. With most families having only one or two children, and knowing how their children's future economic well-being might depend increasingly on educational credentials, parents spent even more on their children's education than in the past, preparing their children for a competitive job market and society.

Chinese parents were not the only ones who spent more on education. Parental or familial spending on education accounted for only less than half of all consumption or spending on education. In 2014, the share of public spending on education was more than that spent by families, accounting for 56 percent of the total, as shown in Figure 6.4. Five years earlier, in 2009, the share of public spending on education as total education spending was only 51 percent.

Using a lifecycle approach in accounting for consumption, private and public consumption for different sources can be identified and differentiated. Figure 6.4 is a snapshot for the year 2014. Total consumption over the age range in 2014 (top line in Figure 6.3) is differentiated here into three categories: education, health, and "other," encompassing the rest. For each category, spending is further differentiated by two sources: private versus public. The amount of public spending per person, for example, is concentrated at the young ages (under 25) and is more than

[12] R. Lee and Mason 2011b.

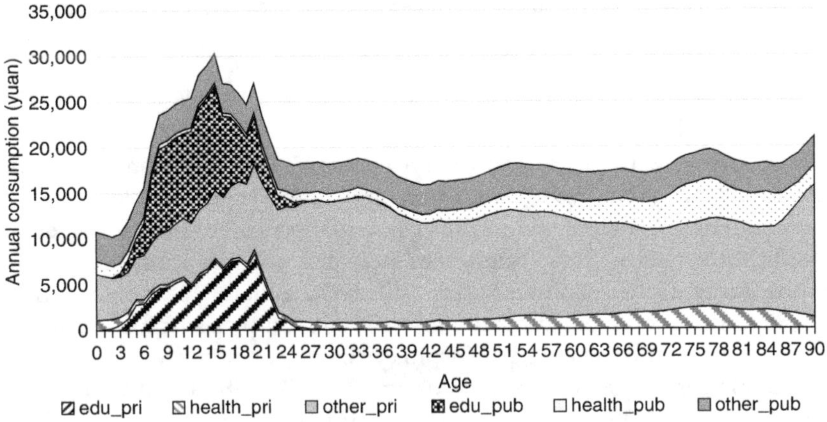

Figure 6.4 Per capita annual consumption by type and source, China, 2014
Sources: Author's calculations based on official Chinese statistics and surveys (see Methodological Notes at the end of this chapter for technical explanations). In 2002 prices. See also Shen Ke 2019.

that generated from private sources. Health care spending occurs throughout all ages but increases with age. Similar to educational spending at the young ages, in 2014 public spending on health care far exceeded the share of spending from private sources. In 2014, per capita public spending on health care made up 60 percent of total per capita spending, and the share of public spending also increased in those five years from 57 percent in 2009.

Aside from education spending among the young ages, the dominant spending category and increases in consumption after 2007 was in the "other" category. This category includes all kinds of consumption except education and health care. After 2007, the rapid increase in these consumption choices – no longer limited to food, clothing, or housing – drove up consumption. The birth of China's consumption generation started with the young, as one would expect. Between 2002 and 2007, and continuing to 2009, consumption among the young and high-earning population aged 20–40 increased faster than among the older age groups. By 2014, while per capita consumption levels appeared to be largely flat after ages in the early 20s, there was a clear difference across ages or generations. Under age 60, the predominant share of spending was in "other" categories and from private sources (Figure 6.4). By the late 2000s, China had become a consumption society with increased spending in dining out, recreation, automobiles, and both domestic and overseas travel (Figure 3.11).

Lifecycle Surplus

Over the lifecycle, there are years when a person's consumption cannot be supported by their own labor income and is hence known as a "dependent." At primary working ages, a person's labor income exceeds consumption needs. The differences between consumption and labor income form what is known as the "lifecycle deficit."[13] At ages when labor income exceeds consumption there is conversely a surplus. Between 2002 and 2014, the age range of surplus years in a person's life course was around 35 years. The average surplus ages were 22–58 in 2002, 21–56 in 2007, 22–57 in 2009, and 21–56 in 2014. Even with increased schooling and reduced labor force participation among young ages in the decades after 1980, as shown in Figure 6.1 and Table 6.1), the average age at which a surplus occurs was still relatively young by international comparison. In China, by people's early 20s, average labor income exceeds average consumption. By comparison, in the early 2000s, the average age at which surplus began was 26 in countries such as the United States, Germany, and Spain.[14] In China, the age when the lifecycle surplus ends and the lifecycle deficit begins – the late 50s – was similar to that in the United States (58), Germany (57), and Spain (57) but earlier than in some less industrialized countries.[15]

In modern societies, the state often assumes the responsibility for all sorts of expenditures, from health care and education to old-age pensions. Using surplus from labor income to meet consumption needs during the dependency years cannot be accomplished solely by an individual or a family. An adult can save for old age in some societies. An infant or a child, however, certainly cannot support themselves. Transfers from surplus to deficit thus make human social organizations indispensable: the family, community, religious and other types of organizations, and increasingly common and importantly the state.

For a society, the ratio of producers and consumers or the dependency ratio is a crucial factor to make up lifecycle deficits and arrange transfers. A society with a higher share of working-age population has a larger aggregate surplus than a population with the same level of per capita surplus level but a smaller share of working-age population. By the same

[13] R. Lee and Mason 2011a; United Nations 2013. [14] Tung 2011.

[15] For instance, lifecycle deficit occurred at age 63 in Nigeria (Olaniyan, Soyibo, and Lawanson 2011), and the same age in five Latin American countries: Ecuador, Honduras, Mexico, Nicaragua, and Peru (Cotlear 2010).

token, a society with a higher share of older population incurs a larger share expenditure or deficit than a population that is younger, with a smaller share of the elderly, with the same level of per capita consumption.

For China, this aggregate level of surplus over its ascendance to prosperity can be calculated. This calculation takes into account the two forces that affect the total lifecycle surplus or deficit in a society: changing per capita labor income and consumption levels, and changes in population age composition. Figure 6.5 tracks changes in China's aggregate level lifecycle surplus for four time points between 2002 and 2014.[16] Along with changes in income and consumption, the size of surplus in the primary working ages increased over time, with the fastest increase occurring between 2009 and 2014 (Figure 6.5). The age shape of the surplus also changed, with the peak shifting sharply toward younger ages, driven by the age profile of labor income (Figure 6.2).

However, rapid increases in consumption and population change have already started to put a dent on the surplus. Figure 6.5 also reveals a faster expansion of lifecycle deficit among the young ages, largely attributable to increased education expenditures from both private and public sources

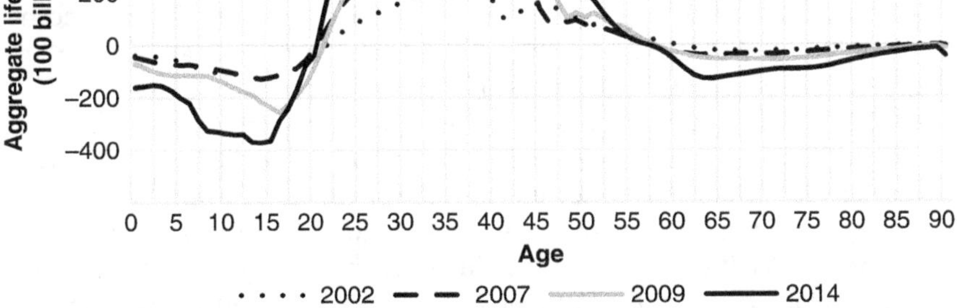

Figure 6.5 Aggregate lifecycle surplus, China, 2002–14
Sources: Author's calculations based on official Chinese statistics and surveys (see Methodological Notes at the end of this chapter for technical explanations). In 2002 prices. See also Shen Ke 2019.

[16] K. Shen, Wang, and Cai 2018a.

(Figures 6.3 and 6.4). Lifecycle deficit in the older ages also increased by 2014, due to increased expenditures in health care. The combined outcome, counting increased income as well as consumption, yields a substantial *reduction* in the size of lifecycle surplus during this period, at both per capita and aggregate levels. At the per capita level, lifecycle surplus increased by 1.2 times between 2002 and 2007. The even larger increase at the aggregate level, by 1.3 times, was due to demographic shifts favorable to lifecycle surplus generation. By the end of this period, between 2009 and 2014, the increase in lifecycle surplus continued but at a much smaller rate of 0.5 times per capita and 0.6 times at the aggregate level. The expansion of lifecycle surplus therefore had already begun shrinking. Due to just the impact of population aging, the size of the surplus, estimated at 7,350 billion yuan in 2014, could be more than halved by the year 2030, to 3,470 billion, and further to less than 500 billion in 2050.[17] Increases in consumption, combined with accelerating population aging, could exhaust China's sizable lifecycle surplus by 2035, as suggested by an estimation based on the experiences of Taiwan.[18]

In addition to labor income, deficits during the lifecycle can also be offset by other income sources, such as savings and asset income. Changes in these sources and their roles in affecting lifecycle surplus are shown in Figure 6.6. The left half of Figure 6.6 summarizes labor income and consumption, both public and private. The right half of the figure shows the other components of the equation in making up lifecycle deficit or surplus: savings, asset income, and net transfers (see Methodological Notes at the end of this chapter for explanations of terms and methods).

Similar to labor income, private savings and asset incomes also increased, and quite rapidly. Both private savings and asset income contributed to the expansion of lifecycle surplus, as shown in Figure 6.6. The negative numbers of the lifecycle deficit, on the left half of the figure, should be read as surpluses which were positive. Between 2002 and 2014, private savings rose 4 times, to 17.2 trillion yuan in 2014. Private asset income rose even more, by 4.6 times, to 9.8 trillion. However, as private consumption accelerated (left half of Figure 6.6), the growth in savings also declined. In contrast to a 160-percent increase in savings between 2002 and 2007, between 2009 and 2014 savings increased by only 40 percent. Private asset income growth slowed down even faster: 200 percent between 2002 and 2007, and only 20 percent between 2009 and 2014. As consumption increased and growth in savings

[17] Shen Ke 2019, 51. [18] Y. Cai et al. 2004.

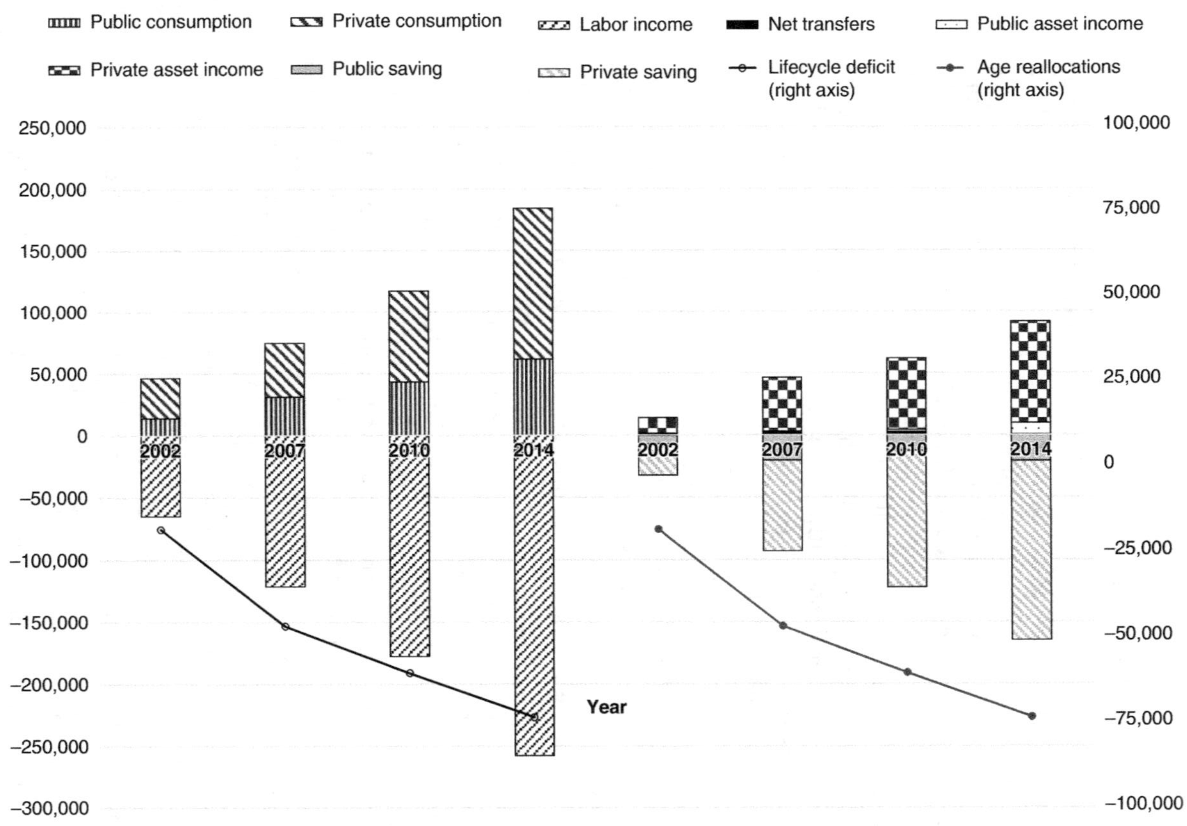

Figure 6.6 Lifecycle deficits and compositions, China, 2002–14 (aggregate, in 100 million yuan, 2009 price)

Sources: Author's calculations based on official Chinese statistics and surveys (see Methodological Notes at the end of this chapter for technical explanations). See also Shen Ke 2019.

and private asset incomes declined, China's rapidly expanded lifecycle surplus during its age of abundance also started to dwindle.

The New Redistributor

To transfer the surplus to cover the lifecycle deficit, the state plays an important role in all modern societies. For China, the state's role as a surplus redistributor went through two distinct stages after the mid-twentieth century. Between the 1950s and the late 1970s, China's state socialist welfare system formed an integral component of its planned economic system. Work organizations in the cities as well as rural collectives in the countryside, in addition to providing jobs and income, delivered a full range of social benefits, including education, health care, and old-age pensions. Although benefit levels were low and there were vast gaps between urban and rural sectors, coverage was generally universal with only limited variations within each sector.

Over the transformation out of the planned economy, China's employment-based and status-differentiated social welfare system slid into a near-death shape. At the turn of the twenty-first century and following the demise of the socialist planned economy in the 1980s and 1990s, the social welfare system was in shambles.[19] With reforms starting in the late 1970s, the organizational basis for benefit delivery of the socialist planned economy collapsed. On the eve of the reforms, virtually all employees in urban China worked in state or collectively owned work organizations; almost everyone in the vast countryside was a member of the people's commune. By the turn of the twenty-first century, the share of the urban labor force employed in state-owned enterprises dropped to less than a half; the people's commune had long become history. China also changed into a highly mobile society, with as many as one in four adults being a so-called migrant. This massive mobility rendered the workplace- and residence-based benefit delivery system utterly incompatible and obsolete. Whereas civil servants and employees in the public sector continued to rely on government support for social benefits, the majority of the Chinese population, including the rapidly grown number of migrants, did not have this privilege.

It did not help that the Chinese state's fiscal power was also in sharp decline two decades into its economic reforms. The share of government revenue as GDP dropped quickly between the late 1970s, from over 30 percent, to a low of barely over 10 percent by the mid-1990s.[20] The decentralization of responsibilities to local governments further resulted

[19] Yip and Hsiao 2009; Frazier 2010. [20] F. Wang, Shen, and Cai 2019a.

in spending cuts on social benefits in poor areas, shifting costs in health care and education more to individuals.[21] In 2002, for instance, only around half of the urban residents were covered by health insurance, and nearly 90 percent of the rural population had no health insurance coverage at all.[22] In 2000, China's population census reported that less than 20 percent of the population aged 60 and over relied on a pension as their main source of livelihood.

The age of abundance gave birth to a new social benefits regime and a return of the Chinese state as the social redistributor. In contrast to the earlier decades of China's post-socialist era, in the 1980s and 1990s, when economic growth took place at the cost of equity, China after the beginning of the twenty-first century shifted its attention to the social and political costs of the fast-growing economic inequality.[23] The government began to reassert its control over the key components of the economy, from retaining substantial ownership in capital-intensive sectors to maintaining control over strategic assets such as land and natural resources.[24] By the mid-2010s, for instance, the majority of the largest Chinese Fortune Global 500 companies were either owned or controlled by the state.[25]

Economic growth, accompanied by a resurgence of state control over key economic resources, enabled the Chinese government to reap the benefits of growth and to generate large revenue streams. The Chinese government's revenue as a share of GDP almost doubled in two decades, from 11.6 percent in 1998 to over 20 percent by 2010, a level it maintained for nearly a decade, until 2018. Moreover, government revenue increased at a rate far outpacing the overall growth in the economy, which was already at a historically high rate. In the decade after 1998, China's GDP unadjusted for inflation expanded by a factor of 3.34 while government revenue rose by a factor of 6.21.[26] In the first decade of the twenty-first century, the average growth rate of government revenue was about twice the economic growth rate (Figure 6.7). The fattened fiscal coffer, largely unexpected, provided the state with the fiscal capacity to increase social benefits spending and to build a post-socialist welfare system.

Developing a new social welfare system was politically necessary. In the closing decades of the twentieth century, China's historical economic

[21] West and Wong 1995. [22] Yip and Hsiao 2009.

[23] Gao, Yang, and Li 2013; Gao 2017; Duckett and Wang 2017; K. Shen, Wang, and Cai 2018b; X. Huang 2020.

[24] Naughton 2017.

[25] Scott Cendrowski, "China's Global 500 companies are bigger than ever – and mostly state-owned," *Fortune*, July 23, 2015. http://fortune.com/2015/07/22/china-global-500-government-owned/

[26] F. Wang 2011b.

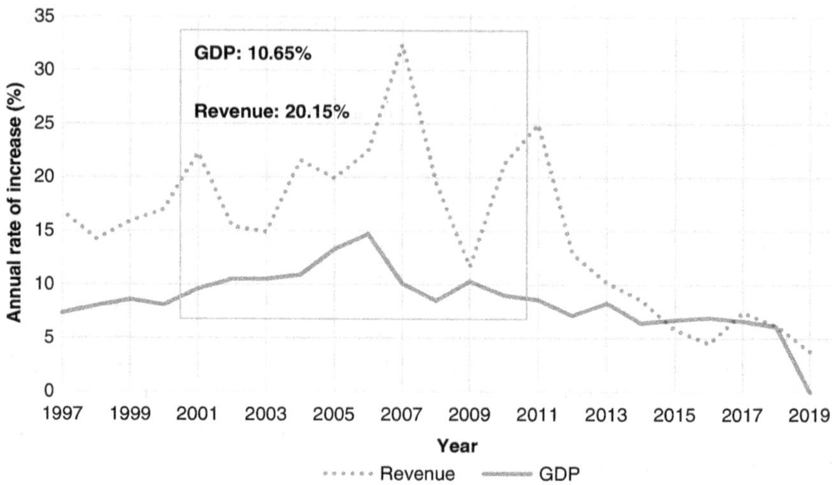

Figure 6.7 Annual rate of growth, economic output (GDP), and government revenue, China, 1997–2019
Source: SYB 2021, tables 3–1 and 7–1 (revenue only includes revenue under budget)

boom also transformed the global map of economic inequality. Rapid economic growth lifted hundreds of millions of people out of poverty, hence helping to close the global gap of inequality among countries.[27] Yet, within China, economic growth and policy changes also turned the country from one of the most equal societies to one of the most unequal. At the turn of the twenty-first century, China's inequality level was not only higher than that in OECD countries but also increased the fastest among emerging economies.[28] Rapidly rising economic inequality threatened the Chinese government's political legitimacy.

The first decade of the twenty-first century witnessed the birth of China's new social welfare regime. In 2001, China mandated public funding for nine years of compulsory education. In an attempt to universalize compulsory education nationwide, the government also devoted resources to improve school infrastructure, alleviate teacher shortages, and set up long-distance education in rural and underdeveloped areas. For higher education, China's State Council adopted a plan of "revitalizing education in the twenty-first century" in order to expand college enrollments. Between 1998 and 2010 annual college enrollments shot up more than sixfold, from 1 million to

[27] Firebaugh and Goesling 2004; Hung and Kucinskas 2011.
[28] OECD 2012; Whyte 2012; Y. Xie and Zhou 2014.

6.6 million, raising the gross enrollment ratio from 9.8 percent to 26.5 percent.[29] In the health sector, in 2003, the government launched a new insurance scheme, the New Cooperative Medical System. It was a program targeted at the previously uninsured rural population, and it focused primarily on covering catastrophic diseases. While there were small individual contributions, the scheme was primarily supported by subsidies from central and local governments. In 2007, a similar program, the Urban Resident Basic Medical System, was established for urban residents without formal employment. This program also covered nonworking urban residents, including children, the elderly, and the unemployed.

With respect to pensions, in 2009 the government established a pilot program, the New Rural Pension Scheme, for rural elderly who previously lacked coverage. For the first time in China's long history, this program offered direct subsidies from the government to a rural pension scheme.[30] This new pension program had two components: a basic pension financed by local and central government, and a personal account based on contributions from enrolled individuals. A similar program for the urban unemployed, the Urban Resident Pension Scheme, was launched in 2011. By 2010, in only seven years, the rural health insurance scheme had covered almost all the rural population. In addition, by 2014 roughly 80 percent of the adult Chinese population were covered by some form of public pension.[31] China's total social spending, defined as the total spending on education, science, culture, health care, and social welfare, increased from a quarter of total government spending in 1998 to over one-third by 2017.

Even with this rapid expansion, the Chinese welfare system at the end of the 2000s remained largely inadequate, highly fragmented, and vastly unequal.[32] Deductibles, reimbursements, and types of coverage varied substantially across health insurance plans. For example, urban formal employees covered under the Urban Employee Basic Medical Insurance had an average inpatient reimbursement rate of 68.2 percent in 2010, in contrast to 47.9 percent for urban unemployed residents under the Urban Resident Basic Medical System and 43.9 percent for rural residents under the New Cooperative Medical System.[33] Pension benefits differed even more drastically due to different pension plans. In 2011, the average monthly pension was 2,914 yuan for civil servants and 1,632 yuan for urban employees. By contrast, the pension was a mere 78 yuan per month for urban unemployed residents and 58 yuan for the rural population.[34]

[29] Yeung 2013. [30] C. Shen and Williamson 2010. [31] W. C.-M. Yip et al. 2012.
[32] K. Shen, Wang, and Cai 2018b; X. Huang 2020. [33] W. C.-M. Yip et al. 2012.
[34] L. Wang, Béland, and Zhang 2014.

China's census in 2020 reported that among the population aged 60 and over, only 36.7 percent of males and 32.8 percent of females reported a pension as their main income source. Urban and rural Chinese again vary sharply in their main sources of income in old age: the share relying on a pension for urban Chinese was 72.4 percent for males and 67.6 percent for females. For rural elderly aged 60 and over, the share was only 12.1 percent for males and 8.8 percent for females.[35]

The same lifecycle approach used earlier in this chapter to illustrate changes in surplus can also be used to assess the distributional effects of China's vastly increased public transfers. Transfers of government spending by gender, generation, and income groups inform the reconfigured roles of the state and at the same time track changes in economic inequality in the country. Studies based on household survey data reported a rather limited role of public transfers in closing the inequality gap.[36] To assess the distributive effects of public transfers, one approach is to divide households by their per capita income levels and examine different types of public transfers received by each income group. These exercises can be conducted at different time points to ascertain changes over time. For instance, in 2010, shortly following the introduction of the new social welfare programs, analyses revealed that China's public spending at the time disproportionally favored the rich and the older population. Individuals from the top income quartile benefited more from public transfers in education, health care, and pensions, with a ratio of 4:1 in comparison to those in the bottom income quartile. The largest source of inequality was found at older ages, where the ratio of receiving public pension transfers between the top and the bottom income quartiles was over 50:1. In addition, regardless of income groups, total public transfers received per person aged 65 and older were almost twice the spending per child aged under 20.[37]

Part of the differences in public transfers received was due to household differences in demographic and social characteristics. Compared with those at the high end of the income distribution, those at the bottom income group have a larger share of children and elders. Moreover, higher income quartiles consist of a larger share of urban residents, and lower income groups are concentrated with rural dwellers. In 2010, nearly three-quarters of households in the top income quartile group resided in urban areas. Chinese residing in urban areas not only had higher educational and occupational attainment, which afforded them greater earning power, they

[35] Calculated by the author from China Population Census 2020.
[36] M. Cai and Yue 2020; Li 2016. [37] K. Shen, Wang, and Cai 2018b.

were also much more likely to receive a multitude of social benefits, a strong urban bias legacy of the socialist system.[38]

Five years after the introduction of the new social welfare programs, public transfers in China continued to favor the more privileged members in society, those in the higher income groups. Figure 6.8 illustrates this pattern of inequality in public transfers. With the three types of public transfers, education, health care, and pensions combined, it was clear that those in the higher income groups received more public transfers per person. In absolute terms, individuals in higher income groups, especially those in the top quartile, received much more at young and old ages, the two ends of the lifecycle. Over almost every age, those in higher income quartiles received more public transfers. For education, the ratio for receiving public transfers between the top and the bottom income quartile groups was 1.2, in health care, 1.4; in pensions, for those aged 60 and over, almost 9:1. With the three items combined, the ratio between the top income quartile group versus the remaining three groups was about 2:1.

Aside from inequalities in public transfer payments across income groups, public transfers were also unevenly distributed across generations and between genders. The elderly received a disproportionately larger share of public transfers than children and the youth. Overall, in 2014,

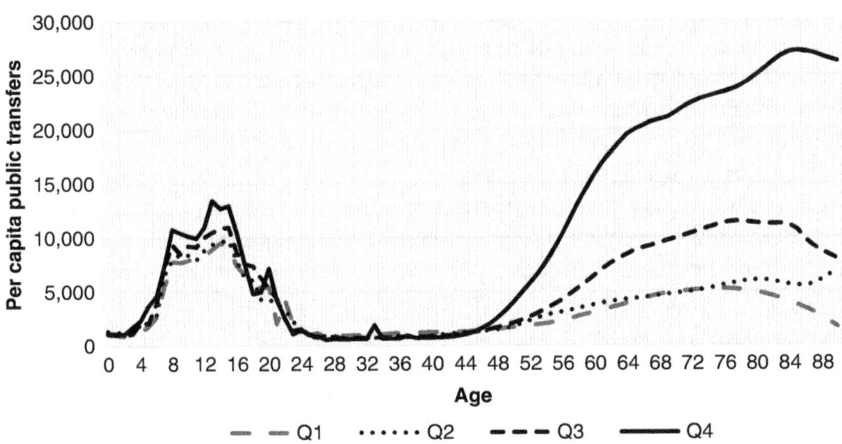

Figure 6.8 Per capita public transfers by income group, China, 2014
Source: Shen, Wang, and Cai 2018b

[38] Whyte 2010.

total public transfers per person aged 65 and older were 1.9 times the spending per child under 20 years old, at an average of 11,272 yuan and 5,807 yuan, respectively. Moreover, the gap between elders and children increased somewhat between 2010 and 2014, concurrent with the expansion of health care and pension programs. The generational imbalances also presented different patterns across income groups; public transfers were biased toward elders for higher income groups, while they favored children in the bottom quartile. For example, in the top income quartile, total public transfers per elderly person were 3.2 times the spending per child. It was 1.8 times for the second quartile. For the third quartile, however, public spending per elderly person was almost equivalent to the spending per child; and in the fourth quartile, on average the elderly only received about 80 percent of the transfers received by children. In education and health care, public transfers were essentially gender neutral and even favored females in the case of education. Public pensions, however, were highly regressive, with women receiving much less than men.[39]

The rapid expansion in social spending in the early 2010s, however, moved in a less regressive direction. The gap between the rich and the poor's public transfers, particularly pensions, was significantly narrowed between 2010 and 2014, though the gap between elders and children widened slightly. These results suggested that the lower income groups and the old benefited more from the recent expansion in social welfare programs; largely attributed to the introduction and improvement in health care and pension programs for urban unemployed residents and rural residents. The ratio of per capita total public transfers between the top and bottom quartiles was 2.2:1 in 2014, dropping from 3.1:1 in 2010. Most of the improvements came from pensions, where the gap between the top and the bottom income groups was reduced from a vast 53:1 in 2010 to about 9:1 in 2014 for those aged 60 and over. As a result, public transfers began to play an important role in reducing income inequalities. The bottom income group received significantly higher public transfers as a share of household income per capita than the other three income groups. The progressive nature of public transfers was strengthened along with social welfare reforms between 2010 and 2014, during which the officially published income inequality, measured by the Gini index, continued its modest decline, from a peak of 0.491 in 2008 to 0.481 in 2010, and further to 0.462 in 2015.[40]

More significant than the absolute value of public transfers for a household in affecting lives is the relative impact of the transfers, or transfers received relative to a household's income level. With this

[39] K. Shen, Wang, and Cai 2018b. [40] F. Wang 2019; Sicular et al. 2020, chap. 1.

measure, it appeared that the emerging social welfare system in China played a notable role in reducing inequality. Relative to per capita household income, the bottom income group benefited the most from public transfers. This was the case at all ages, especially at the two ends of the life course. At young ages, educational transfers were clearly progressive, with the share as per capita household income higher among lower income groups. At the primary and secondary school ages (6–17 years), public transfers received by the bottom income group were four times their per capita income in 2014 on average, as compared to merely 1.8 times in 2010. This boost in educational investment for the poor could have long-term benefits for these children, reducing future income inequalities. For older ages, the bottom quartile income households also received the highest relative share. For seniors older than 65 in the bottom quartile, the ratio of per capita total public transfers received to household income was around 0.5 in 2010. It quadrupled to over 2 in 2014. These changes were consistent with results based on studies using survey data and by comparing Gini indices of household disposable income, pre- and post-transfers.[41]

The redistributive role of the Chinese state, nevertheless, was still rather limited when placed under a globally comparative lens. For instance, among OECD countries, cash transfers cushioned income inequality by 18 percent in 2013, more than three times the magnitude calculated for China.[42] An estimate of the effect of public transfers on reducing income inequality, based on data in 2013, showed a modest role of 8.82 percent, reducing the Gini index of income inequality from 0.5174 (market income) to 0.4720 (disposable income). The type of public transfers that had the largest effect were pensions.[43] In many European countries, the income inequality reducing effect (as measured by the Gini index) ranged between 20 and 40 percent, which was three to five times the magnitude of that seen in China at the time.[44] Even with its promising start, China's emerging social welfare system was still largely inadequate and highly segmented. For instance, in 2014, the benefit generosity ratio for education and health care, measured by benefit level per beneficiary relative to GDP per working-age adult, lagged far behind those of the OECD countries and most countries in Latin America. Whereas the benefit generosity ratio for pensions in China appeared to be close to that in OECD countries, the overall high ratio was largely a result of uneven distribution, in which the minority urban retirees received a high pension while the majority rural elderly received very little.[45]

[41] M. Cai and Yue 2020. [42] OECD 2016; M. Cai and Yue 2020. [43] Li 2016.
[44] Hocquet 2016. [45] Y. Cai, Wang, and Shen 2018.

Can the State Pass This Stress Test?

At the societal level, future surpluses available for transfers depend on two factors. One is individual: the net surplus level per person. The other is aggregate: the changes in population age structure. Demographically, China already faces the challenge of population aging at an accelerating pace. China's highly compressed demographic transition had set in motion a much faster aging process than Western societies. For instance, it took Italy 70 years, Germany 75 years, and France 90 years to see the share of their elderly population aged 65 and over reach 25 percent. It would take China less than 30 years to travel the same distance toward a super-aged society.[46] The share of the Chinese population aged 65 and over nearly doubled within two decades, from about 7 percent in 2000 to 13.5 percent in 2020. The share is expected to exceed 25 percent by 2050.[47]

Population aging in China also has a unique characteristic. A legacy of its 35-year enforcement of the one-child policy left a large portion of families with only one child.[48] A large number of Chinese elderly will enter their old age with only one child, unlike elderly people in the past who could resort to familial sources for old-age support. The weakened family support makes public support of the elderly especially essential. Fertility has been staying below the replacement level since the early 1990s, while lifting birth control has not brought the major fertility rebound the government had hoped for. Even a substantial fertility rebound would only have minimal effect on slowing the aging trend in the short and medium terms. Rapid population aging and mounting pressure to support the rapidly aging population would reduce potential resources for future welfare programs to support the less privileged.[49]

A crucial test for the Chinese state in the coming decades will be its ability to continue its roles as a social welfare provider and a redistributor. An aging population with Chinese characteristics, a social benefits regime that is still inadequate and fragmented, and a downward trend of government revenue growth all make this test daunting. China's population aging has been unfolding and will continue to unfold at an accelerated pace to reach a scale that is unprecedented in its own terms and with few comparable cases in human history. According to the United Nations' projection under the medium fertility scenario (2017), assuming a moderate and gradual fertility recovery, China's population aged 65 and over is expected to increase from 135 million to 246 million between

[46] F. Wang 2011a; Y. Cai, Wang, and Shen 2018. [47] United Nations 2015.
[48] F. Wang, Cai, and Gu 2013; Y. Cai and Wang 2021.
[49] Y. Cai, Wang, and Shen 2018.

2015 and 2030, and to 359 million by 2050, reaching a share of over one in four (26.3 percent) in the total population. A sharp rise in the population in the dependent ages, or the lifecycle deficit ages, leads to rapid increases in pension payouts and health care costs. China's modest welfare system had already shown major signs of strain in the 2010s. For example, a 2017 government report revealed that one of China's 31 provinces was already running a deficit of over $30 billion with its pension fund. In 13 other provinces, their reserves in pension funds were less than one-year's payout.[50] Having exhausted their reimbursement allowance, hospitals were reported to turn to rationing for a range of surgical supplies.[51] Two decades into the promised free nine-year compulsory education for all, there were still areas that could not provide full funding.[52] Slower economic growth after the early 2010s led to a sharp drop in government revenue increase. In contrast to the nearly 20 percent annual growth rate in the 2000s, the government revenue growth rate was barely above 5 percent in the mid-2010s (Figure 6.7).

One benchmark for a stress test of the state's capacity is the share of national economic output required for transferring surpluses to manage the needs in the deficit ages. This benchmark can be projected with two simple inputting parameters: per capita benefit level and population age composition. Benefit level or benefit generosity ratio (BGR) can be measured by the share of benefit expenditure per member of the eligible population as the economic output per working-age adult. Public spending can be represented by spending per person on education, health care, and pensions.[53] Future population changes by age can be projected with assumptions about fertility and mortality changes. For the projections illustrated in this section, the assumption about increases in benefit generosity draws from a rationale that China has set its goal to become a high-income society by 2030. China has also committed to providing

50 "China's pension funds struggling to cope with ageing population-state media," *Reuters*, Dec. 11, 2017. https://reut.rs/45AypdB

51 Coco Feng, "Doctors hurting for supplies as hospitals restrict medical products," *Caixin Global*, Dec. 21, 2017. https://bit.ly/3Q4yVL4

52 According to a government evaluation report that covered 522 counties in 26 provinces, 8 provinces had not "solidified" fiscal mechanisms to guarantee support for mandatory education. https://bit.ly/48VzIqm

53 For education, public spending per student was estimated using data of spending at each level of education, reported in government statistics, and the coverage (i.e. enrollments) by level of education and age, using data from surveys. Age-specific public health care spending included the cost of health care provided by public hospitals and health care purchased by individuals and reimbursed through public programs. The adjusted age-specific public health spending per capita, divided by GDP per working-age adult, gave the values of the age-specific benefit generosity ratio for health care. For pensions, benefit per pensioner and the pension coverage rate by age were both constructed using survey data.

equal access to quality, affordable education and health care, as well as comprehensive pension coverage and reducing fragmentation across subsystems by 2030. If China can realize its goals of economic growth in the next decade and a half, even with an annual growth rate of GDP per capita of 5 to 6 percent, its per capita income could reach the OECD average achieved in 2009 by 2030.[54] Meeting this goal will inevitably lead to an increase in the overall per capita benefit level. Population projections used for this stress test are based on those from the United Nations.[55] These projections included five variants of fertility assumptions to project future population change: medium, high, low, constant, and instant-replacement and one variant of mortality that assumes a general rise of life expectancy over the projection period.[56]

To project future fiscal needs in public transfers, two sets of scenarios could be entertained. The first set would assess the impact of population change only, or the *Aging Only scenarios*. In this case, the benefit level or the benefit generosity ratio by age would be held constant over time, with the only varying parameter being the population age structure. An implicit assumption with this set of scenarios is that the rise in benefit level per beneficiary will keep up with labor productivity growth, but the share will not change. Such projections under *Aging Only scenarios* are useful for examining the implications of current welfare policies due to demographic changes alone.

The second set of scenarios assumes changes in benefit level. These are *Aging and Welfare Expansion scenarios*, where both the benefit generosity ratio and population age structure change over time are considered. The assumption is that by 2030 China's aggregate benefit generosity ratio in

[54] GDP per capita for China, in purchasing power parity, was $15,529 in 2016; and for OECD countries, it was $33,897 on average in 2009. With a 6 percent annual increase rate, in 14 years, China's per capita GDP would be $35,110 (GDP per capita data are from WDI 2018).

[55] United Nations 2015. The UN's population historical estimates and projections were based on its own assessments. Not only were they not necessarily agreeing with the official statistics provided by the Chinese government, but they were also subject to review and revision when new data and/or modeling techniques became available.

[56] As a reference, the UN projections also included a "no change" variation in its published tables that assumed all demographic parameters stay constant from the last observation. Fertility change under various assumptions, which covered a range of uncertainties, could result in different sizes of young cohorts below the age of 40. The projected age structure for people older than 40 (by 2050) was essentially the same under these five fertility variants, because the older cohorts were determined by the same cohort size born before the start of projection and the same assumed mortality rate. The peak number of those aged around 60 by 2050 reflected those large cohorts born in the late 1980s and the early 1990s. The "no change" variant showed an increasingly large divergence for population older than 40 (by 2050) because it assumed a higher mortality than the five fertility variants.

education, health care, and pension sectors would converge toward the average OECD countries' 2009 levels, with age-specific benefit generosity ratio inflated by the same proportion. At the same time, population aging would proceed as assumed in the UN's medium fertility scenario.

Up to the middle of this twenty-first century, the impact of population aging on fiscal burden will largely be predetermined by past demographic changes. Figure 6.9 portrays the long-term nature of this demographic impact. Regardless of fertility assumptions, the fiscal burden in China would rise, as the increased costs in programs for the elderly could not be offset by decreased expenditures on children (all projected changes are in Figure 6.9, except "Medium fertility, Increased BGR"). Any changes in demographic behaviors in the near future, however, could have profound impacts in the long run, beyond the middle of the current century. In the near term, the *Aging Only scenarios* under five different variants of fertility assumption show an interesting resemblance by 2050 – with total public spending making up around 23 percent of GDP, assuming China maintains its benefit generosity level in 2014.

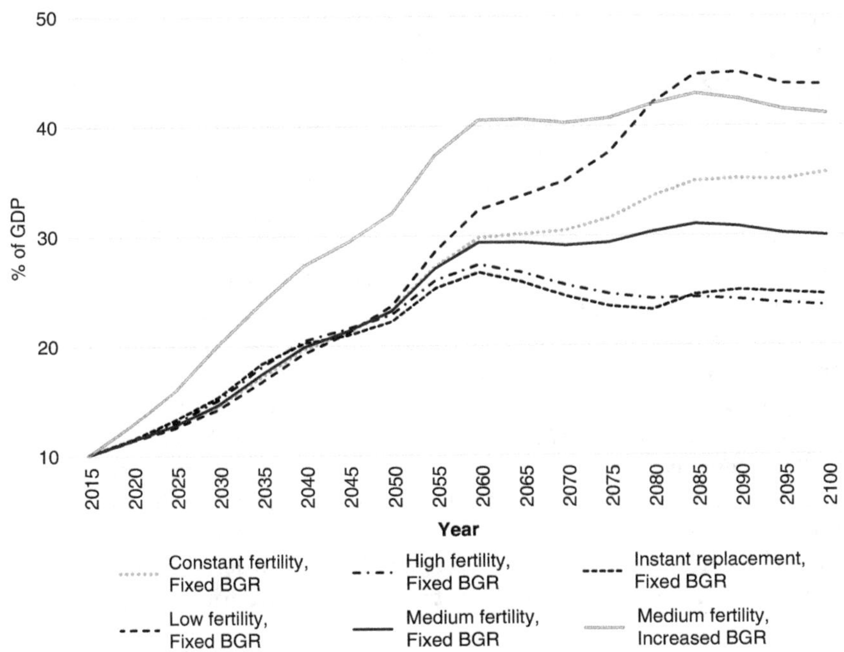

Figure 6.9 Projected public expenditure as share of GDP, China, 2015–2100
Source: Y. Cai, Wang, and Shen 2018

China's demographic trajectories in the near term, in the 2020s and 2030s, could have profound fiscal implications in the long run. The real demographic impact would manifest after 2050. Under the low fertility assumption, total public spending would continue to grow precipitously for the rest of the century; for other higher fertility assumptions, it would increase at a much more moderate pace or decline beyond 2060. The difference between low and high fertility assumptions could be as large as 20 percent of GDP by 2100. Demographic change in the next three-and-a-half decades, in other words, is most likely to lighten the burden of public expenditure on education and increase expenditure on health care moderately, but drive up pensions expenditure massively. Assuming no change in the benefit generosity ratio and with the medium fertility assumption of the UN's projections, the share of GDP to be used for these three types of social welfare programs could increase from 10 percent in 2014 to about 15 percent in 2030 and over 20 percent by 2050.

It is unlikely, however, that with anticipated further increase in per capita income, and with its nascent welfare regime, China can stay at the current benefit level for the coming decades. In fact, public spending in China has already taken another major jump from 2014 to 2020: public education spending as a share of GDP modestly increased from 3.6 percent in 2014 to 3.8 percent in 2015 and 2016, before returning to 3.6 percent afterwards. The increases in public spending on health care and pensions were much more substantial: health care spending rose from 2.8 percent in 2014 to 4.0 percent in 2020; pension spending jumped from 3.6 percent to 5.4 percent. Combined, these three outlays of government fiscal coffer rose to account for 13 percent of GDP, up from just 7.6 percent a decade earlier.[57] These increases were mainly due to rising benefit generosity ratios. What would make a vast difference in fiscal burden in the next three decades are rises in both benefit generosity as well as the elderly population. Assuming China will increase its benefit generosity ratio by 2030 to the average OECD level back in 2009, a reasonable assumption as China aspires to become a high-income society by then, total public spending as a share of GDP could increase to 20 percent by 2030 and to 32 percent by the mid-century, compared with 23 percent under the assumption of constant benefit generosity ratios.

What do these numbers mean in terms of fiscal burden? China's general government revenue – including taxes, social security contributions,

[57] Calculated from SYB 2021, tables 3–1 and 7–1. Health spending follows the definition in the System of National Accounting (SNA), which includes government expenditure on health insurance and reimbursement of expenses.

property income, and other income – had already increased from 18.3 percent of GDP in 2007 to 24.8 percent in 2010, and to 29.2 percent in 2015.[58] Assuming no further increase in the share of general government revenue as GDP, by 2030 nearly half of all government revenue will be needed to support education, health care, and pensions under the scenario of no benefit generosity increase. If China elevates its benefit generosity along the lines of the OECD countries' average in 2009, this social spending could burn through two-thirds of general government revenue in 2030 and over 100 percent by 2050. This trend is obviously unsustainable. The challenge is especially daunting for pensions, which alone could rise to 13.5 percent of GDP by 2050 with no change in benefits, and to above 17 percent with increased benefit generosity. This share implies that by 2050 the pension burden alone could consume over half of the government revenue if the share of China's government revenue as GDP remains fixed.

The inevitable increase in fiscal burdens associated with population aging and welfare expansion poses hard choices for policymakers in China. To meet this rising fiscal demand, the government could either increase revenue or reduce benefit levels. Given the still very low benefit generosity level currently in China, particularly for rural residents and urban unemployed residents, it would be politically and socially unacceptable to lower benefit levels any further. Therefore, the option dwells more on the revenue side of the equation. China already has a high contribution level, with a combined contribution of 28 percent, 20 percent from the employer and 8 percent from the employee, for pensions among urban employees; a contribution rate considered by many to be too burdensome for both employers and employees. China's overall tax and contribution rate, measured as a percentage of profit, for a medium-sized domestic manufacturer was 67.3 percent in 2017. Such a level was also considered among the highest in the world, surpassed by only 11 of the 190 economies studied by the World Bank and PricewaterhouseCoopers.[59] At the same time, however, the share of government revenue as GDP in China is still quite low, around 30 percent, compared to 50 percent or higher in Nordic countries, France, and Belgium. In other words, raising taxes to pay for increased social expenses remains a viable option. In addition, as often discussed, China could also resort to selling off stock shares of state-owned enterprises to increase pension funds.

Increasing government revenue substantially in the future, however, will not be without costs and constraints. Raising taxes used for social spending, while necessary and perhaps unavoidable, could have negative consequences for investment (other than education)

[58] Data from the IMF: https://bit.ly/3Q3t4Wi

[59] PricewaterhouseCoopers 2017.

and consumption, which in turn could affect overall economic growth. Social spending and benefits' choices for the current generation could have profound and long-term effects for intergenerational inequality. Future generations might be overburdened by a large public debt. Still relatively low by international standards, China's debt ratio has already been on a rapid rise. In 2008, on the eve of the global financial crisis, China's total leverage – as measured by a ratio of credit to GDP – was 132 percent. It rose to 160 percent in 2012 after a large government infusion of funds to counter the effects of the global financial crisis. More recently, it rose to 258 percent and is estimated to reach 288 percent by 2021, a level that is well above the global average for emerging economies, which is at 189 percent.[60]

Toward meeting the goal of reducing the pension burden, the most obvious policy option is to postpone retirement age, which at 60 for males and 55 for females currently is rather early considering life expectancy levels and international standards. Raising the retirement age could have the immediate effect of both increasing pension contributions and reducing pension payouts. The effect of this measure, however, could only be gradual and limited in the long term as well. As illustrated by a simulation study, any instant draconian benefit cuts could substantially relieve the fiscal burden. However, such reforms might only result in relatively small gains for future generations, while at a heavy cost for current generations who earn lower wages, hence leading to a net welfare loss for the whole society.[61]

Further expansion of welfare coverage and increases in welfare generosity would inevitably put more stress on the system. Since the early 2010s, China's double-digit economic growth has come to an end, with its annual rate on a continuous downward slide from 10.5 percent in 2010 to less than 7 percent since 2015 (Figure 6.7). Most economists and government officials in China had come to realize that even slower growth was on the horizon. What was more alarming about this economic slowdown was the declining growth of Chinese government's fiscal revenue. During the first decade of the twenty-first century, the annual growth rate of government revenue averaged nearly 20 percent, double the GDP growth. By 2016, the growth rate of government revenue dropped more precipitously, to only 4.5 percent (Figure 6.7). The growth of government spending continued to outpace the growth of government revenue. Economic slowdown and population aging, along

[60] Jane Cai, "Fresh warnings to debt-ridden China of living on borrowed time," *South China Morning Post*, Dec. 10, 2017. https://bit.ly/48UwIKN

[61] Song et al. 2015.

with an inevitable increase in consumption resulting from higher incomes and generational shifts in consumption attitudes, could exhaust economic surplus as early as within the next decade and a half.[62]

China's economic ascendance to an upper-middle income country came with heavy social and environmental sacrifices and challenges. One such challenge was rebuilding a social welfare system from the ruins of its socialist past, a system compatible with both its market economy system and its rapidly increased income level. In the first two decades of the twenty-first century, China indeed made great strides to retool and rebuild its social welfare system. Monumental challenges remain, however, with an unprecedented, rapid population aging process, and a welfare system that emerged only recently and remained highly fragmented. China's success in realizing its aspiration of becoming a high-income society depends largely on how it can manage the challenges of rising fiscal burdens resulting from rapid population aging and continued economic changes. The two challenges China faces, in building up a functional, sustainable, and equitable social welfare system and in addressing rapid population aging, could be overwhelming in future decades.

Methodological Notes

Humans lead lives as consumers, and as producers for a part. At different stages in the life course, a person's consumption exceeds their labor income. During these ages, a lifecycle deficit occurs. This deficit is made up by transfers, asset income, or savings.

The methodological tool used to estimate these lifecycle deficits and surpluses is based on the one from the National Transfer Accounts (NTA) project.[63] The NTA approach was developed to reflect the economic lifecycle common in all human societies and to evaluate how lifecycle deficits are financed, as expressed in the following equation:

$$C(x) - Y^l(x) = \tau^+(x) - \tau^-(x) + Y^A(x) - S(x)$$

[62] Y. Cai et al. 2004; Y. Cai, Wang, and Shen 2018.

[63] R. Lee and Mason 2011a; United Nations 2013. Beginning in 2003 with seven participating countries, by the year 2020 ninety-seven countries and regions around the world had joined the research consortium, covering 6.6 billion of the world population. Full documentation of the project, with its methodologies, data sources, results, and publications, can be found at: www.ntaccounts.org/web/nta/

The left-hand side of the equation, the difference between consumption $C(x)$ and labor income $Y^l(x)$, is defined as the lifecycle deficit. The right-hand side of the equation represents the three sources that can finance the lifecycle deficit: transfer inflows $\tau^+(x)$ net of transfer outflows $\tau^-(x)$, asset income $Y^A(x)$, and dis-savings minus $S(x)$. This equation holds true both at the individual level and at the national level.

All the components, except for labor income, can be distinguished by private or public sources. For instance, consumption can be private or public, as can transfers. Transfer inflows are comprised of two components: in-kind transfers such as public education and health care spending, and cash transfers such as public pension benefits. To examine the distributional effects of public transfers in education, health care, and pensions, one needs to estimate the receipt of public transfers at different ages and for different income groups on a per capita basis.

One main advantage of the NTA approach in comparison with other methodologies is in its consistency between microprofiles and macro aggregates. The age profiles for each component in the equation constructed from microsurvey data, including each type of public transfer, are first smoothed.[64] They are weighted by population age structure to calculate the national total, which is then adjusted proportionately to match the national macro-control reported by government. By combining micro- and macro-level data, the estimates for public transfers from household survey data for instance are in line with government fiscal spending. To compare across income quartiles, this micro-macro-reconsolidation is done separately for each income quartile according to per capita household income in surveys.

Estimations of lifecycle deficit and transfers rely on both micro- and macro-level data. These age-specific profiles are constructed by relying on the aggregate labor income and consumption data from the official government statistics, distributing across ages with the age-specific labor income and consumption patterns from household surveys. For transfers, micro- or household survey data are used to extract information on enrollment in public schools, public health care service utilization, reimbursement for medical expenses, and public pensions. The survey data for China used to produce the results in this chapter are from China Household Income Project surveys (for 2002 and 2007) and from the China Family Panel Studies (CFPS, for 2010 and 2014). Data from the latter surveys are also used to identify a household's position in per capita

[64] The only exception is for education, as age profiles of public education transfers contain many discontinuities, which are not random but are the product of specific ages entering and leaving schools (United Nations 2013).

income distribution, in this case, by quartile.[65] Government administrative records are used to obtain information on public education spending per student by level of education and by province (public spending level per student varies from province to province), as well as national public spending in education, health care, and pensions.

The micro data from household surveys and macro statistics on public social spending are then combined to estimate the age profile of per capita public transfers for various income groups. For education, age-specific per capita public education transfers are obtained by combining public spending per student by education level and by province with age-, level-, and province-specific school enrollment rates, with the last estimated from survey data. Estimating the age-specific public health care transfers is complicated and more subject to error. Public transfers in health care in NTA are the combination of health care purchased by individuals then reimbursed through public health insurance and government-provided health care.[66] The age profile of reimbursed medical expenditures could be estimated from survey data. Neither survey nor government records, however, offer information on the utilization of government-provided health care by age. We resort therefore to estimation of age-specific out-of-pocket medical expenditures based on survey data as substitute, assuming that medical expenditures are proportional to utilization of public health care. Age profiles of public transfers in pensions are obtained directly from survey responses on pension benefits received.

The NTA approach has the advantages of avoiding missing income and consumption based on normal household surveys, as respondents in household surveys, without the benefit of information on consumption expenditure by the government, may underreport their incomes. It also has the advantage of being able to allocate total labor income and consumption across ages, in order to examine an entire lifecycle.

[65] Xie and Hu 2014. [66] R. Lee and Mason 2011a; United Nations 2013.

7 Aftermath

Together with the European Renaissance and the Industrial Revolution, China's economic boom at the end of the twenty-first century was hailed as one of the three most important economic events of the second millennium.[1] This characterization is certainly not an exaggeration, considering that China's economic ascendance transformed the lives of more than one-fifth of humanity and impacted lives in almost every corner of the earth, from soybean growers in the Americas, iron miners in Australia, and cheese makers in Europe, to safari guides in Africa. The number of shoes made in China in a year could fit on the feet of every other person around the globe, and iPhones assembled in China are held in almost one in every three phone owner's hands.[2]

Just as the Chinese abundance arrived largely by surprise, its four-decade-long ascendance after the late 1970s has been accompanied by twists and turns. Any of the twists and turns could have taken China on a different route and to a different end point. The trajectory could hardly be said to have followed any preordained blueprint.

A heady list of "what ifs" could be asked. Any on the list could have set China on a different path.

For instance, what if rural households had not availed themselves of the opportunity to switch from farming to manufacturing in the 1980s and

[1] Such is the view of Larry Summers, former treasury secretary of the United States of America and president of Harvard University, who reflected in his address to students and faculty at Tsinghua University, China, on October 25, 1999: "I am convinced that when the history of the last twenty years of the twentieth century is written, the end of the Cold War will be the second story in that history. The first story will be about the appearance of emerging markets – nowhere more than China places where, when added up across the world, three billion people live and where, for the first time in human history, we're seeing economic growth at rates where standards of living more than doubled within a single decade, and then do it again, and do it again, and do it again. If these trends continue, I believe they will rank in the economic history of the last millennium only with the Industrial Revolution and with the Renaissance." https://china.usc.edu/chinas-role-21st-century-global-economy-1999

[2] Sam Costello, "Where is the iPhone made? It takes a village to build an iPhone," *Lifewire*, Jan. 27, 2021. www.lifewire.com/where-is-the-iphone-made-1999503

1990s? What if, after the massive 1989 protests and bloody crackdown in Beijing, China's supreme leader Deng Xiaoping had simply faded out of the political scene as an old and diminished 87-year-old instead of reigniting the engines of economic reform with his 1992 tour to Shenzhen? What if China had not given in to the conditions – which were deemed considerably harsher than for other developing countries – to become a member of the WTO in 2001? What if the "9/11" attack had not occurred on the US soil, and China – not Al-Qaeda – was targeted as the United States' most threatening enemy at the start of the twenty-first century? And what if Deng had not institutionalized two generations of collective leadership that ensured political stability for fifteen years after his death? Any one of these events might have delayed, or simply derailed, China's ascendance.

Predicting China's rise has been a centuries-old exercise, not least since the famed phrase attributed to Napoleon fully two centuries ago: "Let China sleep. For when she wakes, the world will tremble."[3] These kinds of predictions have little value, as history has shown that they could be either overly pessimistic or optimistic. After all, it took nearly two centuries after Napoleon's alleged utterance for this phenomenal economic boom to occur. As China emerged from the global financial crisis of 2007–08, and following the success of Beijing's first Olympic Games, China's economy resumed the double-digit annual growth it had seen prior to the crisis. Prominent economists made bold predictions that China was going to maintain the same high growth rate for decades.

Among such distinguished economists were those involved in steering China toward a market-based economy and who were well versed in the literature of economics. One such prominent individual was Chicago-trained economist Justin Yi-fu Lin, who became the first chief economist at the World Bank of Chinese origin. Referencing the rapid economic growth trajectories of several East Asian societies, which had maintained their growth after meeting the per capita income levels that China had achieved by the late 2000s, Lin believed as recently as 2011 that "China has the potential to achieve another 20 years of 8 percent growth."[4]

This optimistic projection of China's continued prosperity was not the most bullish. Six years after some of his fellow Nobel Prize laureates doubted whether China could surpass the United States and the European Union within 75 years, Chicago-based Nobel Prize-winning economist, Robert Fogel, made perhaps the most startlingly optimistic

[3] It is disputable, however, whether the French emperor actually uttered these words. See, for instance: www.napoleon.org/en/history-of-the-two-empires/articles/ava-gardner-china-and-napoleon/

[4] J. Y. Lin 2011.

prediction. He predicted in 2010 that the Chinese economy could continue to grow at an annual rate of 10.8 percent for another 30 years; the size of the economy could reach $123 trillion in those three decades, nearly three times the world's total economic output in 2000, and account for 40 percent of the world's total by 2040.

The prediction was not unfounded. Fogel noted that China invested heavily in education, it still had a third of its rural labor force in reserve, and, importantly, the country benefits from what he called "an open political system." While recognizing the demographic challenges China faces, he also believed that the demographic drag in some European countries was more strenuous as they are plagued by very low fertility.[5]

The reality check could not have come any sooner. Just one year after the publication of Fogel's bold projection, China's economic growth rate started its downward trend. The growth rate in 2010, at 10.64 percent, was the final peak in its spectacular four-decade run. Following 2010, the growth rate was never able to return to this level. Instead, a downward slide was consistent and considerable. By the end of the 2010s, the annual growth rate had dropped to just above 6 percent.[6] China's age of abundance propelled by hyper-growth had reached its end.

It is often tempting to refer to the economic miracle realized as a "model." Just as China's achievements during its earlier socialist experiment could hardly be replicated, neither can its recent transformation. Such is the wisdom of Nicholas Eberstadt, when he observed more than four decades ago after examining China's development under Mao:

> the allure of a "model" is that it is a quick answer. If there are quick answers to age-old problems, then somewhere there must also be great, undiscovered secrets .... The sad fact is that there are no "models of development:" there are only lessons to be learned, both through success and failure, for in the final analysis the solution to each country's problem is unique.[7]

So what are the lessons, unique to China, that could have been learned?

Numerous factors, many often unexpected, could lead a prediction to go astray. Forces believed to have driven China's further economic ascendance could have been underappreciated: the size and composition of China's remaining labor force in the countryside, and the severity of a rapid and sustained population aging process. Some were ignored: the impact of the sharply rising inequality that divides the population, and the

[5] Robert Fogel, "$123,000,000,000,000 China," *Foreign Policy*, Jan. 4, 2010. https://foreignpolicy.com/2010/01/04/123000000000000/. A critique of this view was Nicolas Consonery, "A $123 trillion China? Not likely," *Foreign Policy*, Jan. 7, 2010. https://foreignpolicy.com/2010/01/07/a-123-trillion-china-not-likely/.

[6] https://data.worldbank.org/indicator/NY.GDP.MKTP.KD.ZG?locations=CN

[7] Eberstadt 1979, 31.

challenges in population health due to getting old while getting rich. Others could be reversed quickly, such as the belief in an open political system.

China's ascendance came under a uniquely opportune international environment. As China began to move away from its socialist planned economy system in the late 1970s, other countries under socialist rule – from the former Soviet Union to East European countries – were under the same curse of the system and were experimenting with reforms of their own. Only about a decade later, the former Soviet Union collapsed. The end of the Cold War ushered in a new phase of globalization, with global capital chasing cheap labor and high profits at a scale not seen before. By then, other East Asian societies – Japan and the Four Asian Tigers – started to see their rapid economic growth era running out of steam, and labor costs increased.[8] The window of the demographic dividend, which provided inexpensive labor to support an export push development strategy in these societies, was also closing.[9] China, with its abundant labor supply and an opening and export push policy, served as the largest source of good and cheap labor to marry the global capital.[10]

Above all, China entered an age of abundance due to a unique set of domestic historical conditions that simply cannot be recreated. China benefited from what Daron Acemoglu and James A. Robinson call "inclusive institutions" in their book, *Why Nations Fail*. Yet China, as they note, serves as an illustration that history is not destiny. Replacing extractive institutions with an inclusive one:

> is neither automatic nor easy. A confluence of factors, in particular a critical juncture coupled with a broad coalition of those pushing for reform or other propitious existing institutions, is often necessary for a nation to make strides toward more inclusive institutions. In addition some luck is key, because history always unfolds in a contingent way.[11]

[8] The annual growth rate of GDP for Japan, averaging over 10 percent in the 1960s and over 4 percent in the 1970s and 1980s, dropped to only 1.5 percent in the 1990s. In South Korea, the growth rate, averaging 9.5 and 10.5 percent in the 1960s and 1970s, also slowed down, to 8.9 percent in the 1980s and 7.3 percent in the 1990s. Entering the twenty-first century, the annual growth rate further dropped to 4.7 and 2.6 percent for the first two decades. Calculated based on data from: https://data.worldbank.org/indicator/NY.GDP.MKTP.KD.ZG. In Taiwan, after averaging 8 percent in the 1970s, the annual growth rate dropped to around 5 percent in the 1990s and to around 3.5 percent in the 2000s. Calculated based on data from: https://eng.stat.gov.tw/point.asp.

[9] The demographic dividend estimated for Japan turned negative by the early 1980s and to near zero in Taiwan by the turn of the century (A. Mason 2003; F. Wang and Mason 2008).

[10] See Y. Huang 2002 for a study on China's efforts to attract foreign capital, and Hung 2015 on the global capitalism context in that era.

[11] Acemoglu and Robinson 2012, 426–27.

One People, One History, One Person

China's age of abundance arrived due to a happy confluence of several historically unique factors. As documented in Chapter 2 of this book, on the eve of its economic takeoff, China already had a population that was healthy and literate but at the same time trapped in poverty and divided into two classes. The population, suffering from increasingly severe shortages of consumption goods, a product of the planned economy and aggravated by the Cultural Revolution, was hungry and eager for change. The end of the Cultural Revolution served as a critical historical juncture. The decade-long political disruption worsened economic misery. More importantly, it started an era of questioning not just the economic system but also the political rule. That decade of upheaval prepared the social soil for a grand shift. China was blessed with an extraordinary leader to guide it onto a new path. These historical conditions can be summarized into these three elements: one people, the Chinese population; one history, China's disastrous Cultural Revolution; and one person, Deng Xiaoping, China's post-Mao leader who forcefully and skillfully steered China away from the socialist planned economy. All three were essential for China's age of abundance, and none of them is repeatable.

One People: A Divided and Impoverished Population Eager for Change

The population that built China to prosperity, as examined in this book, was the all-important factor. The importance of the population went far beyond its size or age structure to its physical, educational, and social characteristics. On the eve of China's economic takeoff, the country had an income level that squarely belonged to the low-income countries in the world. Much of China's population lived on the margin of subsistence, if not in downright poverty. Yet, largely due to China's two-and-a-half decades of socialist experiment, the population became quite healthy and essentially literate. On the eve of China's economic ascendance, health levels (measured by mortality under age five) and educational levels (measured by female middle school enrollments) were both clearly comparable to those in middle-income societies at that time. These basic physical and educational attributes were essential for economic productivity. A physically compromised person could not have endured long working hours, and an illiterate migrant would have had difficulty reading road signs to travel the land, or to read and receive instructions for work, whether at an assembly line, on a construction site, or in a restaurant, let alone to start a business and become an entrepreneur.

Besides being healthy and literate, the population was also deeply segregated socially and economically. With a socialist industrialization in the absence of accompanying urbanization, the Chinese population was divided into two categories. The overwhelming majority, up to 80 percent of the population who were confined to the countryside, were condemned to secondary citizenship status within their own country and denied access to state-guaranteed employment, income, housing, and other social benefits from childcare to pensions. These people were hence subjected to exploitation and generated profit for those who could exploit them. When given the freedom to leave collective farming but still unable to move easily to cities, they started producing goods to sell to city residents to increase their incomes, and soon they started nonagricultural production in rural industries. These rural enterprises produced not only goods but also people. They bred many of China's first generation of post-socialist capitalists.

For the overwhelming majority of the rural labor force who failed to become capitalists, they became cheap laborers. They were undervalued not just for their lack of education or work ethic or ability to learn quickly; rather, they were the most fervent believers in personal effort and meritocracy. They saw close-up their compatriots' more privileged lives in the cities and aspired to achieve the same, at whatever cost. Once in the cities, these rural-origin migrants carried with them their secondary citizenship status, relegated to jobs with long hours, low pay, and few benefits and rights. The high quality and low cost of these laborers subsidized their counterparts with an urban household registration status, turning China into a world factory, benefiting consumers and financially benefiting capitalists around the world. Their social status suppressed their earning capacity. Though uniquely important, the members of China's vast and underprivileged rural population were not the only ones who longed for change and who contributed to China's economic miracle. While poverty and hunger for change were particularly acute in the countryside, the desire for change was shared by all in China, as observed by Ronald Coase and Ning Wang:

> Only under the crushing pressure of famine and unemployment was private entrepreneurship allowed some breathing room in rural and urban China. But once the floodgate of private entrepreneurship was opened, a series of marginal revolutions, rather than state-led reform initiatives, brought market forces back to the Chinese economy.[12]

[12] Coase and Wang 2012, 200.

One History: Coming Out of the Cultural Revolution

Crises arising from wars, pandemics, famines, and other sources often serve as historical junctures for major upheavals and transformations in human history. The Black Death of the fourteenth century is one such example of an inflection point. It was believed to have altered the socio-economic pyramid in the societies devastated by the disease; redrawn the global geopolitical map, as with the decline of Spain as an economic and political power; and shifted people's worldview, contributing to the Renaissance.[13]

Economic booms in the twentieth century could similarly trace their roots to profound economic and social upheavals. One such example is the "Great Leap Forward" of the US economic growth between 1920 and 1970, and the other, post-war prosperity in Europe, where World War II led to reconstruction and prosperity.[14]

As for the high growth period in the United States, Robert Gordon singled out the two most consequential events in that country's history:

> both the Great Depression and World War II directly contributed to the Great Leap. Had there been no Great Depression, there would probably have been no New Deal with its NIRA [National Industrial Recovery Act] and Wagner Act that promoted unionization and that both directly and indirectly contributed to a sharp rise in real wages and a shrinking in average weekly hours.[15]

The historical juncture for China was the end of the Great Proletarian Cultural Revolution. Lasting between 1966 and 1976, the mass movement consumed more than a third of Mao's rule, which had begun in 1949. It set in motion a mode of "continuous revolution" and self-destruction in China. The often-violent revolution decimated the Chinese state machinery and bureaucratic apparatus. Dispensing with the roles of the Politburo and the Central Committee of the Chinese Communist Party, a "Central Cultural Revolution Group" in Beijing became the most powerful political body. Between January 1967 and September 1968 – in less than two years – "revolutionary committees" replaced all twenty-nine provincial governments across China.

[13] McNeill 1976 (196): "The shift from medieval to renaissance cultural values, needless to say, did not depend on the plague alone; yet the plague, and the generally successful way city authorities managed to react to its ravages, surely contributed something to the general transformation of the European sensibility."

[14] Judt 2005.

[15] Higher wages and shorter working hours helped boost productivity growth. The roles of WWII were different, in that war time production miracles "taught firms and workers to operate more efficiently," and the new capital installed during the war period laid the foundation for increasing productive efficiency both during the after the war; Gordon 2016, 18–19.

The purge and replacement were wide and thorough. Nearly three-quarters of the active members and alternate members of the Central Committee were removed or criticized by 1968. In 1969, the newly formed Communist Party's Central Committee had only 53 of its 279 members, less than one-fifth, as carryovers from the previous Central Committee.[16] China's highest level officials, who fought along Mao to establish the People's Republic and to govern a new China under Communist rule, fell victim to Mao's revolution. Mao's two designated successors perished and became domestic enemies: one died without proper medical care in a detention room and the other in a plane crash in Mongolia. Many officials were physically abused, some beaten to death, and many more were publicly humiliated in mass criticism rallies and parades.

The Cultural Revolution resulted in further economic stagnation on top of an already failing economy and widespread social chaos. Consumer goods, in short supply due to the planned economy and population growth, became even more scarce; food rationing in cities became increasingly widespread and stringent. Lack of employment opportunities led the government to send up to 18 million urban youths to the countryside to be "reeducated by poor and lower-middle (class) peasants."[17] No less devastating, the ten-year class struggles tore the social fabric of the nation, pitting the public against officials, students against teachers, children against parents, and villagers against their neighbors. During this revolution, tens of millions of individuals were persecuted or affected, and millions lost their lives.[18]

At the close of this tumultuous decade, ending with Mao's death, the Chinese people were profoundly disoriented, disappointed, and utterly exhausted. They yearned for change, for a life with greater material prosperity, social stability, and human decency. They were ultimately driven by a deep fear. As William Overholt summarized it, "People are desperate; they fear total social collapse, and they often fear that families will not have enough to eat. Hence they are prepared to follow leadership that they find credible even at the cost of extraordinary social upheaval." And, at the same time, "Pervasive societal fear stimulates leaders to take great risks and people to support leaders who take great risks and impose otherwise unacceptable social stresses."[19] Deng Xiaoping, the Chinese

[16] MacFarquhar and Schoenhals 2006, 293. Of the 45 first and second party secretaries of China's major regions, a level above the province, only 9 were known to be active (Chai 1968).

[17] Bernstein 1977.

[18] Walder and Su 2003; MacFarquhar and Schoenhals 2006; Su 2011; Walder 2014; 2019.

[19] Overholt 2018, 9–10.

leader who guided China out of the Cultural Revolution devastation, summarized it himself: "It [the Cultural Revolution] looked like a bad thing. But ultimately it was a good thing. It made people think, to realize the problems we had. We could implement the policies in the 1970s and 1980s exactly because we learned the lessons from the Cultural Revolution."[20] The Cultural Revolution was a historical juncture, as it was "a terrible era, but out of which has emerged a saner, more prosperous, and perhaps one day a more democratic China."[21]

One Person: Deng Xiaoping

For China, the Cultural Revolution also prepared the stage for the return of the man who led China into the age of abundance. If the Cultural Revolution was the historical juncture, Deng Xiaoping was China's good fortune. A leader with vision, determination, and unparalleled political experience, Deng was a unique historical figure who simply cannot be replicated. Deng's brilliance was not that he initiated private household farming that set in motion rural reforms and agricultural output growth in the late 1970s and early 1980s, nor was it that he anticipated the mushrooming of rural industries that made China a major exporter in the 1980s and early 1990s. His brilliance was that he did not block such initiatives. Instead, he appreciated deep in his mind the value of such bottom-up initiatives. He gathered support and intervened at critical moments to allow and to guide such experiments to spread. He understood China with a uniquely worldly view, a view that neither his predecessors possessed nor his successors possess.

Deng's unique personal history made him a man with worldly views, deep conviction, and unswerving determination. Like Mao, Deng joined the revolution early and at a very young age, survived the Long March, and commanded the revolutionary army to victories. His credentials as a communist were indisputable. Yet, notably, he traveled to France at the age of fifteen, spending six years there, followed by a year in the Soviet Union. Those early experiences in Deng's formative years likely imbued him with a worldview that other leaders, such as Mao himself, who never left China until in his fifties, could never have formed. During his career within the Communist Party, Deng was purged three times, the last time being only months before Mao's death, with all his positions stripped. Deng had been exiled to a tractor factory in a remote province earlier in the Cultural Revolution as the "Number Two Capitalist Roader" in the

[20] Interview with Mike Wallace, "60 Minutes," Sept. 2, 1986. Zhonggong zhongyang wenxian yanjiushi 2004, 1133. Translation by author.

[21] MacFarquhar and Schoenhals 2006, 462.

country. Over four years, he pondered China's future as he bathed and cared for his eldest son, who had become paralyzed after jumping out of a window at his university under the pressure of his father being criticized.

China was fortunate to have Deng because he was not only a man of conviction and determination but also a man of unmatched political experience and competence. As noted by Ezra Vogel in his biography of Deng, "It is doubtful that anyone else then had the combination of authority, depth and breadth of experience, strategic sense, assurance, personal relationships, and political judgement needed to manage China's transformation with comparable success."[22] More than any other leaders of his generation, Deng served closely with Mao as well as with Zhou Enlai, China's first and longest-serving premier. Under Mao, Deng managed party affairs as secretary-general of the Chinese Communist Party prior to the Cultural Revolution. In the mid-1970s, prior to Mao's death and Deng's own third and last fall from power in 1976, Deng was Premier Zhou Enlai's right-hand man, overseeing domestic economic as well as military reorganization and international affairs.

No other leader had such stature and experience in the party as Deng. Others with ideas and vision lacked political skill. Those with political skill lacked vision and determination. Deng's masterful knowledge, personal networks, and political skill enabled him to form alliances and to delegate to surrogates. His grip over political power was so self-assured that when he visited the United States in early 1979 as China's supreme leader to normalize diplomatic relations, he was content to carry the official title of vice-premier. However, to lead China away from socialism, Deng could not act alone. The devastation of the Cultural Revolution afforded Deng the opportunity to form alliances to rally society.

All three of these historical conditions – a population willing and able to work hard; a decade of traumatizing turmoil that made people long for normalcy, with a willingness to compromise and to experiment; and a leader with stature and skill – were essential for realizing China's phenomenal age of abundance. In the absence of any of these, China's history in those four decades would not have been the same. All three conditions are now long gone.

Headwinds

All fast-growing low-income societies enter a phase of slow growth once the forces driving high growth dissipate.[23] These common forces, all

[22] Vogel 2011, 695.

[23] "Rather than having to pioneer new technologies, late-developing countries can import know-how from abroad. They can reap productivity gains simply by shifting workers from underemployment in agriculture to export-oriented manufacturing, where those

inevitable, are demographic, technological, economic, and social. They include a dwindling rural labor force transfer and supply, a shift from manufacturing to service, declining returns to capital investment, cost of indigenous technological development, and increased spending on social welfare benefits.[24] Moreover, as noted by William Overholt – who wrote in 1993 foretelling China to be a new superpower and again in 2022 warning of the end of China's economic success – "the economy had moved from the era of simplicity to an era of complexity."[25] The rather simplistic approaches to generate rapid economic growth, common to successful East Asian economies, are no longer sufficient or even useful in the era of complexity. With the arrival of China's age of abundance and its rising global economic power, the world has also begun to witness unprecedented paranoia of the "China threat," driven by economic concerns as well as domestic politics, in particular in the world's two largest economic powers, the United States and China. China can no longer count on the once favorable international economic environment that was so crucial for its economic rise.[26]

A rapid increase in income and standard of living is typical during the historical transformation from an agrarian economy and a rural-based society to an industrial and post-industrial economy and an urbanized society. Such was the historical experience seen not just in European economies and in the United States but also elsewhere. The experiences of Japan and South Korea, two of China's neighboring countries, are the closest references (Figure 4.1). Yet, having lived through the economic miracles, the per capita income growth rate slowed down substantially once their rapid urbanization was completed. In Japan, for instance, the average per capita income growth rate between 1981 and 2020 was only 1.45 percent, compared to 5.76 percent between 1965 and 1980. In South Korea, it dropped from 7.65 between 1965 and 2000 to 2.85 percent between 2001 and 2020.[27] There is no compelling reason that China can escape from these gravitational forces. To the contrary, into the

imported technologies are utilized. With young generations that are presently engaged in saving enjoying higher incomes than elderly dissavers, such countries are able to finance high levels of investment." Eichengreen, Park, and Shin 2012, 43.

[24] "Eventually the pool of underemployment in rural labor is drained. The share of employment in manufacturing peaks, and growth comes to depend more heavily on the difficult process of raising productivity in the service sector. A larger capital stock means more depreciation, requiring more saving to make this good. As the economy approaches the technological frontier, it must transition from relying on imported technology to indigenous innovation." Ibid., 43.

[25] Overholt 1993; 2018, 52. [26] Hung 2022.

[27] GDP per capita data growth rates calculated from: https://data.worldbank.org/indicator/NY.GDP.PCAP.KD.ZG.

2010s, the core forces that drove China's spectacular economic boom had already begun to weaken, if not disappear.

Just as China's economic boom was not preordained, however, one should also exercise caution before joining the chorus proclaiming China's demise. Even with all the headwinds that the country inevitably faces, there are still many more unknowns than knowns. China today not only has a well-fed and clothed but also an increasingly highly educated population. In 1982, when China conducted its first census after the Cultural Revolution, college-educated individuals were almost impossible to find across its vast landmass: they numbered less than one in a hundred among young people under 35 (Table 7.1). College enrollment capacity prior to the Cultural Revolution was highly limited, available only to a tiny share of the population, and the Cultural Revolution certainly did not help, as shown by the 1982 census. The share of population with a college education actually dropped from 2 percent among those aged 40–44 to less than 0.25 percent.

With China's age of abundance, its population now can enjoy a level of material comfort unprecedented in its history, and they can also afford and have access to most available educational opportunities, though such access is by no means equal to all. The share of population with a college education gradually and steadily improved after 1982, reaching over 5 percent by the year 2000, and 8 percent for those in the youngest age group. The first two decades of the new millennium saw an explosive increase (see Table 6.2 for enrollment numbers). By 2020, over half of

Table 7.1 *Educational transformation of working-age population, China, 1982–2020*

	Year				
Age group	1982	1990	2000	2010	2020
20–24	0.24%	3.13%	8.13%	24.35%	51.90%
25–29	0.62%	3.20%	6.54%	20.00%	40.38%
30–34	0.69%	2.28%	5.52%	14.32%	32.43%
35–39	1.33%	2.21%	5.41%	10.12%	27.19%
40–44	2.01%	2.61%	3.92%	7.50%	18.62%
45–49	1.49%	3.59%	3.23%	7.04%	12.09%
50–54	0.85%	4.49%	3.17%	4.91%	8.01%
55–59	0.56%	3.26%	3.64%	3.90%	6.94%

Note and sources: Percentage of population with college education. China Population Census, various years.

those in their early 20s already had a college education (Table 7.1). Given expansion in enrollment capacities and declining births, the share of college-educated young people is set to increase further in the decades to come. These young college-educated individuals are the new drivers of a post-manufacturing economy, and they are also the transformers of a new society, from their private lives to their participation in public sphere activities.

Countries around the world face similar headwinds in their economic growth, most notably heightened inequality and unprecedented demographic changes. In his study of the rise and fall of the United States' economic growth after 1870, Robert Gordon traces the rise of the US economy using consumption data, an approach used in this book as well. The United States' economic growth, Gordon argues, benefited from great inventions mostly prior to the 1920s. The economic revolution in the "special century" between 1870 and 1970, in Gordon's words, "was unique in human history, unrepeatable because so many of its achievements could happen only once."[28] It is not repeatable because many of the great inventions, from power (electricity) and transportation means (motor vehicles, railways, and jet planes), to medical technologies (X-ray, antibiotics, and cancer treatments) were all from that century. A somewhat similar observation was made by Vaclav Smil, that the four scientific and engineering advances defining a modern civilization, in energies, prime movers, materials, and information flows, all took place between 1865 and 1914. Electronic computing, which has taken place since then, "has made many products and processes cheaper and most of them also more reliable and more convenient to use. But it has not changed the physical and biophysical fundamentals of energy and food production, the two great pillars of any civilization."[29]

China faces both these common and its own unique constraints. The abundant supply of young labor, made cheap by China's political system, could no longer be sustained. Contrary to expectations, China's unfinished urbanization is trapped in its own contradictions. Instead of one, there have been three concurrent urbanization processes manifesting economic constraints as well as social segregation: residential, social, and economic. The unfinished urbanization is therefore unlikely to be a major source of future growth, as was the case in the first two decades of the twenty-first century. Inequalities formed during China's economic boom have already moved from income to wealth, becoming deep-rooted and intergenerational. Accelerated aging, with many families weakened by the ill-conceived one-child policy that was launched after fertility had

[28] Gordon 2016, 1. [29] Smil 2013, 272.

already dropped to a low level, puts increased pressure both on health care and on a still inadequate and highly segregated pension system. With lessons from the Cultural Revolution long forgotten and erased, the once celebrated open political system that allowed entrepreneurship and innovation is shutting down quickly. Though the population is living in material comfort, the political system is succumbing to its old days of rigidity and decay.

Three Urbanizations

In the absence of unexpected scientific and technological revolutions as occurred in the previous era, future growth in China, as elsewhere, will depend largely on current forces. For China, the first candidate is its unfinished urbanization. Could China count on continued urbanization as an engine of economic growth? Industrialization *with* urbanization, a path taken by all countries reaching high living standards, is also an essential characteristic of China's economic ascendance, though with its own characteristics.

China's age of abundance came with its own age of urbanization. At the start of the sustained economic ascendance, the share of China's urban population stood at only 18 percent, a share that had stayed unchanged for a decade, between 1968 and 1978. In the four decades between 1980 and 2020, the share of the Chinese population defined as urban more than tripled, from only 20 percent to nearly 64 percent (Figure 7.1, middle line). It took China only 30 years to increase its share of the urban population from 20 to 50 percent between 1980 and 2010, a process that took Japan 35 years, from 1920 to 1955, and the United States 60 years, from 1860 to 1920.[30]

China's seemingly compressed urbanization process in the last two decades, however, disguises its entire seventy-year history. It was not until 2011, more than three decades after China's reopening to the outside world, that China could finally claim itself to be an industrialized society. This milestone is no longer measured by the composition of economic output. As far back as in 1978, or even the 1960s, China's industrial output already made up close to half of the total economic output calculated.[31] China then, however, was by no means an industrialized society. The overwhelming majority of the population still lived

[30] www.census.gov/history/www/programs/geography/urban_and_rural_areas.html. Also in Smil 2013, 337; Gordon 2016, 98. The urbanization level in Japan was reported at 18 percent in 1920.

[31] The industrial sector accounted for 46.8 percent of total economic output and agriculture only 35.4 percent. In 1960, agricultural output counted for 46.3 percent, before dropping to the lowest share in 1968, 31.1 percent (SYB 1986).

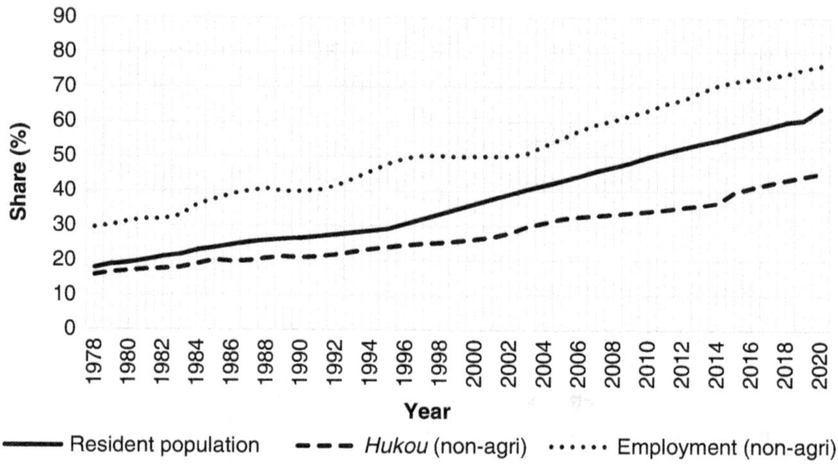

Figure 7.1 China's three urbanizations, 1978–2020
Sources: Residential urban: SYB 2019, table 2–1; Employment: SYB 2019, table 4–2; *Hukou*: National Commission of Health and Birth Control 2015, table 14-1, 1978–2014, and annual statistical communique, National Bureau of Statistics, 2020: https://finance.sina.com.cn/china/gncj/2021-05-11/doc-ikmxzfmm1763811.shtml

and worked in the countryside. In 2011, for the first time in Chinese history, over 50 percent of all the population lived in urban areas. Sensing urbanization tracked with China's prosperity, policymakers in China placed their hope of continued economic prosperity on China's unfinished urbanization, as more than 35 percent of Chinese were still counted as rural by 2020.[32]

Counting on continued urbanization as an engine to sustain China's economic growth appears to be a misplaced bet. The abundant outflows of young people from the countryside have already largely dried up, following more than two decades of out-migration and a sustained fertility decline many decades over. Instead of a continued new supply from rural China, hundreds of millions of new urban residents, many of them still migrants, now need to be treated the same as the locals, to receive the same rights and benefits as the old urban residents.

[32] So much so that in 2012, Premier Li Keqiang asked the World Bank to collaborate with China's Development Research Center of the State Council for a comprehensive and elaborative study. Many, though not all, of the recommendations of the report seem to have influenced policymaking since the report's publication in 2014. https://elibrary.worldbank.org/doi/abs/10.1596/978-1-4648-0206-5.

China hence faces not just one, but three concurrent urbanizations. Along with the officially published statistic of urbanization, which is based on residence (residential), are two other urbanization processes: one social, defined by a person's type of household registration; and the other economic, by their type of employment, whether in or outside the farming sector. Not all residents classified as urban have the same social status. Among those left to be urbanized, or the labor force to be transferred out of the countryside, the labor pool available for transfer from the countryside to the cities is vastly overestimated.

Measured by types of economic activities, in 2020 China no longer had 40 percent of the population left to be urbanized. By the late 2010s, as shown in Figure 7.1, the number of people employed in urban China already surpassed that in rural China.[33] Nationwide, as measured by employment type, nearly 80 percent of the labor force was reported to be employed in non-farm sectors.[34] The share of China's labor force employed off the farm had increased sharply in three decades: from 30 percent in 1979, to 50 percent in 2000, 63 percent in 2010, and close to 80 percent by the late 2010s (Figure 7.1, top line).

Who was still left in farming? The characteristics of those remaining in farming reveal that China's massive migration and urbanization era is at its end. The remaining rural labor force is disproportionately older and female. These characteristics were already evident by the late 2010s, as reported in China's 2020 census. Compared with 1990, when over 60 percent of young males and over 70 percent of females were in the farming sector, the shares dropped sharply over a period of three decades, to only around 10 percent by 2020. The share of those employed in the farming sector was above 50 percent for females aged 55 and over, and over 30 percent for males (Figure 7.2).

Farming is not only getting older; it is also increasingly a female-dominant profession. The sex ratio of the rural labor force, calculated as females over males, shows a clear sign of feminization of farming labor. At every age from the late 20s, more females than males remained in farming. The ratio of females to males in 2020 was about 1.2 for the 40–44 age group and rose to above 1.5 by age 50–54 (Figure 7.2). While young men and women left the countryside to escape farming, older women continued to shoulder the responsibility for farming and caring for other family members as well.

[33] In 2018, 434.19 million people were employed in cities, compared with 341.67 million in rural areas (SYB 2019, table 4–1).

[34] The China Population Census 2020 reported that only 20.56 percent of employed persons were in agriculture-related sectors (calculated from table 4–5 of the census tabulations).

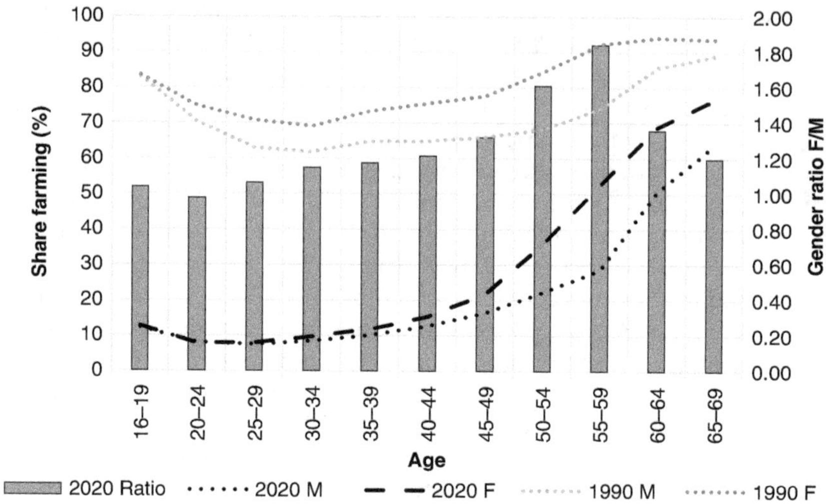

Figure 7.2 Leaving farming: share of employment in farming, 1990 and 2020
Sources: Calculated from China Population Census 1990, table 6–9; and 2020, table 4–5.

Four decades of sustained fertility decline in China's countryside will further shrink the future labor force pool from rural China. Fertility measured by total fertility rate was at 6.38 in 1970 and plummeted to 2.48 in 1980. Rural fertility fluctuated in the 1980s and remained at the same level in 1990 as in 1980. Along with massive out-migration, by the mid-1990s rural fertility dropped quickly to below the level of replacement of about two births per couple. In the first two decades of the twenty-first century, rural fertility further dropped to below 1.5.[35] Combined, low fertility and a smaller population of women of childbearing age resulting from earlier fertility decline, promises lead to even smaller birth cohorts from rural China in the decades to come.

Unlike the shrinking pool of out-migrants from rural China, the stock of migrants already in Chinese cities pose a different set of challenges. China's urban population, over 60 percent or 850 million, are still classified into two categories. In 2019, 26.8 percent of China's urban residents, or about 230 million, still did not have a household registration at their place of residence (Figure 7.1, bottom line).[36] These were the rural migrants in

[35] Whyte, Wang, and Cai 2015, fig. 2.
[36] The reported number of people with "inconsistencies between locations of residence and household registrations" was even larger, close to 300 million in 2018 (SYB 2019, table 2–3).

cities who still held what is known as the "agricultural" household registration status or a status of "nonagricultural" from a different locale. Over China's recent urbanization process, the gap between this "hukou" urbanization and "residential" urbanization has widened. If measured by residents with a local or "nonagricultural" household registration, China's urbanization level at the end of 2010s was at 45.4 percent, not around 65 percent.

Despite the widening gap between social and residential urbanization, a substantial number of Chinese have changed their household registration from "agricultural" to "nonagricultural" status over the four decades since 1978. The change was especially rapid between 2000 and 2019. Due to out-migration and administrative reclassification, in the short five years between 2000 and 2005, 93,976 Chinese villages disappeared, nearly 13 percent of the total in 2000.[37] Between 2000 and 2019, 367 million people, more than the entire population of the United States, became new urban residents. Nearly three-quarters of them, 274 million, became urban residents due to changed household registration status. Most of these new urban residents, however, dwell in townships and small- to medium-sized cities; large cities are still mostly off-limits to them.

Even China's recently arrived urban residents remain unable to shed their secondary citizenship status. Reintegration of the two categories of the Chinese population, those with and without nonagricultural household registration status, has been a long and arduous process. It began with opening city gates for rural residents to sell their products, to move into small townships in the mid-1980s, and to obtain a resident permit in the larger cities. Even by the late 1990s, changing household registration for rural residents was limited to small townships. The first major relaxation did not come until 1998, when the central government allowed a few categories of individuals to change their registration from agricultural to nonagricultural status in cities, not just in small townships.[38] In the 2000s, rural residents were allowed to change their household registration to towns and small cities. Medium-sized cities (0.5–1 million residents), and to some extent large cities (1–5 million), relaxed these rigid restrictions only in the 2010s. In 2014, nearly six decades after China institutionalized the urban-rural classifications, China's State Council announced a unified resident permit system nationwide, eliminating the agricultural designation and more importantly, promising to offer the same social services to all long-term residents in their places of registration.

[37] SYB 2006, table 13–3.

[38] These allowances included family unions, businesses, and purchasing urban commercial housing, which at the start of the urban housing reform needed buyers with money. https://baike.baidu.com/item/户籍改革 (*hukou* reforms)

For China, the true challenge may no longer be in whether a person is classified as agricultural or nonagricultural. Nor is it in how to further increase the share of the urban population, drawing from the dwindling share of the labor force that is still in the countryside. The true challenge is how to "digest," or to incorporate, the hundreds of millions of residents in cities with a secondary citizenship status. As of 2020, 376 million Chinese were still counted as "floating population," namely having a place of residence and a place of household registration in different locales. Moreover, 261 millions of these new urban residents still did not have a "nonagricultural" or urban household registration status. That's more than 1 in 4 and 1 in 5.5 persons in China, respectively.[39]

For the more than 250 million Chinese without an urban residential status in 2020, most of them live in cities where many social benefits are still out of their reach. Among these migrants were 135 million migrant laborers working in Chinese cities,[40] double the size of the employees in state- or collectively owned organizations (60.87 million) and twice the size of those in limited liability companies (65.55 million). As of 2021, policy changes dictated that cities with a population of up to 3 million open registration for newcomers without restrictions. The state still deemed it necessary, however, to continue residential designation in cities with populations greater than 5 million. To qualify for household registration status changes in these cities, one is judged by a point-system, a system modeled after the system countries such as Canada or Australia use for international migration.[41] Combined, with nearly 300 million residents in 21 cities with a population of 7 million and more, in 2020 these superlarge cities still encompassed about one-third of all Chinese urban residents.[42] Rural migrants who reside in these large cities are still outsiders, and they are not entitled to the same social services as residents with a local registration status.

Vast regional disparities in social benefits impede this last stage of Chinese social reintegration. Social benefits remain highly localized. In 2010, for instance, public spending per primary school student in China's richest city, Shanghai, was 7.5 times (750% greater) that in the larger and poorer province of Henan. Public spending per preschooler was 20 times more in Shanghai than in the city of Chongqing.[43] In 2020, per student public expenditure for middle school education in Shanghai and Beijing was 2.4 and 3.7 times the national average, respectively, compared with

[39] Shares calculated from China Population Census 2020 reports. https://finance.sina.com.cn/china/gncj/2021-05-11/doc-ikmxzfmm1763811.shtml
[40] www.stats.gov.cn/tjsj/zxfb/202004/t20200430_1742724.html
[41] An example to illustrate this point-system is in Zhang 2012.
[42] http://finance.people.com.cn/n1/2021/0923/c1004-32234160.htm
[43] Shen, Wang, and Cai 2018b, 149.

less than 70 percent of the national average in the provinces of Liaoning, Guizhou, and Yunnan.[44] In the same year, per person pension fund payouts in Shanghai and Beijing were 7.8 and 3.3 times the national average, respectively, compared with less than 80 percent of the national average in nearly ten provinces.[45]

China's fiscal system distributes funds locally, putting the burden of providing social benefits on local governments. In 2020, for instance, local government revenue made up only slightly over half of total government revenue (both local and central governments), at 54.7 percent. Yet almost all social service expenditures are local: 95.4 percent for education, 96.6 percent for social security and unemployment, and 98.2 percent for health care.[46] A substantial share of local government revenue, 25.4 percent, came from "non-taxation" revenue, such as land sales. Such revenue is less subject to transfers to other locales. To remove the role of *hukou* in segregating the population and perpetuating inequality, and to facilitate mobility, basic social services will have to be nationalized. The equitable distribution of social benefits across Chinese provinces and cities is a daunting challenge. It will require both vast financial resources and savvy political courage and will become increasingly challenging as the central government's coffers tighten and as local governments' revenues dry up.[47]

Inequality: Resetting Starting Lines

At the start of China's ascendance to material prosperity, Deng Xiaoping both incentivized and assured the Chinese public with his comforting words in 1978, "let some people get rich first."[48] As a consummate politician and a pragmatist, he resorted to the same political wisdom as he used to deal with political reforms and the later return of Hong Kong: letting those in the future figure out the solutions should they be needed. Deng did not and could not say what would happen after some people had gotten rich.

Four decades after the gate to richness was let open, it was not just a few Chinese who became rich. The population as a whole has reached an upper-middle income level, measured by global standards. Some have achieved an affluence beyond their wildest dreams. Just as the pace of

44 www.gov.cn/zhengce/zhengceku/2021-12/01/content_5655192.htm
45 Calculated from *China Social Statistical Yearbook 2021*, table 7–4. www.tjcn.org/tjnj/SSS/40398.html
46 Calculated based on SYB 2021, tables 7–2 and 7–3.
47 Revenues from land sales, for decades a major source of local government revenue for all sorts of spending from infrastructure to social services, were centralized in 2021. Cheng Siwei and Luo Meihan, "China moves to take collection of land sales income out of local government hands," *Caixin Global*, Jun. 7, 2021. https://bit.ly/402SwjB
48 Yang 1998, 390.

prosperity far exceeded expectations, so did the rise of inequality. China's record-setting economic ascendance was paired with a yawning income gap.[49] Within two decades after the race to richness began, China also became one of the most unequal countries in the world. Measured by the Gini index of income inequality, the inequality level rose from 0.3 in 1980 to more than 0.45 in 2002 (Figure 7.3). China's income inequality level surpassed the level in high-income societies and rivaled the highest in the world, found in Latin America and sub-Saharan Africa. As summarized in a study by Piketty, Yang, and Zucman, "(T)he top 10 percent income share rose from 27 percent to 41 percent between 1978 and 2015; the bottom 50 percent share dropped from 27 percent to 15 percent. China's inequality levels, previously approximating Nordic countries, are now approaching US levels."[50] In 2021, it was estimated that the share of the top 10 percent of individuals in total wealth reached nearly 70 percent. Between 1995 and 2021, the share of personal wealth of the bottom 50 percent of the population more than halved, from 16 percent to merely 6 percent.[51]

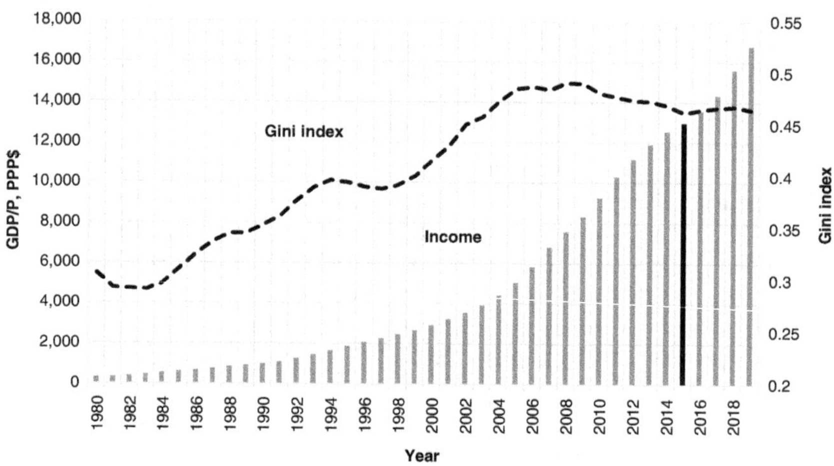

Figure 7.3 Growth with inequality, China, 1980–2018
Sources: Income, GDP per capita, PPP (current international $), 1980–89: IMF Economic Outlook 2016; post-1989: WDI; Gini: SYB, www.unicef.cn/figure-27-national-gini-index-20032017, www.ceicdata.com/zh-hans/china/resident-income-distribution/gini-coefficient (2018, 2019)

49 Sicular et al. 2020; F. Wang 2007.
50 Piketty, Yang, and Zucman 2019, 2469.
51 Mo 2022.

Improvements in standards of living certainly were not evenly shared throughout China's vast society. China's premier Li Keqiang drove home this point at the closing session of the annual People's Congress in June 2020. Dampening the Chinese pride in the fact that it had become an upper-middle income society with a per capita income of close to $10,000, Premier Li's reminder that 40 percent of China's population, slightly over 600 million people, earned less than $2,000 annually, created quite a stir.[52]

Into the twenty-first century, China's economic inequality also underwent a fundamental transformation. First, inequality spread throughout society more evenly, reducing the sources of inequality from socialist legacies. Rising inequality in the early phase of China's transformation followed closely the legacies of its socialist past. A large share of the rising inequality was due to increased inequality between urban and rural areas (which first narrowed then expanded), across geographic regions, industries, and often, work organizations. Inequalities were associated with one's identity in society: where a person was born and where a person was employed. By 2000, nearly half of all observed income inequality among Chinese urban employees could be accounted for by location of residence, sector of employment, and notably work organizations, not personal attributes such as educational attainment, gender, and age. These inequalities were categorical inequalities.[53]

By the late 2000s, after peaking at close to 0.5 on the Gini index, overall income inequality started to level off to a moderate decline (Figure 7.3). This reversal, however, should not be interpreted simply as a positive indicator. Along with increased geographic and labor market mobility, inequality due to categorical sources such as geographic regions declined.[54] At the same time, that reduction was more than offset by increases in within-category inequality. Households and individuals in other words are more likely to experience the same economic inequalities regardless of where they live and work.

More importantly, by the turn of the twenty-first century, economic inequality in China had quickly shifted from income to wealth inequality, a form of inequality that is much more structural. Unlike income

[52] Sidney Leng, "China confirms more than 40 per cent of population survived on just US$141 per month in 2019," *South China Morning Post*, Jun. 15, 2020. https://bit.ly/46UbtqF. A later clarification by a leading scholar of income inequality, Li Shi, gives the number of people with less than $2,000 annual income in 2019 at 310 million, or only about 22 percent of China's population. About half of China's population, 710 million people, were estimated to have an annual income level lower than $4,000. Li Shi, "Shouru wenti yingxiang zhong di shouru jieceng xiaofei," *Caixin*, Sept. 3, 2020. https://opinion.caixin.com/2020-09-03/101600664.html.

[53] F. Wang 2007. [54] Sicular et al. 2020, 24–25.

inequality, vastly increased inequality in wealth resets starting lines for the population and establishes a structural basis that transmits inequality across generations.[55] Between 2002 and 2013, for instance, household wealth was estimated to have increased at a rate of 17 percent annually, far outpacing income and GDP growth. The Gini index of wealth inequality was estimated at between 0.63 and 0.72, also far higher than that in income.[56] By the early 2010s, the richest 1 percent of Chinese were estimated to own one-third of all the wealth, compared to the bottom 20 percent owning only 1 percent. The ratio between the top 10 percent and the bottom 10 percent of the population in household wealth reached 33:1 in 2012, compared to the income ratio of 13:1.[57] As with income inequality, China's level of wealth inequality was approaching that of the United States. However, unlike the United States, where wealth and wealth inequality took decades if not centuries to accumulate, China achieved all of these (high inequality levels) in just a couple of decades.

In a country where just a half-century ago private wealth was unheard of, China has become the land of millionaires and billionaires. At the start of the century, in 2004, there were only three reported billionaires in China. About a decade later, that number rose sharply, to 213, making China the country with the second largest number of billionaires in the world. That number was still not quite half of the number of billionaires in the United States, which had 536.[58] By early 2021, the number of Chinese billionaires increased to 626, a number not far behind the United States, which counted 724. China had nearly 500 more billionaires than India, third on the list of billionaires globally. Japan, China's neighbor and the third largest economy in the world, had only 40.[59] With a per capita income level that was still no more than one-quarter of the United States', China produced nearly the same number of billionaires in a couple of decades as the country that has had centuries of capitalist economic growth and is known as one of the most unequal societies in the world.[60]

At the bottom of Chinese society, the picture is entirely different. China's march toward prosperity came with hundreds of millions of people leaving abject poverty. That success, however, has not and will

[55] F. Wang 2019. [56] Sicular et al. 2020, 26. [57] Y. Xie and Jin 2015.

[58] F. Wang 2019, 28.

[59] Giacomo Tognini, "The countries with the most billionaires 2021," *Forbes*, Apr. 6, 2021. https://bit.ly/3QljMGF

[60] Per capita income (PPP) in 2019 reported by the World Bank for China was $16,790 and for the United States was $66,080. WDI. By current US dollars, the difference is more than six times ($65,297 for the United States versus $10,216 for China). https://data.worldbank.org/indicator/NY.GDP.PCAP.CD?locations=US

not be sufficient to eliminate relative poverty, a form of poverty that continues to cripple human development for a large share of the Chinese population. One segment of this population is the tens of millions of children in rural China, who make up the majority of China's next generation, and who are eating better, getting taller, and receiving more years of schooling in an environment much better than their parents' generation. A large number of them, however, has also grown up with early-childhood adversities. Scott Rozelle, a leading scholar of rural development, estimates that in the early 2010s, about 60 percent of rural Chinese elementary school children suffered from either anemia, uncorrected poor vision, or intestinal worm infection. These early life adversities affecting cognitive development, learning, and physical health have lifelong consequences.[61]

Many of the children in rural China, offspring of migrants, were left behind by their parents. China's great age of migration, driven by its urban-rural two systems legacy, created a "left-behind" generation of children. By the mid-2010s, the estimated number of these children, defined as those residing in a village or township but not living with both parents, was close to 70 million. Combined with the over 30 million children of migrants in the cities, the number equaled 100 million. In 2015, these children made up 40 percent of all children in China.[62] Children were "left-behind" either with one parent, or typically, with grandparents and other relatives, when their parents went to work in factories, construction sites, retail shops, restaurants, security details, and janitorial services in cities. The parents sought more plentiful employment opportunities with better wages than were found in farming. Migrant parents could not bring their children with them due to their low wages, lack of social benefits, and the high cost of living in cities. Children of migrants did not have access to city schools until the late 1990s. Even after compulsory education was extended beyond nine years, a migrant child still had to return to their place of origin to take exams for entrance to college. While not conclusive, a wealth of studies reported detrimental effects of children growing up in the absence of their parent or parents: from lifelong cognitive development, to health status, to educational outcomes.[63]

Like their parents, China's left-behind children were not meant to be left in the countryside forever. Rather, these children never learned farming and departed the countryside for cities after completing their junior high school education. As new migrants, they inherited outsider status from their parents, becoming the second generation of outsiders. Whereas their parents' generation worked in factories and construction sites, many of these second-generation migrants have taken up platform

[61] Rozelle and Hell 2020; Murphy 2020, 109. [62] Chan 2019. [63] Murphy 2020.

jobs in the service sector, working as delivery persons or drivers for ride-hailing companies. Their role is indispensable for China's growth in e-commerce, but the jobs they hold are those in which income is tied to piecework, with nonexistent or meager benefits. Unlike their parents or grandparents' generations, this generation of migrant workers never learned farming and can not return to the villages, as many such villages have disappeared. Unlike their parents, who grew up amidst material scarcity and poverty, China's new migrants were born in the era of the Internet; everyone had a cellphone in hand from an early age. These young migrants will not put up with outright discrimination.

Getting Old While Becoming Rich

In 1980, a fifteen-year-old child in rural China would most likely have had four to five siblings.[64] The child would have easily reached adulthood thanks to access to clean water, basic food stuff, and a primary school education, if not a couple of years of middle school. School was free but a bit primitive. Classrooms likely were not equipped with proper desks and stools. Textbooks, if available, were outdated. And teachers themselves had not much more education than the students. The child would have never seen or even heard of a thing called television, never taken a train or even a bus. The child's family would have been allocated some land to farm; any additional work had to be found elsewhere.

In 2020, a comparable fifteen-year-old child in rural China on average had most likely only one sibling, living in a household with no more than two other persons.[65] They had watched television as long as they could remember. All of the child's peers had completed primary school education and almost everyone went to middle school as well. In contrast to four decades ago, when 1 in 20 had a chance to get into a college, now half in their age group had access to a higher education institution. For a fifteen-year-old in urban China, however, they were one of more than 6 million only children in their birth cohort, and one of the more than 225 million only children born during the three-and-a-half decades under China's one-child rule.[66]

64 The total fertility rate in rural China fifteen years prior to 1980, in 1965, was 6.6, and the first time the level dropped to below 5 was 1973. The rural fertility level dropped to below 3 in 1988 and to 1.65 by 2005 (Whyte, Wang, and Cai 2015).

65 In 1982, the average household size a fifteen-year-old lived in was 5.8, urban and rural China combined. By 2010, the number dropped to barely 4. The average family household size for all persons dropped from 4.4 to 3.1 (K. Shen et al. 2021). Between 2010 and 2020, the average household size saw another sharp drop, by nearly half a person, to 2.6. www.stats.gov.cn/english/PressRelease/202105/t20210510_1817185.html

66 These are conservative estimates. The number of births in 2005 was about 12.5 million, and over the thirty-five years between 1980 and 2015 – when the one-child policy was

China mortgaged its future heavily to achieve rapid economic growth. One such heavy toll was the environment. Growth, especially in the earlier decades, resulted in China's polluted air, rivers, lakes, and soil. The most consequential long-term mortgage, however, was taken out on the Chinese population itself, by limiting a large share of families to only one child per couple. At the turn of the twenty-first century, nearly two-thirds of all Chinese couples were restricted to having only one child.[67] The ill-conceived and extreme birth control policy, unparalleled in the world, lasted for three-and-a-half decades, more than one generation.[68] Couples who complied with the one-child policy when the policy was launched in the late 1970s had already reached their 60s when the policy was lifted in 2015. As more and more parents of these only children step into their old age in the next decades, the strains imposed on them as well as on their children, at such a massive scale, will be unprecedented in Chinese and in world history. Robots, artificial intelligence, and other technological inventions may help lessen physical burdens, but they are unlikely to replace the emotional bonds across generations and among human beings.

On the eve of China's economic transformation, the specter of severe material scarcity loomed large, and a large number of youths were coming of age. From the late 1970s and into the 1980s, cohorts born in the early 1960s – in the wake of the Great Leap famine – started to reach schooling and employment age. And soon they would grow to be young parents themselves. Under a planned economy system that was increasingly unable to generate economic opportunities, the rapidly growing population was deemed a burden, even a threat. Feeding more babies would take away resources that could be used for investment. Perhaps in part emboldened by the relatively easy success of fertility reduction in the 1970s, Chinese leaders in the late 1970s conceived a drastically different and extremely short-sighted birth control policy: limiting each couple to one child. Whereas the progenitors were well aware of the long-term negative consequences imposed by this extreme policy upon Chinese families and the whole of society, they were convinced and tried to convince everyone that such a desperate policy was necessary.

lifted – it was over 550 million. The one-child policy subjected over 60 percent of Chinese couples to having only one child (Gu et al. 2007). With a conservative estimate of 50 percent of births being only children, there would be over 6 million only children among the fifteen-year-olds in 2020 and about 225 million only children born over the 35-year time span.

[67] An overview of the policy can be found in Gu et al. 2007.

[68] For a quick overview of the policy's history, see F. Wang, Gu, and Cai 2016. A discussion of the policy's origin is in F. Wang, Cai, and Gu 2013, and a review of the policy's consequences is in Y. Cai and Wang 2021.

Unbeknownst to these Chinese planners, or scholars specializing in demographic studies, the rapid population growth the world witnessed in the second half of the twentieth century was but a brief chapter of human population history. Following improvements in health and social changes, especially with respect to gender relations, fertility declined worldwide, regardless of a society's culture, religion, or income levels. More than half of the world's population today are living in countries with a fertility level that will not maintain the country's population size. China will step into an era of population decline well before 2030, a decline that is not caused by wars, famines, or epidemics. Unlike previous interruptions in population growth, the pending decline will continue unabated, with no end in sight.[69]

For China, the commonly cited concern is "getting old before getting rich." In 2010, for instance, when China passed the mark of being an aging society, its per capita income level was only 55 percent of the level for Japan when its population aging reached that level, only 38 percent of that for South Korea, and 44 percent for Taiwan.[70] As the demographic dividend that propelled China's economic boom diminishes, a population aging process unprecedented in Chinese history has set in. The share of the population aged 65 and over rose from less than 5 percent in the early 1980s to 7 percent around the turn of the century, and to over 13 percent in 2020. Driven by both the rapid fertility decline in the 1970s and the continued low fertility level since the early 1990s, population aging in China is accelerating. The share of the population aged 65 and over is expected to reach roughly 20 percent by 2030 and 25 percent by 2040. This rapid pace, with the share of the elderly population increasing from 9 percent to 25 percent in as few as 28 years, sets a world record. The same increase would take 70 years for Italy, 75 years for Germany, 90 years for France, 110 years for Britain, and 130 years for the United States, if the latter ever reaches that stage. Even China's fast-aging East Asian neighbors could not match such a record: it took Japan 35 years, and in South Korea it is projected to take 30 years.[71]

China is not just "getting old before getting rich" but also "getting old while becoming rich." Between 2000 and 2020, the share of China's elderly aged 65 and over nearly doubled from 7 to 13 percent; the per capita income level rose from less than $1,000 to over $10,000 (current US$).

[69] F. Wang 2011a.

[70] An aging society is defined as having more than 7 percent of the population aged 65 and above. China's share was 9 percent in 2010. GDP per capita is from Maddison 2007, in 1990 International Geary-Khamis dollars.

[71] UN World Population Prospect 2010, www.un.org/en/development/desa/population/publications/pdf/trends/WPP2010/WPP2010_Volume-I_Comprehensive-Tables.pdf

Considering purchasing power parity, the per capita income rose by nearly six times in two decades.[72] China's age of abundance, which began in the countryside, first and foremost brought a quick and massive improvement in food supply. As the population has become healthier, as seen in the rapid increase in their average height as well as in further increases in life expectancy, new health risks and diseases, rarely occurring in China's past, have also emerged. Poor nutrition during childhood years and the sudden availability of an abundant and varied supply of foods has led to a rapid increase in obesity, hypertension, and certainly, diabetes. Excessive consumption of tobacco and alcohol, made possible by increased income, has also resulted in increased lung and liver diseases and deaths due to lung cancers.

Moreover, with the influx of dairy products, processed foods, and sweetened soft drinks and snacks, recent generations of Chinese children are growing up facing new health risks later in life. As noted in Chapter 3, the proportion of overweight school children aged 7–18 shot up by 28 times between 1985 and 2000, with obesity increasing by 4 times. The obesity increase was particularly pronounced among boys, likely attributable to the prevailing son-preference, combined with the large number of only children who were sons. By the early 2000s, obesity rates in Chinese cities reached 12.9 percent among boys aged 7–9 and 9.1 percent among those aged 10–12. In the mid-1980s, these rates were only between 1 and 2 percent, respectively. At the young age of 7–9, 25.4 percent of boys and 17 percent of girls were considered overweight or obese.[73] In contrast to earlier generations, whose early-life health risks were mostly attributable to lack of nutrition, those who were raised during China's age of abundance face a whole different type of early-life health risks.

Just as China's explosive economic growth was completely underestimated nearly four decades ago, so was the explosive increase in population with chronic illness. In its first report on China's health sector, in 1984 the World Bank anticipated chronic disease to be a major health challenge in the decades to follow. The report projected that by the year 2010, 110 million or 10.8% of its population aged 15 and over would have hypertension (140/90 mm Hg).[74] The projection missed by more than 130 million people, or more than 50 percent. In the early 2010s, 244.5 million adults (23.2 percent) aged 18 and over had hypertension, with another 435 million (41.4 percent) having pre-hypertension, according to Chinese guidelines.[75]

[72] https://data.worldbank.org/indicator/NY.GDP.PCAP.PP.CD?locations=CN
[73] Ji, Sun, and Chen 2004, 103–08. [74] World Bank 1984, 97.
[75] www.ahajournals.org/doi/full/10.1161/CIRCULATIONAHA.117.032380

Changes in causes of death foretell challenges to health care and the inevitable increases in costs associated with health care. The three main causes of death in China are all noncommunicable diseases (NCDs) – cancer, cardiovascular diseases, and cerebrovascular diseases – and they are already on the rise. These diseases are chronic and involve much higher costs for treatment and care, and they drain resources for those of working age. In 1990, these three types of NCDs accounted for about 60 percent of all deaths among the urban population and 45 percent among the rural population. The share increased to 66 and 52 percent by 2000, and to 69 and 66 percent in 2010. By 2020, these causes combined accounted for more than 70 percent of all deaths, for both urban and rural populations. Not only have these noncommunicable deaths risen to account for 7 in 10 deaths, the rural population has also caught up to converge with the urban population, with the same share of deaths resulting from these noncommunicable diseases (Figure 7.4).

This increase in the share of deaths caused by noncommunicable diseases is due to two sources: increased incidences among the population of such diseases and, importantly, a changing population age composition. As cancer and, in particular, cardiovascular and cerebrovascular diseases are more likely to develop later in life, an older population is also more likely to have an increased incidence of these illnesses, resulting in more deaths. With the number of elderly people continuing to increase,

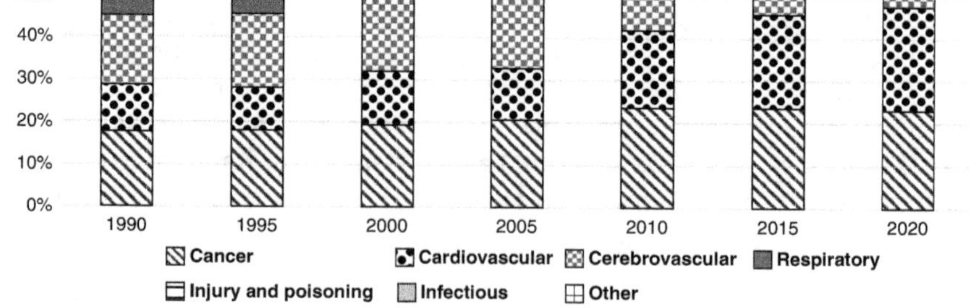

Figure 7.4 Changing causes of death, rural China, 1990–2020
Source: HSYB, various years

an even higher share of deaths in the future will also likely result from these NCDs.

A population that becomes affluent expects social benefits and services commensurate to its increased standard of living. With an aging population, health care and public pensions are the most needed. These services will be especially important for the Chinese population which will age, increasingly, to old-old age. In contrast to aging societies elsewhere in the world, a very large share of Chinese parents have only one child, and a considerable number of Chinese have grown up without siblings. The fiscal demand from the government to fund health care and pensions could be daunting, as detailed in the previous chapter of this volume.

A Chinese Renaissance?

A confluence of unique historical conditions propelled China to its age of abundance. As this age draws to a close, a familiar scene has reemerged. Decades of growth, made possible primarily by the state easing its tight grip, has allowed the state to regain its power that appeared to be slipping away. The state has rebounded in ways that are different from the failed planned economy days. Gone are government-set production quotas and price levels, and the overwhelming majority of employees are no longer on government payrolls. Judged by these measures, the state administrative power does not seem to be in direct control of the economy, and China has moved to a market-based economy. Yet these indicators only paint a partial and, in fact, a superficial picture.

The Empire Strikes Back

The first half of China's age of abundance, between the early 1980s and early 2000s, featured a rapid decline in state fiscal power. The share of government revenue as GDP dropped from 25 percent in 1980 to merely 10 percent in 1995, before rising to 13.36 percent in 2000. In the latter half of the abundance era, however, the share had risen to 22.2 percent by 2015 and remained at that level thereafter. This share, as analyzed and compared by economist Barry Naughton, had already risen well above that among middle-income nations and was on par with the average taxation level in high-income OECD countries.[76] As the comparisons in

[76] Naughton 2017, 6. Both numbers exclude social security revenues. The average level for 30 OECD countries was 22.14 percent. Adding social insurance revenues, which was 6.9 percent of the GDP, China's overall government revenue of 28.6 percent of GDP in 2015, according to Naughton's calculations, was way above the 21.5 percent level of middle-income countries.

the previous chapter show, the level of social benefits in China is still substantially below that in OECD countries. Despite the state's capacity and intention, its role in redistribution and responsiveness to popular demands is not that of a regime considered to be socialist.[77]

In a race between state and society, as far as wealth expansion goes, the state has come out far ahead. The country as a whole has become much more affluent. However, compared to the amount of wealth in private hands, the state has done much better. So, is China socialist? Based on measures such as government-controlled assets and fiscal revenue, the answer from Naughton was in the affirmative. While the Chinese state no longer maintains virtual total control over the means of production, the government still has substantial assets in its hands. Land is still owned by the state, as are many other types of assets such as banks and state-owned enterprises. By the early 2010s, the value of government assets relative to GDP, calculated at over 300 percent, was still much higher than that in other countries. Subtracting government liabilities, the ratio of net government assets to GDP stood at 114 percent in 2013.[78]

This ratio was only a "midpoint" of the state's return. At the turn of the century, in 2000 state net assets accounted for only 80 percent of the nominal GDP. This share rose to 117 percent in 2009, 146 percent in 2015, and then to 165 percent in 2019. While private Chinese citizens also became wealthier, the state did so at a faster pace. Nongovernment wealth increased sharply, by 16.75 times between 2000 and 2019, outpacing that of GDP growth, by 9.84 times in nominal terms. Yet it lagged behind the increase in government wealth, which rose by a staggering 20.35 times. During the two decades of vast wealth increase in China, the ratio of private wealth to government wealth actually declined, from 3.83 in 2000 to 3.15 in 2019.[79]

A major source of the government's expanded wealth portfolio is derived from the large companies it owns. No one could have expected that after decades of reforms aimed at dismantling the planned economy system, China's state sector would actually rise to unprecedented global dominance. Back in 1997, of the over 260,000 large- and medium-sized enterprises owned by the state, nearly 40 percent were in the red, with a total loss of 66.6 billion yuan. The total government fiscal revenue for the same year was only 865.1 billion yuan. A decade later, by 2008, enterprise reforms reduced the number of state-owned firms sharply by nearly 60 percent to only 110,000.[80] The number of employees in state-owned organizations

[77] Ibid., 22. [78] Ibid., 9, table 1.

[79] Calculated based on national wealth numbers estimated and reported in K. J. Lin et al. 2020; GDP numbers are from various years of the SYB.

[80] K. J. Lin et al. 2020.

was halved between 1995 and 2008 from over 112.6 million to 57.4 million. The share of urban employees in state-owned organizations dropped from 83.1 percent in 1995 to 30.5 percent in 2010, and fell further to only 14.7 percent in 2018 (Table 5.1).

A smaller number of enterprises and employees is not equivalent to a weaker state economic power. To the contrary, at the start of the 2010s, the number of state-owned enterprises increased again; and more prominently, so did the importance of the state sector in China's economy. The value of assets in state-owned enterprises relative to GDP stood at 145 percent in 2011, when their revenues accounted for over a quarter of all China's GDP. In Russia, by comparison, the shares were only 64 and 16 percent, respectively.[81] Both countries had gone through reforms, but China's state control over the economy would make the former leader of the socialist camp look pale in comparison.

China's state sector has also risen to global prominence, a prominence that could not have been dreamed of merely a couple of decades ago. The Chinese state now owns and controls a high share of the largest companies in the world. Entering the twenty-first century, ten Chinese companies joined the list of Fortune Global 500 companies, accounting for merely 2 percent. By 2020, the number of Chinese companies on this list rose to 124, accounting for nearly a quarter of all listings; exceeding the 121 companies headquartered in the United States and the 53 in Japan.[82] Almost all of these Chinese companies are state owned: 49 in 2005, 75 in 2010, and 102 in 2015.[83] In 2005, only three Chinese companies made the list of the top 100 largest companies in the Fortune Global 500 club, and none was among the top 10. By 2020, Chinese companies made up nearly a quarter of the largest 100 global companies; 22 of the 24 being state owned. Since 2010, all three of the Chinese companies ranking in the top ten in the world have been owned by the Chinese state.[84]

The might of the Chinese state in the global economy comes as both a blessing and possibly a curse. Direct control over the critical sectors of the economy – energy, materials, transportation and communication, and banking – gives the Chinese state unrivaled power in steering the national economy and in positioning itself in global economic competition. These state-owned enterprises' profits can also be used to shore up national pension deficits for an aging population.

Yet these massive corporations came with their own problems. While their monopoly positions afforded them certain advantages, the firms

[81] Kroeber 2016, 100. [82] Kennedy 2020.

[83] K. J. Lin et al. 2020. The number of Chinese state-owned enterprises rose to 117 on the Fortune Global 500 list in 2014. In 2017, the number dropped slightly, to 102.

[84] http://fortune.com/global500/list/

were far from being efficiently run. An easy comparison is to look at the large and privately owned Chinese enterprises, which made up 27 percent of the 124 China-based companies on the Fortune Global 500 list. In 2020, these privately owned enterprises had 16 percent of the total assets of all Chinese companies on the list. Yet they took in a 22-percent share of revenue in the year before, with a profit margin two times and an average return to assets three times that of state-owned companies.[85] With a 3.5-percent profit margin, Chinese state-owned enterprises lagged far behind Canada (9.1%), the United States (8.9%), Switzerland (8.3%), Britain (5.9%), and France (4.3%).

In the long term, the economic impact of these state-owned companies is not limited to inefficiency but to their stifling roles for the entire industries they operate in, as the economist Milton Friedman famously summarized, "the surest way to destroy an industry is to protect it with state monopoly."[86] The state's monopolistic grip over large state-owned enterprises is by no means the only or the most destructive force. State monopolies allowed these firms to pay higher wages and benefits, seeding income inequality. Absent competition, state-owned firms have little incentive for innovation or efficiency. And quite often, ordinary consumers and producers are forced to pay higher prices for everything, from raw materials to energy and utilities, precisely because these state-backed firms have unchallenged monopoly power. A hazard perhaps greater than inefficiency and inequality is how the state monopoly undermines the functioning of the market, a market not just for exchanging goods but also for generating ideas and useful knowledge and for stimulating innovation.

A Cultural Revival?

Four decades of sustained fast economic growth have improved the livelihoods of one-fifth of the human race, with China having regained its stature as a rich and powerful country. The changes are not only material; many are cultural as well. Palaces, temples, and other historical monuments, demolished during the Cultural Revolution, have been repaired and rebuilt and put on the list of UNESCO World Heritage sites. Dramas about imperial court life and intrigue often saturate the Chinese mass media, watched by hundreds of millions year after year. Folk rituals and festivals have returned. New archaeological discoveries

[85] Kennedy 2020. The average profit margin in 2019 was 7 percent for private companies versus 3.5 percent for state-owned enterprises, and the average return to assets 3.7 percent versus 1.2 percent.

[86] Quoted in Coase and Wang 2012, 192.

are celebrated. Even long-buried ruins, such as the palace grounds of the Qin emperor, burned to the ground over 2,000 years ago, were recreated. A great cultural revival appears to have arrived. Is China's age of abundance also its age of renaissance?

The European Renaissance, which began in the Italian city of Florence in the fourteenth century and lasted for nearly two centuries, was far more than just material abundance. It was a "rebirth" of the Greek and Roman culture in politics, science, and humanity. The Renaissance was about the idea of democracy, of exploring nature, and ultimately it was humanistic, about empowering the individual. Humanism was the intellectual basis of the Renaissance.[87] With the Renaissance, Italy "beamed a radiance out beyond its own frontiers, a light that spread to every corner of the world." In the words of the French historian Fernand Braudel, "That radiance, that distribution of cultural goods from Italy, can be seen as the mark of an exceptional destiny, evidence so overwhelming that it gives the true measure of a multidimensional history."[88] The transformative and long-lasting impact of the Renaissance for the world was far more than the material glory, as also summarized by Braudel:

> The glory of the intellect may appear to us more than the glory of wealth. For century after century, Italy provided a living example, a spectacle of intellectual prowess, agility, and originality, a series of contradictory cultural revolutions, as freedom was followed by order, progress by interruption, radiance by obscurity [. . .] here was one of the most dazzling sequences of displays of intelligence since the world began.[89]

Similarly, the Industrial Revolution in the late eighteenth century, along with the attendant modern economy, had its roots in the Enlightenment. This particular era set in motion "a culture of practical improvement, a belief in social progress, and the recognition that useful knowledge was the key to their realization."[90] But the Enlightenment was considerably more. It ushered in other elements,

> the idea of political power as a social contract, formal limits on the executive branch, freedom of expression, intellectual contestability, religious tolerance, basic human legal rights, the realization that exchange was a positive-sum game, the virtuousness of economic activity and trade, the sanctity of property rights, and the folly of mercantilist notions that placed the state (and not the individual) as the ultimate object of society.[91]

[87] Nauert 2006.
[88] Braudel 2019, 11. I am indebted to Gianpiero Dalla Zuanna and Maria Castiglioni for gifting this book to me and for their suggestions on literature of the Renaissance.
[89] Braudel 2019, 17. [90] Mokyr 2017, 267. [91] Ibid.

China's age of abundance also began with its own enlightenment. Each element of the Enlightenment listed above was invoked, as a reaction to the dark decade of the Cultural Revolution, and by extension, the flaws of China's three-decade-long communist attempt and the Maoist Cult. During the Cultural Revolution, Mao was worshipped as a deity: his teachings became the absolute truth. Only with Mao's death was it possible to bring the dark decade to a close. Returning to power in 1977, Deng spent his first year demystifying the religious-like treatment of Mao. The fateful speech he delivered in December 1978 concluding the 3rd Plenum of the CCP's 11th Congress considered the official launch of China's reforms and was entitled "Emancipating minds, seeking truth from facts, and looking to the future."[92] Among Deng's first reform measures were reinstating college entrance exams, recognizing and praising contributions by scientists, welcoming foreign experts, and sending officials as well as students overseas to study. Prior to the creation of a market of goods, first a market of ideas was created. Emancipation of the mind and a market of ideas served China well. Without these overhauls, China would not have entered its era of material abundance. Debates would have continued on whether the cat was white or black, or whether China was going socialist or capitalist. Yet that period of enlightenment only existed briefly, mostly in the 1980s.

China's modern history offers vivid examples of ebbs and flows of thought control and mind emancipation. This book so far has used many graphs, drawing from official statistics. It is appropriate to end this book with a final one. During China's socialist years, and prior to the era of the Internet and social media, printed media in the form of books, magazines, and newspapers were the sole outlets. To publish a book required a publication number, tightly controlled by the state. The number of book titles and pages printed per capita (Figure 7.5) record China's emancipation of the mind after Mao's death. The number of books increased from under 13,000 titles in 1977 to about 32,000 in 1982; and the number of pages printed per person increased from 12 to 22. The number of titles more than doubled again to 80,224 by 1990, while the number of pages printed per person has remained largely the same since the 1980s (not shown in the figure).

The surge in the number of books published in 1958 and 1959 (Figure 7.5), prior to the post-Mao emancipation, was from when Mao encouraged free speech and criticism of the Communist Party to allow

[92] Yang 1998, 134; Vogel 2011. Vogel notes how seriously Deng himself took this speech. "Rarely did Deng write out notes for a speech, but for this meeting on December 2 he took out three pages of notes with some 1,600 Chinese characters (about eight hundred words) and explained to those responsible for the draft what he expected in terms of the speech's style, content, and outline." (242)

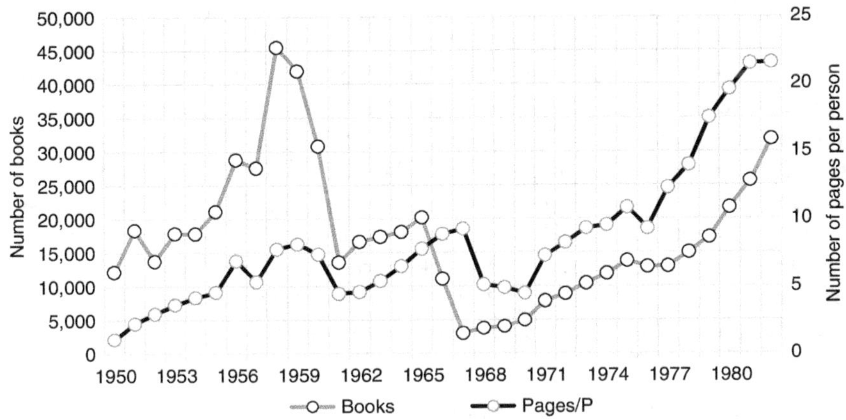

Figure 7.5 Total book titles published and pages per capita printed, China, 1950–80
Source: Calculated from SYB 1983

"one hundred flowers" to bloom. That bloom did not end well. The "anti-rightists" campaign, following a brief period of free speech, sent more than 350,000 intellectuals to labor camps. With that purge, the number of book titles declined by 70 percent and pages printed per person declined by more than 40 percent in the two years between 1959 and 1961 (Figure 7.5). China's Great Leap famine-induced scarcity could have played a role, but the sharp drop starting before the famine was clearly the outcome of politics.

The role of politics in censorship and publication was evident again just a few years later in 1967. The number of book titles printed reached its nadir in the entire period between 1950 and 1980, during the Chinese socialist era. In that year, with no famine or extreme economic hardship, fewer than 3,000 titles were printed for a nation of 800 million people, down from over 20,000 two years previously, in 1965. The nadir in the number of titles printed took place at the zenith of the Cultural Revolution, when a sweeping cultural cleansing was underway. The irony, however, was that the number of pages printed did not drop. To the contrary, it surged to the highest level since the founding of the People's Republic, with more pages printed per person, a record that was not surpassed until 1977. It was not that the Chinese people did not have materials to read. Everyone was just reading Chairman Mao's Little Red Books. China did not fare well during those periods of political censorship and cultural poverty.

The Chinese state under Communist Party rule was not the first regime to exercise a tight control over book printing and distribution. More than five centuries earlier, in 1485, the Ottoman sultan Bayezid II issued an edict banning printing in Arabic, while printing with Gutenberg movable type technology spread in European cities, four decades after its invention in 1439. That ban lasted for two-and-a-half centuries.[93] Such a ban, though lasting for over two centuries, was not the first nor the cruelest. China's first emperor, Qin Shi Huangdi, set that record: he is remembered not only for unifying China and building the Great Wall but also for ordering texts to be burned in 213 BCE and 460 scholars buried alive in 212 BCE, a most chilling legacy of authoritarian rule.

Returning to a New Normal

China entered this age of abundance with a population that was ready and eager to work in the aftermath of the failed socialist planned economy exacerbated by the Cultural Revolution and under the guidance of a rare leader. In the absence of any of these three historic opportunities, the Chinese miracle would not have materialized. As discussed earlier, none of these conditions, however, can be recreated. More than four decades after the start of China's post-socialist reforms, the Cultural Revolution and the material scarcity plaguing one-quarter of humanity are both long-gone histories, fading into memory.

With the improvement in the population's living standards came the expansion of state power. Instead of an open political system noted by Robert Fogel as one of the forces driving China's continued economic ascendance, in the decade after his writing in 2010, the Chinese political system has turned increasingly inward and closed. Partial political institutionalization, which supplied a source for stability and facilitated economic growth, was stalled and reversed, at the same time as the economic growth rate slowed down in the 2010s. The end of an era has descended.[94] Material abundance, achieved by the hard work and ingenuity of the Chinese population, has enabled a fifth of humanity to live in the comfort of an upper-middle income society. This same abundance is now used by the state to claim new legitimacy to exercise control amidst public complacency.

Though beginning with an emancipation campaign in the wake of the Cultural Revolution, China seems to have returned to a state of normalcy. It has returned to a normalcy where the state reasserts its control over the population and to a normalcy by which stability once again takes

[93] Acemoglu and Robinson 2012, 213–14. [94] Minzner 2018.

precedence over everything else, at almost any cost. Material abundance is paving the way of a new national mental frame, a national mental frame no longer set in revolution and liberating the world's poor but in national revival and nationalism. The state's dominance in the economy has made the Chinese state more confident to reign in a free market of ideas. In the eyes of the power holders, the market of ideas stands in contradiction to a state-led, market-based economy.

Whereas China's age of ascendance began with its own enlightenment, that period of opening up was short-lived. The power holders' fear of losing control has often driven its censoring of ideas and containing of a market of ideas. Such fear and control, which once led China to a technological standstill and to social suffocation, is once again depriving China of opportunities for innovation and ideas, and of institutional reforms. As economists Coase and Wang note, "As remarkable as the Chinese market transformation is, capitalism with Chinese characteristics is impoverished by the lack of a free market of ideas; this deficiency has become the most restrictive bottleneck in China's economic and social development."[95]

Will China be able to break such a bottleneck? Has China once again returned to its own traditional roots of governance? Examining China's long history of political governance, sociologist Xueguang Zhou considers this a likely scenario. For a country with both a vast landmass and a long history of centralized rule, stability has long been a national priority in governance. Between the choice of stability or efficiency, stability always takes precedence. Having achieved a level of material abundance unimaginable merely a generation ago, China has traveled through an age of abundance and entered a new phase of complacence. In the absence of legal-rational authority, state power bureaucratization with its opaque policy setting will lead to stagnation, a recurrent theme throughout Chinese history.[96] Nearly a half-century after bidding farewell to the godlike leader Mao, the country seems to be once again willing to put up with another era of charismatic authority.

"Socialism is the longest detour to capitalism." That was the phrase often heard in the late 1980s, when the worldwide socialist experiment came to an end with the crumbling of the Berlin Wall and the collapse of the Soviet Union. It took China three decades of a socialist detour before finally venturing on the road of capitalism.

As China exits its age of abundance, one wonders: Was China's four-decade-long encounter with capitalism just another detour, a detour back to socialism, socialism with Chinese characteristics?

[95] Coase and Wang 2012, 199. [96] Zhou 2022.

References

China Population Census National Bureau of Statistics of China. Various years. *Tabulation on the Population Census of the People's Republic of China*. Beijing: China Statistics Press.

ESYB Ministry of Education of China. Various years. *Educational Statistics Yearbook of China*. Beijing: China Statistics Press.

HSYB National Commission of Health. Various years. *China Health Statistical Yearbook*. Beijing: Peking Union Medical College Press.

SYB National Bureau of Statistics of China. Various years. *China Statistical Yearbook*. Beijing: China Statistics Press. www.stats.gov.cn/english/Statisticaldata/yearbook/

WDI World Bank. Various years. *World Development Indicators*. Washington DC: World Bank.

Acemoglu, Daron, and James A. Robinson. 2012. *Why Nations Fail: The Origins of Power, Prosperity, and Poverty*. New York: Crown.

Ang, Yuen Yuen. 2016. *How China Escaped the Poverty Trap*. Ithaca, NY: Cornell University Press.

Ash, Robert. 2006. "Squeezing the Peasants: Grain Extraction, Food Consumption and Rural Living Standards in Mao's China." *The China Quarterly* 188: 959–98. http://www.jstor.org/stable/20192701

Banister, Judith. 1987. *China's Changing Population*. Stanford, CA: Stanford University Press.

Banister, Judith, and Kenneth Hill. 2004. "Mortality in China 1964–2000." *Population Studies* 58 (1): 55–75. http://www.jstor.org/stable/4148247

Banister, Judith, and Samuel H. Preston. 1981. "Mortality in China." *Population and Development Review* 7 (1): 98–110. https://doi.org/10.2307/1972767

Baum, Emily. 2020. "Medicine and Public Health in Twentieth-Century China: Histories of Modernization and Change." *History Compass* 18 (7): e12616. https://doi.org/10.1111/hic3.12616

Beckert, Sven. 2014. *Empire of Cotton: A Global History*. New York: Vintage.

Bernstein, Thomas P. 1977. *Up to the Mountains and Down to the Villages: The Transfer of Youth from Urban to Rural China*. New Haven, CT: Yale University Press.

Bloom, David E., and Jeffrey G. Williamson. 1998. "Demographic Transitions and Economic Miracles in Emerging Asia." *World Bank Economic Review* 12 (3): 419–55.

Bloom, David, David Canning, and Jaypee Sevilla. 2003. *The Demographic Dividend: A New Perspective on the Economic Consequences of Population Change*. Santa Monica, CA: RAND Corporation. https://doi.org/10.7249/MR1274

Brandt, Loren, and Thomas G. Rawski, eds. 2008. *China's Great Economic Transformation*. Cambridge: Cambridge University Press. https://doi.org/10.1017/CBO9780511754234

Braudel, Fernand. 2019. *Out of Italy: Two Centuries of World Domination and Demise*. Translated by Siân Reynolds. Reprint. New York: Europa Compass.

Cai Fang, Wang Dewen, and Du Yang. 2008. *Zhongguo nongcun gaige yu bianqian* 中国农村改革与变迁 (Reform and change in rural China). Shanghai: Shanghai renminbi chubanshe.

Cai, Meng, and Ximing Yue. 2020. "The Redistributive Role of Government Social Security Transfers on Inequality in China." *China Economic Review* 62 (August): 101512. https://doi.org/10.1016/j.chieco.2020.101512

Cai, Yong, and Feng Wang. 2021. "The Social and Sociological Consequences of China's One-Child Policy." *Annual Review of Sociology* 47: 587–606. https://doi.org/10.1146/annurev-soc-090220-032839

Cai, Yong, Feng Wang, and Ke Shen. 2018. "Fiscal Implications of Population Aging and Social Sector Expenditure in China." *Population and Development Review* 44 (4): 811–31. www.jstor.org/stable/45174458

Cai, Yong, Feng Wang, Ke Shen, Ding Li, and Xiwei Wu. 2004. "China's Age of Abundance: When Might It Run Out?" *Journal of the Economics of Ageing* 4: 90–97. http://dx.doi.org/10.1016/j.jeoa.2014.02.001

Campbell, Cameron. 1997. "Public Health Efforts in China before 1949 and Their Effects on Mortality: The Case of Beijing." *Social Science History* 21 (2): 179–218. https://doi.org/10.2307/1171273

Chai, Winberg. 1968. "The Reorganization of the Chinese Communist Party, 1966–1968." *Asian Survey* 8 (11): 901–10. https://doi.org/10.2307/2642373

Chan, Kam Wing. 1994. *Cities with Invisible Walls: Reinterpreting Urbanization in Post-1949 China*. Hong Kong: Oxford University Press.

2012. "Migration and Development in China: Trends, Geography and Current Issues." *Migration and Development* 1 (2): 187–205. https://doi.org/10.1080/21632324.2012.739316

2019. "China's Precious Children." *Eurasian Geography and Economics* 60 (5): 616–33. https://doi.org/10.1080/15387216.2019.1691034

Chen Guili and Wu Chuntao. 2009. *Xiaogang cun de gushi* 小岗村的故事 (The story of Xiaogang village). Beijing: Huawen chubanshe.

Cheng, Hong, Dezhuang Hu, and Hongbin Li. 2020. "Wage Differential between Rural Migrant and Urban Workers in the People's Republic of China." *Asian Development Review* 37 (1): 43–60. https://doi.org/10.1162/adev_a_00140

Cheng, Tiejun, and Mark Selden. 1994. "The Origins and Social Consequences of China's Hukou System." *The China Quarterly*, no. 139: 644–68. www.jstor.org/stable/655134

Coale, Ansley J., and Judith Banister. 1996. "Five Decades of Missing Females in China." *Proceedings of the American Philosophical Society* 140 (4): 421–50. www.jstor.org/stable/987286

Coase, Ronald, and Ning Wang. 2012. *How China Became Capitalist*. Basingstoke, UK: Palgrave Macmillan.

Cotlear, Daniel, ed. 2010. *Population Aging: Is Latin America Ready?* Washington, DC: World Bank Publications.

Du, S. F., H. J. Wang, B. Zhang, F. Y. Zhai, and B. M. Popkin. 2014. "China in the Period of Transition from Scarcity and Extensive Undernutrition to Emerging Nutrition-Related Non-Communicable Diseases, 1949–1992." *Obesity Reviews* 15 (S1): 8–15. https://doi.org/10.1111/obr.12122

Duckett, Jane, and Guohui Wang. 2017. "Why Do Authoritarian Regimes Provide Public Goods? Policy Communities, External Shocks and Ideas in China's Rural Social Policy Making." *Europe-Asia Studies* 69 (1): 92–109. https://doi.org/10.1080/09668136.2016.1274379

Eberstadt, Nick. 1979. *Poverty in China*. Bloomington, IN: International Development Institute.

Eichengreen, Barry, Donghyun Park, and Kwanho Shin. 2012. "When Fast-Growing Economies Slow Down: International Evidence and Implications for China." *Asian Economic Papers* 11 (1): 42–87.

Fang, Hanming, Quanlin Gu, Wei Xiong, and Li-An Zhou. 2015. "Demystifying the Chinese Housing Boom." In Martin Eichenbaum and Jonathan Parker, eds., *NBER Macroeconomics Annual 2015*, Vol. 30, 105–66. Cambridge, MA: National Bureau of Economic Research. https://EconPapers.repec.org/RePEc:nbr:nberch:13595

Fei, Xiaotong. 1986. *Small Towns in China: Functions, Problems and Prospects*. Beijing: New World Press.

Feng, Xiaojun. 2017. "Manufacturing Conflict: The Experience of a World Factory in a Changing China." *Modern China* 43 (6): 590–619.

Firebaugh, Glenn, and Brian Goesling. 2004. "Accounting for the Recent Decline in Global Income Inequality." *American Journal of Sociology* 110 (2): 283–312. https://doi.org/10.1086/421541

Floud, Roderick, Kenneth Wachter, and Annabel Gregory. 1990. *Height, Health and History: Nutritional Status in the United Kingdom, 1750–1980*. Cambridge: Cambridge University Press.

Fogel, Robert W. (William). 1994. "Economic Growth, Population Theory, and Physiology: The Bearing of Long-Term Processes on the Making of Economic Policy." *American Economic Review* 84 (3): 369–95. www.jstor.org/stable/2118058

2004a. *The Escape from Hunger and Premature Death, 1700–2100: Europe, America, and the Third World*. Cambridge: Cambridge University Press.

2004b. "Health, Nutrition, and Economic Growth." *Economic Development and Cultural Change* 52 (3): 643–58. https://doi.org/10.1086/383450

Frazier, Mark W. 2010. *Socialist Insecurity: Pensions and the Politics of Uneven Development in China*. Ithaca, NY: Cornell University Press.

Gallagher, Mary E. 2014. "China's Workers Movement and the End of the Rapid-Growth Era." *Daedalus* 143 (2): 81–95. https://doi.org/10.1162/DAED_a_00274

Gao, Qin. 2017. *Welfare, Work, and Poverty: Social Assistance in China*. New York: Oxford University Press.

Gao, Qin, Sui Yang, and Shi Li. 2013. "The Chinese Welfare State in Transition: 1988–2007." *Journal of Social Policy* 42 (4): 743–62. https://doi.org/10.1017/S0047279413000329

Gewirtz, Julian. 2017. *Unlikely Partners: Chinese Reformers, Western Economists, and the Making of Global China*. Cambridge, MA: Harvard University Press.

Glaeser, Edward, Wei Huang, Yueran Ma, and Andrei Shleifer. 2017. "A Real Estate Boom with Chinese Characteristics." *Journal of Economic Perspectives* 31 (1): 93–116. https://doi.org/10.1257/jep.31.1.93

Gordon, Robert J. 2016. *The Rise and Fall of American Growth: The U.S. Standard of Living since the Civil War*. The Princeton Economic History of the Western World. Princeton, NJ: Princeton University Press.

Gruber, Johnathan, and David Wise. 2001. "An International Perspective on Policies for an Aging Society." NBER Working Paper 8103. Cambridge, MA: National Bureau of Economic Research. www.nber.org/papers/w8103

Gu, Baochang, Wang Feng, Guo Zhigang, and Zhang Erli. 2007. "China's Local and National Fertility Policies at the End of the Twentieth Century." *Population and Development Review* 33 (1): 129–47. www.jstor.org/stable/25434587

Guo Shutian and Liu Chunbing. 1990. *Shiheng de Zhongguo* 失衡的中国 (An imbalanced China). Shijiazhuang: Hebei renmin chubanshe.

Guojia Weisheng he Jihuashengyu Weiyuanhui 国家卫生和计划生育委员会 (National Commission of Health and Birth Control). 2015. *Zhongguo weisheng he jihuashengyu tongji nianjian* 中国卫生和计划生育统计年鉴 (China yearbook of health and birth control). Beijing: China Union Medical College Press.

Gustafsson, Bjorn, Terry Sicular, and Xiuna Yang. 2020. "China's Emerging Global Middle Class." In Sicular et al., *Changing Trends in China's Inequality*, 75–108.

Harris, Chauncy D. 1982. "The urban and industrial transformation of Japan." *Geographical Review* 72 (1): 50–89.

Hocquet, Jean-Yves. 2016. "Social Protection and Employment: Partnership or Rivalry. Report of EU-China Social Protection Reform Project." www.sprp-cn.eu/reporting.htm

Howell, David L. 1995. *Capitalism from Within: Economy, Society, and the State in a Japanese Fishery*. Berkeley: University of California Press.

Huang, Jianxin. 2017. *Social Mobility and Entrepreneurship of Migrant Workers*. Beijing: Social Sciences Academy Press (China).

Huang, Xian. 2020. *Social Protection under Authoritarianism: Health Politics and Policy in China*. Oxford: Oxford University Press.

Huang, Yasheng. 2002. *Selling China: Foreign Direct Investment during the Reform Era*. Cambridge Modern China Series. Cambridge: Cambridge University Press. https://doi.org/10.1017/CBO9780511815164

2008. *Capitalism with Chinese Characteristics: Entrepreneurship and the State*. Cambridge; Cambridge University Press.

2012. "How Did China Take Off?" *Journal of Economic Perspectives* 26 (4): 147–70. www.jstor.org/stable/23290284

Hung, Ho-fung. 2015. *The China Boom: Why China Will Not Rule the World*. New York: Columbia University Press.

2022. *Clash of Empires*. Cambridge: Cambridge University Press.

Hung, Ho-fung, and Jaime Kucinskas. 2011. "Globalization and Global Inequality: Assessing the Impact of the Rise of China and India, 1980–2005." *American Journal of Sociology* 116 (5): 1478–1513. https://doi.org/10.1086/657456

Ji, Cheng-ye, Jun-ling Sun, and Tian-jiao Chen. 2004. "[Dynamic analysis on the prevalence of obesity and overweight school-age children and adolescents in recent 15 years in China]." [Original article in Chinese.] *Zhonghua liuxingbingxue zazhi* 25 (2): 103–8. https://pubmed.ncbi.nlm.nih.gov/15132859/

Judt, Tony. 2005. *Postwar: A History of Europe since 1945*. New York: Penguin Press.

Kennedy, Scott. 2020. "The Biggest But Not the Strongest: China's Place in the Fortune Global 500." (blog) Center for Strategic and International Studies, Aug. 18. www.csis.org/blogs/trustee-china-hand/biggest-not-strongest-chinas-place-fortune-global-500

Knight, John, Shi Li, and Haiyuan Wan. 2020. "The Increasing Inequality of Wealth in China." In Sicular et al., *Changing Trends in China's Inequality*, 109–44.

Kornai, J.-Anos. 1980. *Economics of Shortage*. Amsterdam: Elsevier Science.

Kroeber, Arthur R. 2016. *China's Economy: What Everyone Needs to Know*. New York: Oxford University Press.

Lavely, William, James Lee, and Wang Feng. 1990. "Chinese Demography: The State of the Field." *Journal of Asian Studies* 49 (4): 807–34. https://doi.org/10.2307/2058237

Lee, Ching Kwan. 1998. *Gender and the South China Miracle: Two Worlds of Factory Women*. Reprint 2019. Berkeley: University of California Press. https://doi.org/10.1525/9780520920040

Lee, James, and Feng Wang. 1999. *One Quarter of Humanity: Malthusian Mythology and Chinese Realities, 1700–2000*. Cambridge, MA: Harvard University Press.

Lee, James, Cameron Campbell, and Feng Wang. 2002. "Positive Check or Chinese Checks?" *Journal of Asian Studies* 61 (2): 591–607. https://doi.org/10.2307/2700301

Lee, Ronald. 2003. "The Demographic Transition: Three Centuries of Fundamental Change." *Journal of Economic Perspectives* 17 (4): 167–90. https://doi.org/10.1257/089533003772034943

Lee, Ronald, and Andrew Mason. 2011a. "Lifecycles, Support Systems, and Generational Flows: Patterns and Change." In Lee and Mason, *Population Aging and the Generational Economy*, 79–106.

eds. 2011b. *Population Aging and the Generational Economy: A Global Perspective*. Cheltenham, UK: Edward Elgar.

Li, Shi. 2016. "Redistributive Effects of Social Security System in China. Report of EU-China Social Protection Reform Project." www.sprp-cn.eu/reporting.htm

Liang, Zai. 2016. "China's Great Migration and the Prospects of a More Integrated Society." *Annual Review of Sociology* 42 (1): 451–71.

Lin, Justin Yifu. 2011. "China and the Global Economy." *China Economic Journal* 4 (1): 1–14. https://doi.org/10.1080/17538963.2011.609612

Lin, Justin Yifu, and Yang Yao. 2001. "Chinese Rural Industrialization in the Context of the East Asian Miracle." In Joseph E. Stiglitz and Shahid Yusuf, eds., *Rethinking the East Asian Miracle*. Oxford: Oxford University Press, 143–96.

Lin, Justin Yifu, Fang Cai, and Zhou Li. 1996. *The China Miracle: Development Strategy and Economic Reform*. A Friedman Lecture Fund Monograph. Hong Kong: Chinese University Press.

Lin, Karen Jingrong, Xiaoyan Lu, Junsheng Zhang, and Ying Zheng. 2020. "State-Owned Enterprises in China: A Review of 40 years of Research and Practice." *China Journal of Accounting Research* 13 (1): 31–55. https://doi.org/10.1016/j.cjar.2019.12.001

Lu, Feng. 2012. "Wage Trends among Chinese Migrant Workers: 1979–2010." *Chinese Journal of Social Sciences*, no. 7: 47–68.

Lu, Yao, and Feng Wang. 2013. "From General Discrimination to Segmented Inequality: Migration and Inequality in Urban China." *Social Science Research* 42 (6): 1443–56. https://doi.org/10.1016/j.ssresearch.2013.06.006

Ma, Hengyun, Jikun Huang, Frank Fuller, and Scott Rozelle. 2006. "Getting Rich and Eating Out: Consumption of Food Away from Home in Urban China." *Canadian Journal of Agricultural Economics/Revue Canadienne d'agroeconomie* 54 (1): 101–19. https://doi.org/10.1111/j.1744-7976.2006.00040.x

MacFarquhar, Roderick, and Michael Schoenhals. 2006. *Mao's Last Revolution*. Cambridge, MA: Belknap Press.

Maddison, Angus. 2007. *Chinese Economic Performance in the Long Run*. 2nd Ed., revised and updated, 960–2030 AD. Paris: OECD Development Centre.

Man, Joyce Yanyun, ed. 2011. *China's Housing Reform and Outcomes*. Cambridge, MA: Lincoln Institute of Land Policy.

Mason, Andrew. 2003 "Population Change and Economic Development: What Have We Learned from the East Asia Experience?" *Applied Population and Policy* 1 (1): 3–14.

Mason, Karen Oppenheim. 1997. "Explaining Fertility Transitions." *Demography* 34 (4): 443–54. https://doi.org/10.2307/3038299

McNeill, William H. 1976. *Plagues and Peoples*. New York: Anchor.

Mendels, Franklin F. 1972. "Proto-Industrialization: The First Phase of the Industrialization Process." *Journal of Economic History* 32 (1): 241–61. www.jstor.org/stable/2117187

Meng, Xin. 2007. "Wealth Accumulation and Distribution in Urban China." *Economic Development and Cultural Change* 55 (4): 761–91. https://doi.org/10.1086/516761

Minzner, Carl. 2018. *End of an Era: How China's Authoritarian Revival Is Undermining Its Rise*. New York: Oxford University Press.

Mo, Zhexun. 2022. "What's New about Inequality in East Asia?" *WID – World Inequality Database* (blog). https://wid.world/news-article/whats-new-about-inequality-in-east-asia/

Mokyr, Joel. 2017. *A Culture of Growth: The Origins of the Modern Economy*. Princeton, NJ: Princeton University Press. https://doi.org/10.2307/j.ctt1wf4dft

Murphy, Rachel. 2020. *The Children of China's Great Migration*. Cambridge: Cambridge University Press.

Nauert, Charles G. 2006. *Humanism and the Culture of Renaissance Europe*. Updated edition. Cambridge: Cambridge University Press.

Naughton, Barry J. 1996. *Growing Out of the Plan: Chinese Economic Reform, 1978–1993*. Cambridge: Cambridge University Press.

2006. *The Chinese Economy: Transitions and Growth*. Cambridge, MA: MIT Press.

2013. *Wu Jinglian: Voice of Reform in China*. Cambridge, MA: MIT Press.

2017. "Is China Socialist?" *Journal of Economic Perspectives* 31 (1): 3–24. https://doi.org/10.1257/jep.31.1.3

Niu Ruofeng. 1992. "Lun woguo gongnong guanxi shiheng yu fazhan guan de zhuanbian"论我国工农关系失衡与发展观的转变 (On the imbalance of industrial-agricultural relationships and reorientation of developmental perspective). *Nongye jingji wenti* 农业经济问题 (2): 3–8.

OECD (Organisation for Economic Co-operation and Development). 2012. "Inequality: Recent Trends in China and Experience in the OECD Area." In *China in Focus: Lessons and Challenges*, 16–34. Paris: OECD.

2016. "Income inequality remains high in the face of weak recovery." Income Inequality Update. www.oecd.org/social/OECD2016-Income-Inequality-Update.pdf

Oi, Jean C. 1999. *Rural China Takes Off: Institutional Foundations of Economic Reform*. Berkeley: University of California Press.

Overholt, William H. 1993. *The Rise of China: How Economic Reform Is Creating a New Superpower*. W.W. Norton.

2018. *China's Crisis of Success*. Cambridge: Cambridge University Press.

Peng Sen and Chen Li. 2008. *Zhongguo jingji tizhi gaige zhongda shijian* 中国经济体制改革重大事件 (Major events in China's economic reform). Beijing: Zhongguo renmin daxue chubanshe.

Peng, Xizhe. 1987. "Demographic consequences of the Great Leap Forward in Chinese provinces." *Population and Development Review* 13 (4): 639–70.

Piketty, Thomas, Li Yang, and Gabriel Zucman. 2019. "Capital Accumulation, Private Property, and Rising Inequality in China, 1978–2015." *American Economic Review* 109 (7): 2469–96. https://doi.org/10.1257/aer.20170973

Polanyi, Karl. 1980. *The Great Transformation: The Political and Economic Origins of Our Time*. 20th printing edition. Boston: Beacon Press.

PricewaterhouseCoopers. 2017. "Paying Taxes 2017." www.pwc.com/al/en/publications/paying-taxes-2017.html

Qian, Yingyi. 2017. *How Reform Worked in China: The Transition from Planto Market*. Cambridge, MA: MIT Press.

Reher, David S. 2011. "Economic and Social Implications of the Demographic Transition." *Population and Development Review* 37 (s1): 11–33. https://doi.org/10.1111/j.1728-4457.2011.00376.x

Riskin, Carl. 1987. *China's Political Economy: The Quest for Development since 1949*. Oxford: Oxford University Press.

Roberts, Kenneth D. 1997. "China's 'Tidal Wave' of Migrant Labor: What Can We Learn from Mexican Undocumented Migration to the United States?" *International Migration Review* 31 (2): 249–93. https://doi.org/10.2307/2547220

Rogaski, Ruth. 2014. *Hygienic Modernity: Meanings of Health and Disease in Treaty-Port China*. Berkeley: University of California Press.

Rozelle, Scott, and Natalie Hell. 2020. *Invisible China: How the Urban-Rural Divide Threatens China's Rise*. Chicago: University of Chicago Press.

Shen, Ce, and John B. Williamson. 2010. "China's New Rural Pension Scheme: Can It Be Improved?" *International Journal of Sociology and Social Policy* 30 (5/6): 239–50. https://doi.org/10.1108/01443331011054217

Shen Ke. 2019. *Renkou laolinghua, daiji fenpei yu caizheng fudan* 人口老龄化、代际分配与财政负担 (Population aging, intergenerational redistribution and fiscal burden). Beijing: Shehui kexue wenxian chubanshe.

Shen, Ke, Feng Wang, and Yong Cai. 2018a. "China's Age of Abundance: Tracking Changes with NTA Analyses." Paper presented at the 12th NTA Global Conference, Mexico City, Mexico, July, 2018.

2018b. "A Benevolent State against an Unjust Society? Inequalities in Public Transfers in China." *Chinese Sociological Review* 50 (2): 137–62. https://doi.org/10.1080/21620555.2017.1410432

Shen, Ke, Yong Cai, Feng Wang, and Zhan Hu. 2021. "Changing Society, Changing Lives: Three Decades of Family Change in China." *International Journal of Social Welfare* 30 (4): 453–64. https://doi.org/10.1111/ijsw.12492

Shirk, Susan L. 1993. *The Political Logic of Economic Reform in China*. Berkeley: University of California Press.

Sicular, Terry, Shi Li, Ximing Yue, and Hiroshi Satō, eds. 2020. *Changing Trends in China's Inequality: Evidence, Analysis, and Prospects*. New York: Oxford University Press.

Smil, Vaclav. 1986. "Food Production and Quality of Diet in China." *Population and Development Review* 12 (1): 25–45. https://doi.org/10.2307/1973350

2003. *China's Past, China's Future: Energy, Food, Environment*. New York: Routledge.

2013. "The Last Eighty Years: Continuities and Change." *Population and Development Review* 38: 265–79. www.jstor.org/stable/23655298

Solinger, Dorothy J. 1999. *Contesting Citizenship in Urban China: Peasant Migrants, the State, and the Logic of the Market*. Berkeley: University of California Press.

2022. *Poverty and Pacification: The Chinese State Abandons the Old Working Class*. Lanham, MD: Rowman & Littlefield.

Song, Zheng, Kjetil Storesletten, Yikai Wang, and Fabrizio Zilibotti. 2015. "Sharing High Growth across Generations: Pensions and Demographic Transition in China." *American Economic Journal: Macroeconomics* 7 (2): 1–39. https://doi.org/10.1257/mac.20130322

Olaniyan, Olanrewaju, Adedoyin Soyibo, and Akanni O. Lawanson. 2011. "Consumption and Income over the Lifecycle in Nigeria." *African Population Studies* 25 (1). https://doi.org/10.11564/25-1-270

Steckel, Richard H. 1995. "Stature and the Standard of Living." *Journal of Economic Literature* 33 (4): 1903–40. www.jstor.org/stable/2729317

Steckel, Richard H., and Roderick Floud. 1997. *Health and Welfare during Industrialization*. Chicago: University of Chicago Press.

Su, Yang. 2011. *Collective Killing in Rural China during the Cultural Revolution*. Cambridge: Cambridge University Press.

2023. *Deadly Decision in Beijing: Succession Politics, Protest Repression, and the 1989 Tiananmen Massacre*. Cambridge: Cambridge University Press.

Tanner, James Mourilyan. 1990. *Foetus into Man: Physical Growth from Conception to Maturity*. Revised and enlarged edition. Cambridge, MA: Harvard University Press.

Tao Ran and Su Fubing. 2021. "Jingji zengzhang de 'Zhongguo moshi': liang ge beize lilun jiashuo he yi ge xitongxing fenxi kuangjia" 经济增长的'中国模式': 两个备择理论假说和一个系统性分析框架 (A "China model" of economic growth: Two alternative hypotheses and one integrated framework). *Bijiao/Comparative Studies* 114. http://bijiao.caixin.com/2021-07-06/101736863.html

Tsuya, Noriko O., Wang Feng, George Alter, James Z. Lee, Tommy Bengtsson, Cameron Campbell, Satomi Kurosu et al. 2010. *Prudence and Pressure: Reproduction and Human Agency in Europe and Asia, 1700–1900*. Cambridge, MA: MIT Press.

Tung, An-Chi. 2011. "Consumption over the Lifecycle: An International Comparison." In Lee and Mason, *Population Aging and the Generational Economy*, 136–60.

United Nations, Population Division. 2013. *Measuring and Analysing the Generational Economy: National Transfer Accounts Manual*. New York: United Nations.

2015. "The World Population Prospects: 2015 Revision." Report. www.un.org/en/development/desa/publications/world-population-prospects-2015-revision.html

Vogel, Ezra F. 1993. *The Four Little Dragons: The Spread of Industrialization in East Asia*. Cambridge, MA: Harvard University Press.

2011. *Deng Xiaoping and the Transformation of China*. Cambridge, MA: Belknap Press.

Walder, Andrew G. 2000. "China's Transitional Economy." In J. T. Li, Anne S. Tsui, and Elizabeth Weldon, eds., *Management and Organizations in the Chinese Context*, 63–83. London: Palgrave Macmillan. https://doi.org/10.1057/9780230511590_4

2014. "Rebellion and Repression in China, 1966–1971." *Social Science History* 38 (4): 513–39.

2019. *Agents of Disorder: Insider China's Cultural Revolution*. Cambridge, MA: Harvard University Press.

Walder, Andrew G., and Jean C. Oi, eds. 1999. *Property Rights and Economic Reform in China*. Stanford, CA: Stanford University Press.

Walder, Andrew G., and Yang Su. 2003. "The Cultural Revolution in the Countryside: Scope, Timing and Human Impact." *The China Quarterly*, no. 173: 74–99. www.jstor.org/stable/20058959

Wang, Fei-Ling. 2004. "Reformed Migration Control and New Targeted People: China's Hukou System in the 2000s." *The China Quarterly*, no. 177: 115–32. www.jstor.org/stable/20192307

2005. *Organizing through Division and Exclusion: China's Hukou System*. Stanford, CA: Stanford University Press.

Wang, Feng. 2003. "Housing Improvement and Distribution in Urban China: Initial Evidence from China's 2000 Census." *China Review* 3 (2): 121–43. www.jstor.org/stable/23461907

2007. *Boundaries and Categories: Rising Inequality in Post-Socialist Urban China*. Stanford, CA: Stanford University Press.

2011a. "The Future of a Demographic Overachiever: Long-Term Implications of the Demographic Transition in China." *Population and Development Review* 37: 173–90. www.jstor.org/stable/41762404

2011b. "The End of 'Growth with Equity'? Economic Growth and Income Inequality in East Asia." https://www.eastwestcenter.org/publications/end-growth-equity-economic-growth-and-income-inequality-east-asia

2019. "China's Uphill Battle against Inequality." In Dorothy J. Solinger, ed., *Polarized Cities: Portraits of Rich and Poor in Urban China*, 23–42. Lanham, MD: Rowman & Littlefield.

Wang, Feng, and Andrew Mason. 2008. "The Demographic Factor in China's Transition." In Loren Brandt and Thomas G. Rawski, eds., *China's Great Economic Transformation*, 136–66. Cambridge: Cambridge University Press. https://doi.org/10.1017/CBO9780511754234.006

Wang, Feng, Yong Cai, and Baochang Gu. 2013. "Population, Policy, and Politics: How Will History Judge China's One-Child Policy?" *Population and Development Review* 38: 115–29. www.jstor.org/stable/23655290

Wang, Feng, Baochang Gu, and Yong Cai. 2016. "The End of China's One-Child Policy." *Studies in Family Planning* 47 (1): 83–86. www.jstor.org/stable/24720399

Wang, Feng, Ke Shen, and Yong Cai. 2019a. "Expansion of Public Transfers in China: Who Are the Beneficiaries?" *Journal of the Economics of Ageing* 14 (January): 100194. https://doi.org/10.1016/j.jeoa.2019.100194

Wang, Feng, Ke Shen, and Yong Cai. 2019b. "One city, three peoples: Migration, immigration, and the making of global Shanghai." Paper presented at the Conference on Immigration and the Transformation of Chinese Society, University of Manchester, Manchester, UK, April 25–26.

Wang, Feng, Xuejin Zuo, and Danching Ruan. 2002. "Rural Migrants in Shanghai: Living under the Shadow of Socialism." *International Migration Review* 36 (2): 520–45. www.jstor.org/stable/4149463

Wang, Feng, Yong Cai, Ke Shen, and Stuart Gietel-Basten. 2018. "Is Demography Just a Numerical Exercise? Numbers, Politics, and Legacies of China's One-Child Policy." *Demography* 55 (2): 693–719. https://doi.org/10.1007/s13524-018-0658-7

Wang, Lijian, Daniel Béland, and Sifeng Zhang. 2014. "Pension Fairness in China." *China Economic Review* 28: 25–36. https://doi.org/10.1016/j.chieco.2013.11.003

Weber, Isabella M. 2021. *How China Escaped Shock Therapy*. Abingdon, UK: Routledge.

West, Loraine A., and Christine P. W. Wong. 1995. "Fiscal Decentralization and Growing Regional Disparities in Rural China: Some Evidence in the

Provision of Social Services." *Oxford Review of Economic Policy* 11 (4): 70–84. https://doi.org/10.1093/oxrep/11.4.70

Whyte, Martin King. 1995. "The Social Roots of China's Economic Development." *The China Quarterly*, no. 144: 999–1019. www.jstor.org/stable/655289

2010. *One Country, Two Societies: Rural-Urban Inequality in Contemporary China*. Cambridge, MA: Harvard University Press.

2012. "China's Post-Socialist Inequality." *Current History* 111 (746): 229–34. https://doi.org/10.1525/curh.2012.111.746.229

Whyte, Martin King, Feng Wang, and Yong Cai. 2015. "Challenging Myths about China's One-Child Policy." *The China Journal*, no. 74: 144–59. https://doi.org/10.1086/681664

Williamson, John. 2000. "What Should the World Bank Think about the Washington Consensus?" *The World Bank Research Observer* 15 (2): 251–64. www.jstor.org/stable/3986418

World Bank. 1983. "China – Socialist Economic Development: The Economy, Statistical System, and Basic Data" (English). A World Bank country study. Washington, DC: World Bank. http://documents.worldbank.org/curated/en/192611468769173749/The-economy-statistical-system-and-basic-data

1984. "China – The Health Sector" (English). A World Bank Country Study. Washington, DC: World Bank. http://documents.worldbank.org/curated/en/480551468743746436/China-The-health-sector

Wu, Jinglian. 2005. *Understanding and Interpreting Chinese Economic Reform*. Mason, OH: Texere.

Wu, Xiaogang, and Donald J. Treiman. 2004. "The Household Registration System and Social Stratification in China: 1955–1996." *Demography* 41 (2): 363–84. www.jstor.org/stable/1515171

Wu, Yang-feng, Guan-sheng Ma, Yong-hua Hu, Yan-ping Li, Xian Li, Zhao-hui Cui, Chun-ming Chen, and Ling-zhi Kong. 2005. "[The current prevalence status of body overweight and obesity in China: Data from the China National Nutrition and Health Survey]." [Original article in Chinese.] *Zhonghua yufang yixue zazhi* 39 (5): 316–20. https://pubmed.ncbi.nlm.nih.gov/16266540/

Xia, Qingjie, Shi Li, and Lina Song. 2020. "Consumption Inequality in Urban China." In Sicular et al., *Changing Trends in China's Inequality*, 267–96.

Xie, Pengxin, Fuxi Wang, and Yanyuan Cheng. 2017. "How Did Chinese Migrant Workers Fare in Labour Dispute Mediation? Differentiated Legal Protection and the Moderating Role of the Nature of Dispute." *Journal of Industrial Relations* 59 (5): 611–30. https://doi.org/10.1177/0022185617716730

Xie, Yu, and Jingwei Hu. 2014. "An Introduction to the China Family Panel Studies (CFPS)." *Chinese Sociological Review* 47 (1): 3–29. https://doi.org/10.2753/CSA2162-0555470101.2014.11082908

Xie, Yu, and Yongai Jin. 2015. "Household Wealth in China." *Chinese Sociological Review* 47 (3): 203–29. https://doi.org/10.1080/21620555.2015.1032158

Xie, Yu, and Xiang Zhou. 2014. "Income Inequality in Today's China." *Proceedings of the National Academy of Sciences* 111 (19): 6928–33. https://doi.org/10.1073/pnas.1403158111

Yang Jisheng. 1998. *Deng Xiaoping shidai* 邓小平时代 (The era of Deng Xiaoping). Beijing: Zhongyang bianyi chubanshe.

Yeung, Wei-Jun Jean. 2013. "Higher Education Expansion and Social Stratification in China." *Chinese Sociological Review* 45 (4): 54–80. https://doi.org/10.2753/CSA2162-0555450403

Yip, Winnie, and William Hsiao. 2009. "China's Health Care Reform: A Tentative Assessment." *China Economic Review* 20 (4): 613–19. https://doi.org/10.1016/j.chieco.2009.08.003

Yip, Winnie Chi-Man, William C. Hsiao, Wen Chen, Shanlian Hu, Jin Ma, and Alan Maynard. 2012. "Early Appraisal of China's Huge and Complex Health-Care Reforms." *The Lancet* 379 (9818): 833–42. https://doi.org/10.1016/S0140-6736(11)61880-1

Zhang, Li. 2012. "Economic Migration and Urban Citizenship in China: The Role of Points Systems." *Population and Development Review* 38 (3): 503–33. www.jstor.org/stable/41857403

Zhonggong zhongyang wenxian yanjiushi 中共中央文献研究室 (Chinese Communist Party Research Office of Historical Records), ed. 1998. *Deng Xiaoping sixiang nianpu*邓小平思想年谱 1975–1997 (Chronicles of Deng Xiaoping thought 1975–1997) Beijing: Zhongyang wenxian chubanshe.

2004. *Deng Xiaoping nianpu* 邓小平年谱, 1975–1997 (Chronicles of Deng Xiaoping 1975–1997). Beijing: Zhongyang wenxian chubanshe.

Zhou, Xueguang. 2000. "Economic Transformation and Income Inequality in Urban China: Evidence from Panel Data." *American Journal of Sociology* 105 (4): 1135–74. www.jstor.org/stable/3003890

2022. *The Logic of Governance in China*. Cambridge: Cambridge University Press.

Zong, Xin-Nan, and Hui Li. 2014. "Physical Growth of Children and Adolescents in China over the Past 35 Years." *Bull World Health Organ* 92 (8): 555–64.

Index

For EU product safety concerns, contact us at Calle de José Abascal, 56–1°, 28003 Madrid, Spain or eugpsr@cambridge.org.

www.ingramcontent.com/pod-product-compliance
Lightning Source LLC
LaVergne TN
LVHW011811200926
848484LV00005B/1149

* 9 7 8 1 0 0 9 4 4 4 8 9 7 *